Ageless Artistry

A NEWCOMER'S GUIDE TO CLASSIC WESTERN PAINTINGS FROM 1400 TO 1900

SAMANTHA BRIGHT

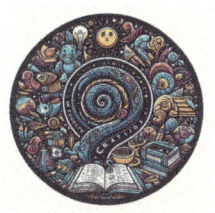

CURIOSITY CREATIONS

ISBN: 979-8-89321-000-2

Published by Curiosity Creations
Deleware, USA

www.CuriosityCreationsBooks.com

CONTENTS

Introduction: A Journey Through Western Art   1

The Art   3

The Arnolfini Portrait — Jan van Eyck   5

Primavera (Allegory of Spring) — Sandro Botticelli   7

The Birth of Venus — Sandro Botticelli   9

The Garden of Earthly Delights — Hieronymus Bosch   11

The Last Supper — Leonardo da Vinci   13

Mona Lisa — Leonardo da Vinci   15

The Creation of Adam — Michelangelo Buonarroti   17

The School of Athens — Raphael   19

The Sistine Madonna — Raphael   21

The Raising of Lazarus — Rembrandt Harmenszoon van Rijn   23

Judith Beheading Holofernes — Artemisia Gentileschi   25

The Anatomy Lesson of Dr. Nicolaes Tulp — Rembrandt Harmenszoon van Rijn   27

The Philosopher in Meditation — Rembrandt Harmenszoon van Rijn   29

Moses and The Brazen Serpent — Peter Paul Rubens   31

The Night Watch — Rembrandt Harmenszoon van Rijn   33

Las Meninas — Diego Velázquez   35

Girl with a Pearl Earring — Johannes Vermeer   37

The Embarkation for Cythera — Jean-Antoine Watteau   39

The Swing — Jean-Honoré Fragonard   41

Yard with Lunatics (Corral de locos) — Francisco Goya   43

The Raft of the Medusa — Théodore Géricault   45

Wanderer Above the Sea of Fog — Caspar David Friedrich   47

The Apotheosis of Homer — Jean-Auguste-Dominique Ingres   49

The Death of Sardanapalus — Eugène Delacroix   51

Liberty Leading the People — Eugène Delacroix   53

The Fighting Temeraire Tugged to Her Last Berth to be Broken Up , 1938 — Joseph Mallord William Turner   55

Kindred Spirits — Asher B. Durand   57

Ophelia — John Everett Millais   59

Washington Crossing the Delaware — Emanuel Leutze   61

The Gleaners — Jean-François Millet 63

The Third-Class Carriage — Honoré Daumier 65

The Barge Haulers on the Volga — Ilya Repin 67

Whistler's Mother (Arrangement in Grey and Black No. 1) — James McNeill Whistler 69

Impression, Sunrise — Claude Monet 71

Luncheon of the Boating Party — Pierre-Auguste Renoir 73

Bathers at Asnières — Georges Seurat 75

Ivan the Terrible and His Son Ivan — Ilya Repin 77

The Lady of Shalott — John William Waterhouse 79

The Bedroom — Vincent van Gogh 81

Starry Night Over the Rhône — Vincent van Gogh 83

Sunflowers — Vincent van Gogh 85

Irises — Vincent van Gogh 87

The Starry Night — Vincent van Gogh 89

Haystacks (Series) — Claude Monet 91

At the Moulin Rouge — Henri de Toulouse-Lautrec 93

The Scream — Edvard Munch 95

The Sleeping Gypsy — Henri Rousseau 97

The Kiss (Lovers) — Gustav Klimt 99

Midnight Ride of Paul Revere — Grant Wood 101

The Artists **103**

Jan van Eyck 105

Sandro Botticelli 105

Hieronymus Bosch 106

Leonardo da Vinci 107

Michelangelo Buonarroti 108

Raphael (Raffaello Sanzio da Urbino) 110

Peter Paul Rubens 111

Artemisia Gentileschi 112

Diego Velázquez 113

Rembrandt Harmenszoon van Rijn 114

Johannes Vermeer 116

Jean-Antoine Watteau 117

Jean-Honoré Fragonard 118

Francisco Goya 119

Caspar David Friedrich 120

Joseph Mallord William Turner 121

Jean-Auguste-Dominique Ingres 123

Théodore Géricault 124

Asher B. Durand 125

Eugène Delacroix 126

Honoré Daumier 128

Jean-François Millet 129

Emanuel Leutze 130

John Everett Millais 131

James McNeill Whistler 132

Claude Monet 133

Pierre-Auguste Renoir 135

Ilya Repin 136

Henri Rousseau 137

John William Waterhouse 138

Vincent van Gogh 140

Georges Seurat 141

Gustav Klimt 142

Edvard Munch 143

Henri de Toulouse-Lautrec 145

Grant Wood 146

Introduction: A Journey Through Western Art

Art has always been a reflection of the human experience, capturing the imagination, emotions, and beliefs of people across time. In compiling a collection of Western art, we are confronted with the enormity of the task: how does one distill centuries of artistic achievement into a single volume? Any selection of art is inherently subjective. No book can claim to encapsulate the entire breadth and depth of Western art history, as countless masterpieces remain unmentioned. However, this book seeks to provide a broad overview of the major artistic movements and influential works that have shaped the Western artistic tradition. The journey of Western art is a complex, evolving narrative. From the early realism of Jan van Eyck's Arnolfini Portrait in the 15th century to the bold emotional expressions of Vincent van Gogh's Starry Night in the 19th century, this book charts the evolution of style, technique, and vision. Along the way, we will explore the major artistic movements that emerged over the centuries, each reflecting the changing sensibilities and philosophies of the time.

The Renaissance: Rediscovering Classical Ideals

Our exploration begins with the Renaissance, a period when artists in Italy and Northern Europe sought to revive the classical ideals of ancient Greece and Rome. Jan van Eyck's meticulous attention to detail in the Arnolfini Portrait exemplifies the Northern Renaissance's emphasis on realism and texture. Meanwhile, in Italy, artists like Sandro Botticelli brought mythological subjects to life with works such as Primavera and The Birth of Venus, where the human form is celebrated in its idealized beauty.

The High Renaissance, represented by masters like Leonardo da Vinci and Michelangelo, marks a peak in the technical mastery of the human figure and perspective. Da Vinci's The Last Supper and Mona Lisa capture both psychological depth and compositional balance, while Michelangelo's Creation of Adam, part of the Sistine Chapel frescoes, demonstrates his unparalleled skill in rendering the human body. Raphael's The School of Athens synthesizes these ideals, with its harmonious composition and depiction of philosophers symbolizing the merging of art, philosophy, and science.

The Baroque and Rococo: Drama and Ornate Elegance

As the Renaissance gave way to the Baroque period in the 17th century, the focus shifted to dramatic intensity and emotional realism. Rembrandt van Rijn is a defining figure of the era, known for his deep explorations of human psychology and the use of chiaroscuro (the contrast between light and dark), as seen in works like The Night Watch and The Anatomy Lesson of Dr. Nicolaes Tulp. Artemisia Gentileschi's Judith Beheading Holofernes embodies the Baroque's flair for drama, with its vivid portrayal of violence and emotion.

In the Rococo period that followed, we see a lighthearted, ornamental style emerge, exemplified by the playful sensuality of Jean-Honoré Fragonard's The Swing and the idyllic beauty of Jean-Antoine Watteau's The Embarkation for Cythera. Rococo was the art of aristocratic leisure, often focusing on themes of love and nature.

The Enlightenment and Romanticism: Reason and Emotion

The 18th century Enlightenment, with its emphasis on reason and science, brought about a shift in subject matter. Neoclassical artists like Jean-Auguste-Dominique Ingres, in works such as The Apotheosis of Homer, drew inspiration from the simplicity and order of classical antiquity, reflecting the Enlightenment's intellectual ideals.

However, by the 19th century, Romanticism arose as a reaction against this rationalism, emphasizing emotion, nature, and individualism. Caspar David Friedrich's Wanderer Above the Sea of Fog captures the Romantic fascination with the sublime—nature's power and beauty, often dwarfing the individual. Eugène Delacroix, with works like Liberty Leading the People, expressed the political passions of the time, portraying revolutionary fervor with bold colors and dynamic compositions.

Realism, Impressionism, and Beyond: Breaking New Ground

The mid-19th century saw a movement toward realism, as artists sought to depict the world as it was, without embellishment. Jean-François Millet's The Gleaners and Honoré Daumier's The Third-Class Carriage portray the dignity of everyday life and the hardships of the working class, aligning with the social changes brought about by industrialization.

Simultaneously, the Impressionists, led by figures like Claude Monet and Pierre-Auguste Renoir, revolutionized painting by focusing on the fleeting effects of light and color. Monet's Impression, Sunrise gave the movement its name, with its loose brushstrokes and emphasis on atmosphere rather than detail. The post-Impressionists, including Vincent van Gogh, further pushed these boundaries, exploring emotional depth through bold, expressive color, as seen in The Starry Night and Sunflowers.

The Modern Era: Innovation and Experimentation

As the 20th century approached, Western art continued to evolve in exciting new directions. Edvard Munch's The Scream captured the existential anxiety of the modern age, while Henri Rousseau's The Sleeping Gypsy conjured dreamlike visions that foreshadowed the surrealism of the coming decades. The decorative sensuality of Gustav Klimt's The Kiss and the stark realism of Grant Wood's Midnight Ride of Paul Revere each represent unique expressions of modern concerns and aesthetics.

In tracing the history of Western art through these works, we glimpse the vast and varied ways that artists have responded to the world around them. This book is not a comprehensive history, nor could it be, but rather an introduction to some of the most influential and transformative works in Western art. Each painting is a window into the time in which it was created, and together, they offer a rich tapestry that continues to inspire and provoke thought today.

As we move through the ages, from the structured perfection of the Renaissance to the emotive power of Romanticism, and from the precise realism of the Baroque to the expressive abstraction of modern art, we can see how each movement builds upon or reacts against the one before it. This continuous dialogue between past and present is what makes the study of art so endlessly fascinating.

THE ART

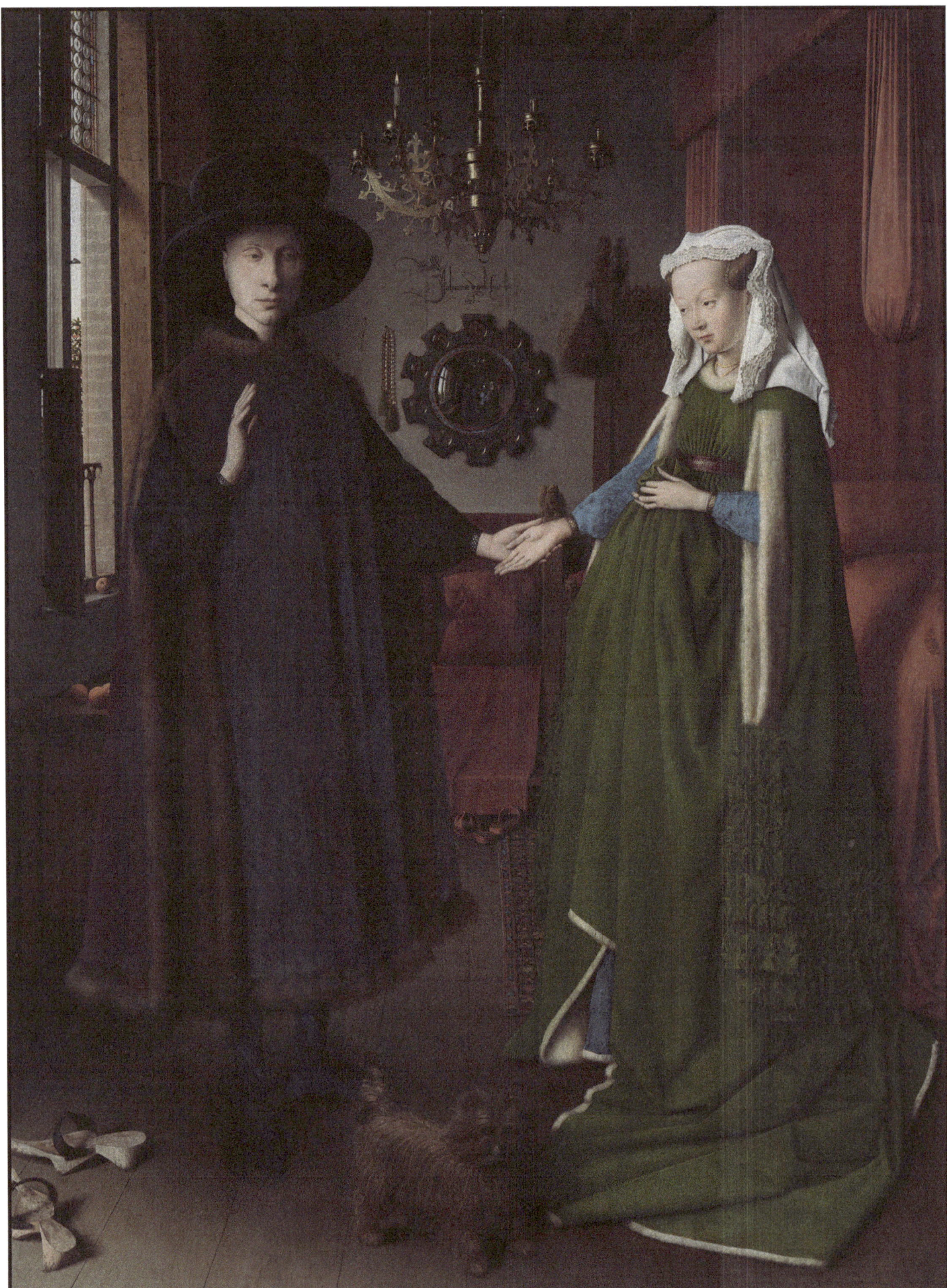

The Arnolfini Portrait

Jan van Eyck

Date of Creation: 1434.

Art Movement or Style: Northern Renaissance.

Medium and Technique: Oil on oak panel.

Dimensions of the Painting: 82.2 cm × 60 cm (32.4 in × 23.6 in).

Current Location: The National Gallery in London.

Historical and Cultural Context
The Arnolfini Portrait was created during a time of great wealth and cultural growth in the Burgundian Netherlands. It is one of the earliest examples of oil painting in Europe and is famous for its detailed representation of a wealthy merchant and his wife, possibly as a form of a marriage contract.

Subject Matter and Themes
The painting is thought to depict the Italian merchant Giovanni di Nicolao di Arnolfini and his wife, possibly in their home in the Flemish city of Bruges. Themes include marriage, wealth, and domestic life.

Artistic Significance
This painting is celebrated for its exquisite detail, use of oil paints, and mastery of light. It is also noted for its use of perspective and the mirror that reflects the room, including the figures of two men who may be witnesses to the marriage.

Critical Reception and Interpretations
The Arnolfini Portrait has been subject to various interpretations, including that it is a document of the couple's marriage, a reflection of wealth and social status, or a memorial portrait of the wife who may have died. The mirror in the painting, decorated with scenes of the Passion of Christ, suggests a spiritual and moral reflection as well.

Visual Analysis
The painting is known for its realistic depiction of the interior and the figures. Van Eyck's attention to detail is evident in the textures of fabrics, the reflective surfaces of the mirror and the chandelier, and the naturalistic rendering of objects. The couple stands in a stiff, formal pose, typical of the time. Noteworthy is the use of light and shadow, which adds depth to the room, and the complex symbolism present in the objects, like the single candle lit in the chandelier or the dog at the couple's feet.

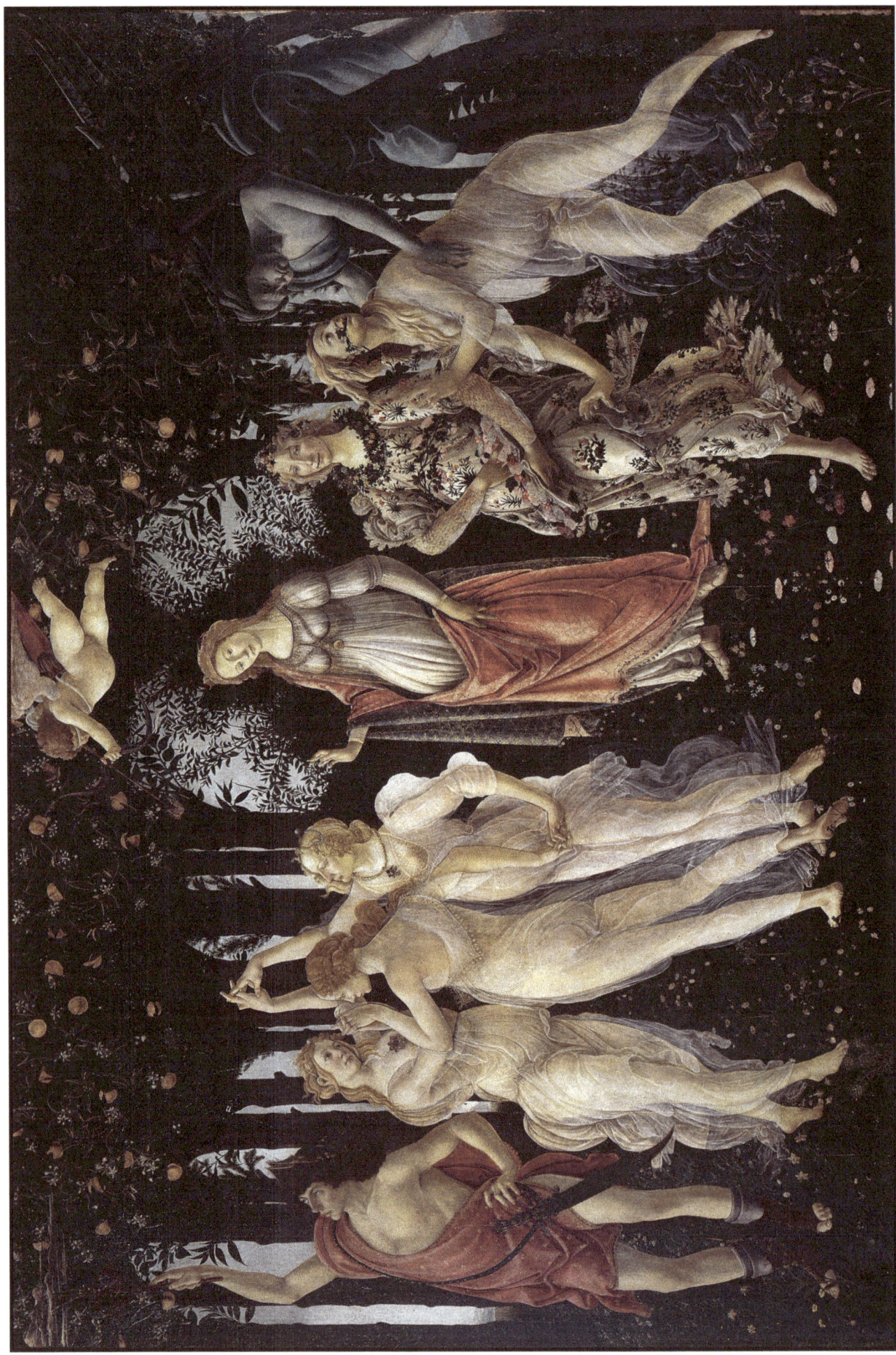

Primavera (Allegory of Spring)

Sandro Botticelli

Date of Creation: Around 1482.

Art Movement or Style: Early Renaissance

Medium and Technique: Tempera on panel.

Dimensions of the Painting: Approximately 202 cm × 314 cm (80 in × 124 in).

Current Location: The Uffizi Gallery in Florence, Italy.

Historical and Cultural Context
Primavera is one of the most popular works of the Florentine Renaissance. It was painted during the early Renaissance, a period that witnessed a revival of interest in classical mythology and philosophy, which is reflected in the painting's subject matter.

Subject Matter and Themes
The painting features figures from classical mythology and is believed to represent the lush growth of spring. Themes include love, the beauty of nature, and classical mythology.

Artistic Significance
Primavera is considered one of the greatest works of the Early Renaissance for its beauty, complex iconography, and its representation of the ideals of the era. It is a prime example of the use of allegory and mythological subjects during the Renaissance.

Critical Reception and Interpretations
The painting has been subject to numerous interpretations over the years. Some believe it was meant to depict the ideal of Neoplatonic love, while others interpret it as a representation of the lushness and fertility of spring. Its exact meaning remains a topic of scholarly debate.

Visual Analysis
The painting is renowned for its vivid colors, graceful forms, and the detailed depiction of figures and flora. It features Venus at the center, with the Three Graces dancing in a circle, Mercury dissipating the clouds on the left, and the dark figure of Zephyrus pursuing the nymph Chloris, whom he transforms into Flora, the goddess of spring, covering the right side. The figures are set against a dark wooded background that highlights their ethereal and delicate forms. The composition is symmetrical and balanced, with a clear focus on Venus, aligning with the classical ideals of beauty and harmony.

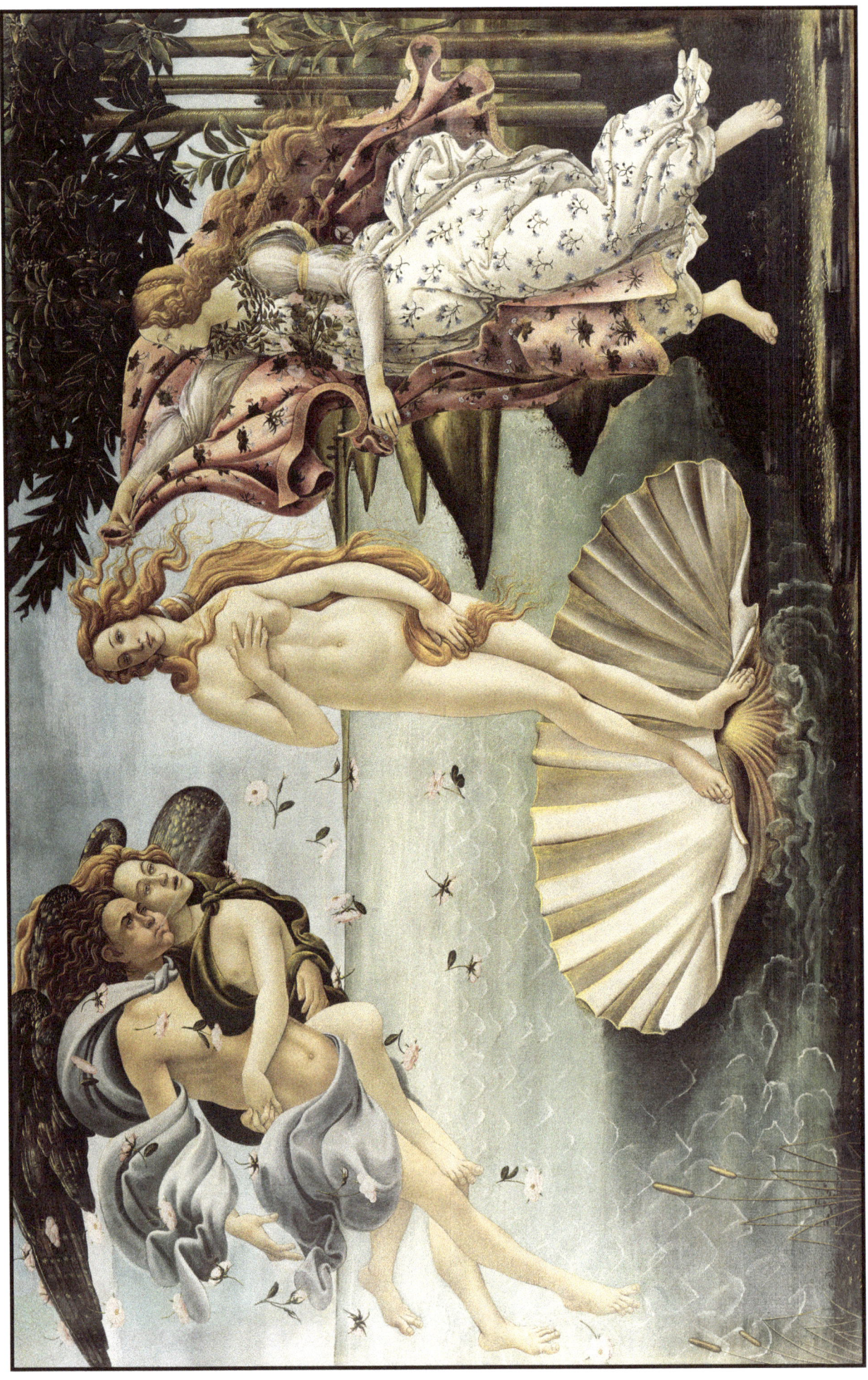

The Birth of Venus

Sandro Botticelli

Date of Creation: Circa 1484-1486.

Art Movement or Style: Early Renaissance

Medium and Technique: Tempera on panel.

Dimensions of the Painting: 172.5 cm × 278.9 cm (67.9 in × 109.6 in).

Current Location: The Uffizi Gallery in Florence, Italy.

Historical and Cultural Context
The Birth of Venus was created during the Italian Renaissance, a period of renewed interest in classical philosophy and mythology. The painting reflects the humanist values of the time, portraying a mythological subject with grace and beauty.

Subject Matter and Themes
The painting depicts the goddess Venus emerging from the sea as a full-grown woman, as described in classical mythology. Themes include beauty, divine love, and the rebirth of classical antiquity's ideals.

Artistic Significance
This work is one of the most famous paintings of the Renaissance and exemplifies the period's aesthetic values. It marked a departure from the religious themes that dominated the art of the Middle Ages and is celebrated for its grace, composition, and the idealized beauty of its figures.

Critical Reception and Interpretations
The Birth of Venus has been subject to various interpretations, often related to the humanistic and neoplatonic views of the Medici court that Botticelli was associated with. Some see it as a symbol of the synthesis between Christian and classical traditions.

Visual Analysis
The painting is renowned for its soft, flowing lines and the ethereal beauty of Venus, who stands modestly in the center. The figures on the left are Zephyrus and Aura, who blow the goddess towards the shore, and on the right, one of the Horae, goddesses of the seasons, who reaches out to clothe her. The use of aerial perspective and the detailed rendering of nature and the human form are characteristic of Botticelli's style. The figures are idealized, and the overall effect is one of serene beauty and harmony.

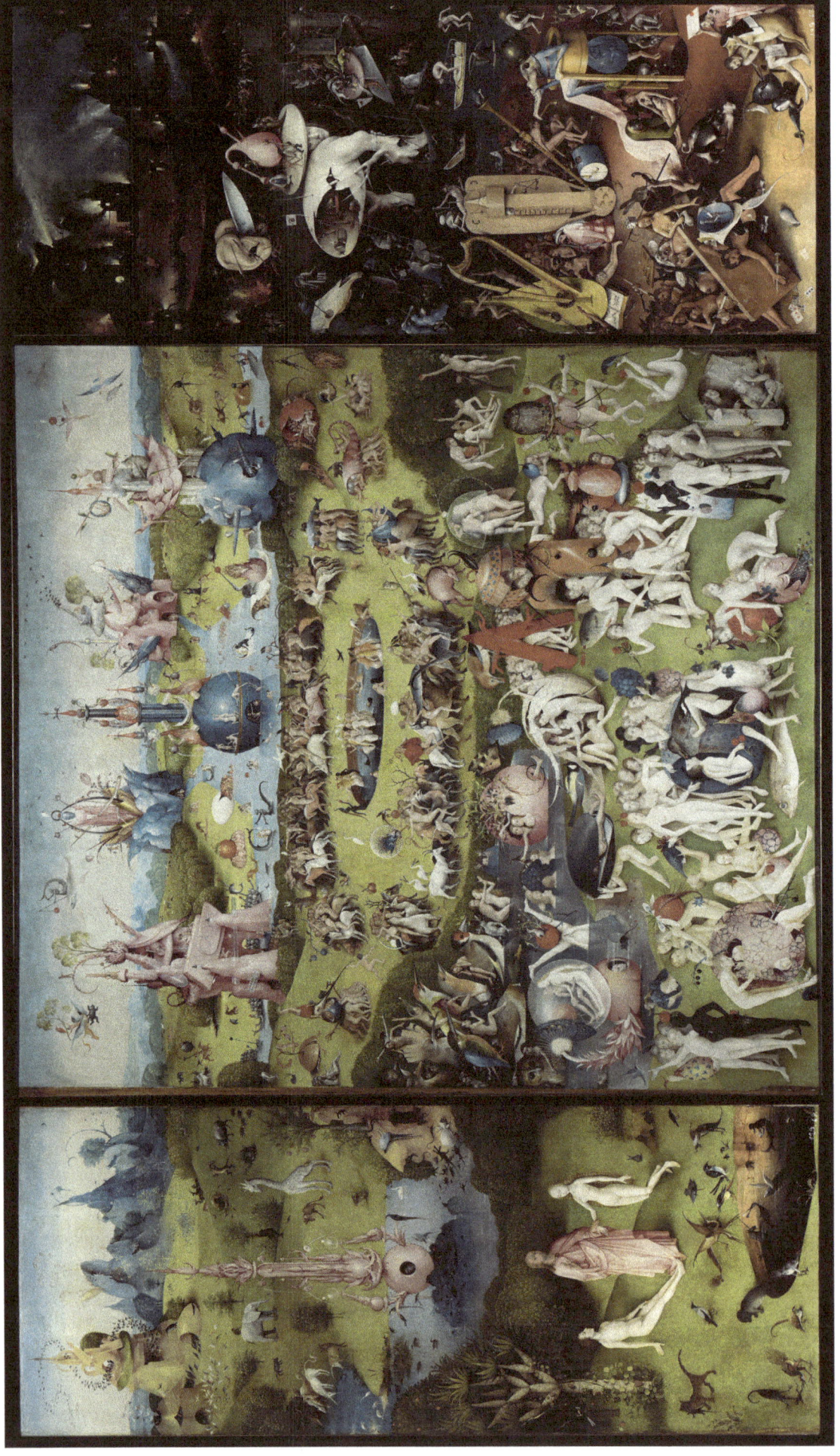

The Garden of Earthly Delights

Hieronymus Bosch

Date of Creation: Circa 1490–1510.

Art Movement or Style: Northern Renaissance.

Medium and Technique: Oil painting on oak panels.

Dimensions of the Painting: 205.5 cm × 384.9 cm (81 in × 152 in) when fully opened.

Current Location: The Museo del Prado in Madrid, Spain.

Historical and Cultural Context
The painting was created during the Northern Renaissance, a period of great social and religious change in Europe. It reflects the era's complex attitudes towards sin, salvation, and the morality of human pleasure.

Subject Matter and Themes
The triptych depicts three scenes: the left panel shows God presenting Eve to Adam, the central panel depicts a fantastical scene of earthly delights, and the right panel shows the torments of hell. Themes of human sin, morality, paradise, and damnation are prevalent.

Artistic Significance
The Garden of Earthly Delights is considered one of Bosch's seminal works, renowned for its detailed, imaginative scenes and complex symbolism. It is a benchmark for the use of triptych in Renaissance art and is one of the most famous and intriguing works of the Northern Renaissance.

Critical Reception and Interpretations
The painting has been subject to numerous interpretations, ranging from a warning on the perils of life's temptations to an alchemical allegory. Its complexity has led to extensive scholarly debate.

Visual Analysis
The work is notable for its extensive use of symbolism, meticulous attention to detail, and the imaginative representation of fantastical creatures and landscapes. Bosch's use of color and light creates a vivid contrast between the panels, enhancing their narrative and thematic power.

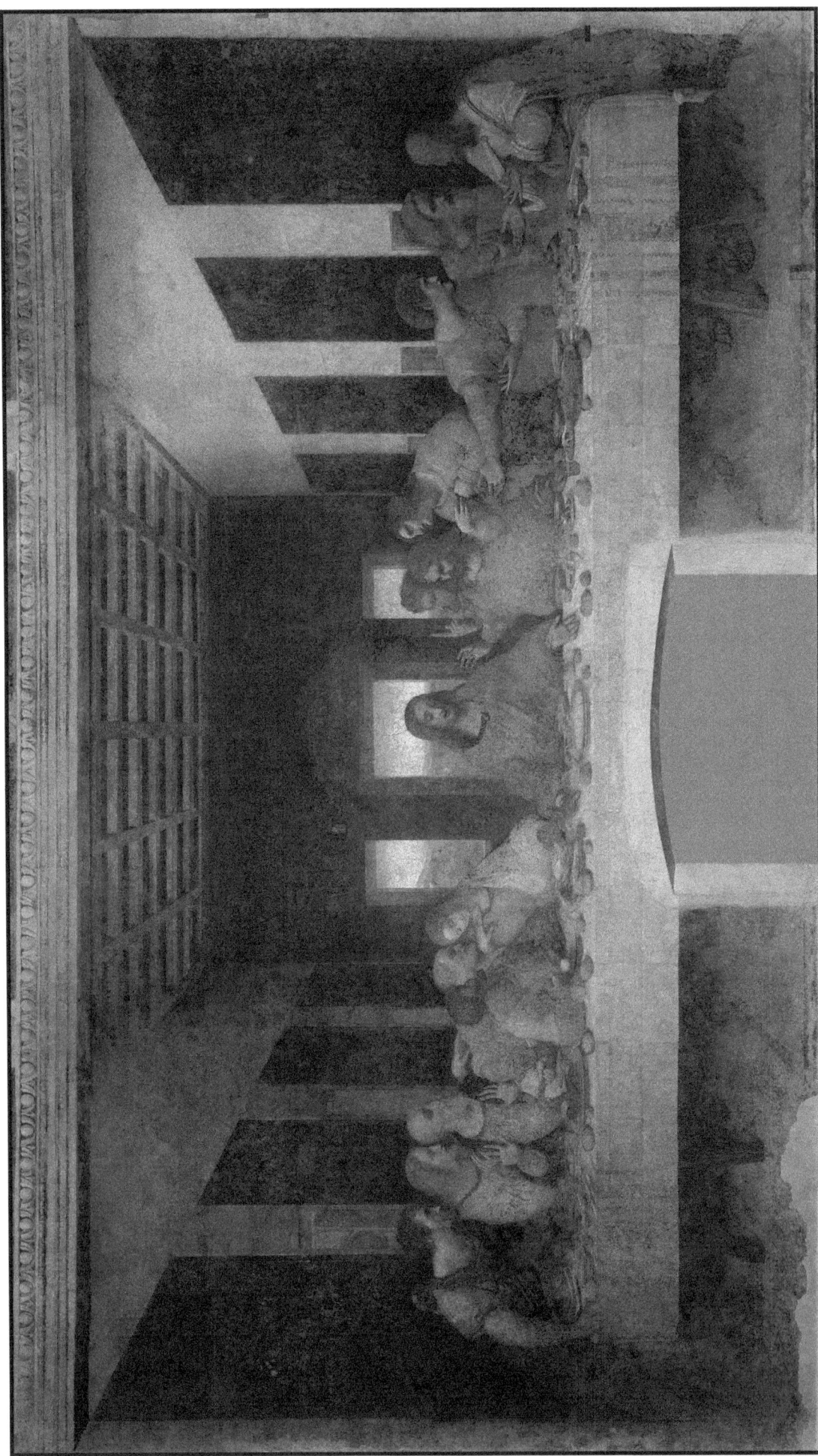

The Last Supper

Leonardo da Vinci

Date of Creation: Between 1495–1498.

Art Movement or Style: Italian Renaissance.

Medium and Technique: Fresco (modified). Leonardo da Vinci used a technique that involved applying tempera paints upon a dry plaster wall, which was a departure from the traditional fresco technique of painting onto wet plaster. This choice contributed to the artwork's deterioration over time.

Dimensions of the Painting: The mural measures 460 cm × 880 cm (180 in × 350 in).

Current Location: The refectory of the Convent of Santa Maria delle Grazie in Milan, Italy.

Historical and Cultural Context
The Last Supper was commissioned as part of a renovation of the church and its convent buildings by Leonardo's patron Ludovico Sforza, Duke of Milan. The painting represents the scene of the Last Supper of Jesus with his apostles, as told in the Gospel of John, 13:21. It was a time of great religious and artistic exploration, with the Renaissance emphasizing a rebirth of classical learning and a focus on humanism.

Subject Matter and Themes
The painting depicts the moment Jesus has just announced that one of the Apostles would betray him. The themes are betrayal, the divinity of Jesus, and the reaction of the individual apostles to the announcement, which is conveyed through their varied emotional responses.

Artistic Significance
The Last Supper is one of the most iconic and influential works in the history of art. It is significant for its dramatic and humanistic portrayal of a key moment in the Christian narrative. Leonardo's innovative use of perspective and chiaroscuro (the contrast of light and shadow) was revolutionary.

Critical Reception and Interpretations
Since its creation, the painting has been subject to various restorations and interpretations. It has been admired for its composition and Leonardo's skill in depicting the emotional reactions of the figures. The work has also been analyzed for hidden meanings, including possible references to Jesus' relationship with the apostles and the presence of Mary Magdalene, which is a subject of debate among art historians.

Visual Analysis
The Last Supper is a masterful example of one-point perspective, with all perspective lines leading to the figure of Jesus at the center, which establishes him as the focal point. The composition is balanced with equal numbers of disciples on either side of Jesus and their expressions and gestures are rendered in a way that captures their individual reactions to the news of the betrayal. The use of light and shadow, particularly around the figures, gives them a three-dimensional quality and enhances the drama of the scene.

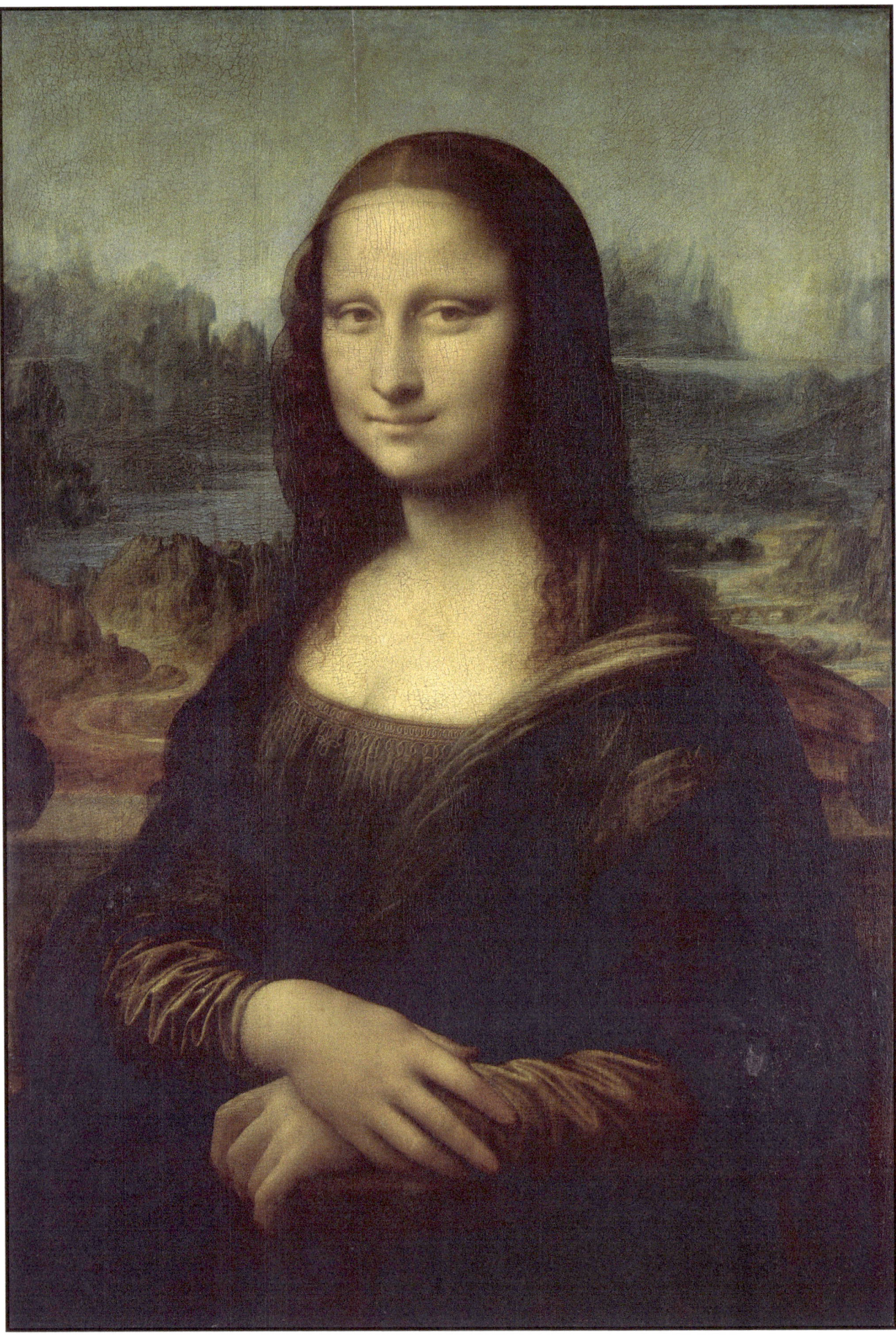

Mona Lisa

Leonardo da Vinci

Date of Creation: Between 1503-1517.

Art Movement or Style: High Renaissance.

Medium and Technique: Oil on white poplar wood panel.

Dimensions of the Painting: 77 cm × 53 cm (30 in × 21 in).

Current Location: The Louvre Museum in Paris, France.

Historical and Cultural Context

The *Mona Lisa* is thought to depict Lisa Gherardini, the wife of Florentine merchant Francesco del Giocondo. It's famous for its portrayal of the sitter's elusive expression, which seems both alluring and aloof. The painting's fame is amplified by its various thefts and vandalisms over the years, as well as the mystery surrounding the identity of the subject and the intent of the artist.

Subject Matter and Themes

The subject is a portrait of a woman, believed to be Lisa Gherardini. Themes often associated with the *Mona Lisa* include the nature of human happiness, the mystique of femininity, and the complexity of human emotion conveyed through expression.

Artistic Significance

The *Mona Lisa* is considered an archetypal masterpiece of the Italian Renaissance, and it has been described as "the best known, the most visited, the most written about, the most sung about, the most parodied work of art in the world."

Critical Reception and Interpretations

The *Mona Lisa* has been praised for its sophistication, its depiction of emotion, the innovative use of sfumato (a technique of allowing tones and colors to shade gradually into one another, producing softened outlines or hazy forms), and for the enigmatic nature of its subject's expression.

Visual Analysis

The painting is renowned for its exquisite detail, the serene landscape that frames the subject, and the soft blending of colors. The sitter's famously enigmatic expression, often described as a smile, has intrigued viewers for centuries. Leonardo's use of atmospheric perspective can also be seen in the background, giving the painting a remarkable sense of depth.

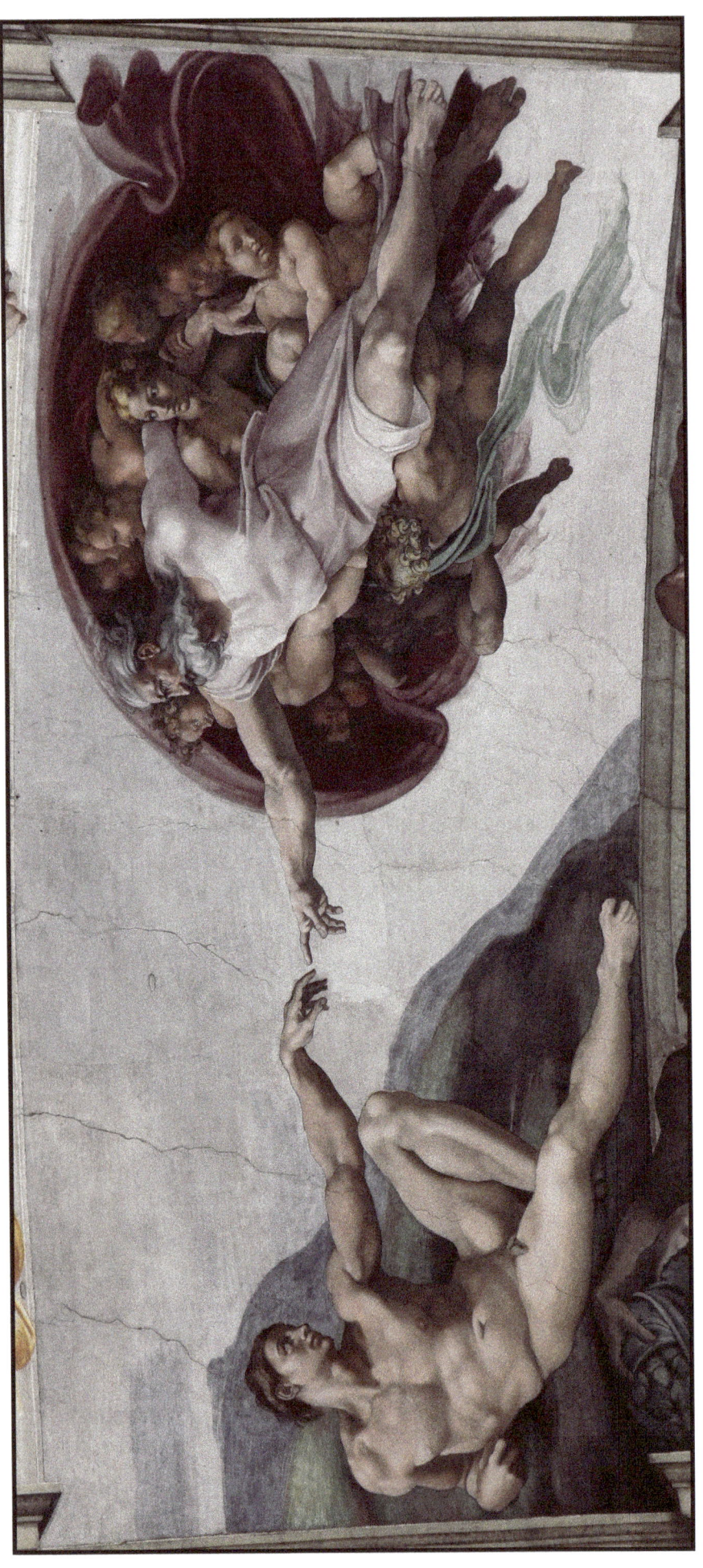

The Creation of Adam

Michelangelo Buonarroti

Date of Creation: 1508-1512.

Art Movement or Style: High Renaissance

Medium and Technique: Fresco.

Dimensions of the Painting: Approximately 280 cm × 570 cm (110 in × 220 in).

Current Location: Sistine Chapel, Vatican City.

Historical and Cultural Context

This is part of the larger scheme of the Sistine Chapel ceiling painted by Michelangelo, commissioned by Pope Julius II. The work falls within the period of the High Renaissance, characterized by an emphasis on harmony, balance, and the integration of classical ideals with Christian themes. This era in art saw a profound interest in humanism, which is strongly reflected in Michelangelo's human-centric depiction of biblical scenes.

Subject Matter and Themes

The painting depicts the biblical story from the Book of Genesis in which God gives life to Adam, the first man. The almost-touching hands of God and Adam have become iconic, symbolizing the birth of mankind and the transmission of divine spark. Themes include creation, divine intervention, the beauty of the human form, and the connection between the divine and humanity.

Artistic Significance

This fresco is one of the most renowned artworks of the Renaissance and remains a pivotal image in the history of Western art. Its significance lies in Michelangelo's innovative approach to depicting the human body, imbued with both movement and emotion, which exemplified the Renaissance ideals of human potential and beauty. The dynamic composition and the dramatic interaction between the figures reflect a deep understanding of anatomy and express profound theological concepts through art.

Critical Reception and Interpretations

The Creation of Adam has been subject to various interpretations over the centuries, ranging from its reflection on human nature and divine influence to more contemporary readings that consider neuroanatomical figures in the depiction of God and the angels around him, suggesting Michelangelo's interest in human anatomy. Critics and historians have praised the fresco for its artistic mastery and profound symbolism.

Visual Analysis

The fresco is characterized by the strong use of chiaroscuro, the contrast between light and dark, to model the figures in three dimensions. The composition is centered around the nearly touching hands of God and Adam, creating a focal point that draws the viewer's eyes. God is depicted as an elderly, yet powerful figure, enveloped by a group of angels, while Adam is shown as a muscular yet passive figure, illustrating the Renaissance ideal of the perfect human form. The background is relatively subdued, directing attention to the figures themselves and emphasizing the interaction between the divine and the human.

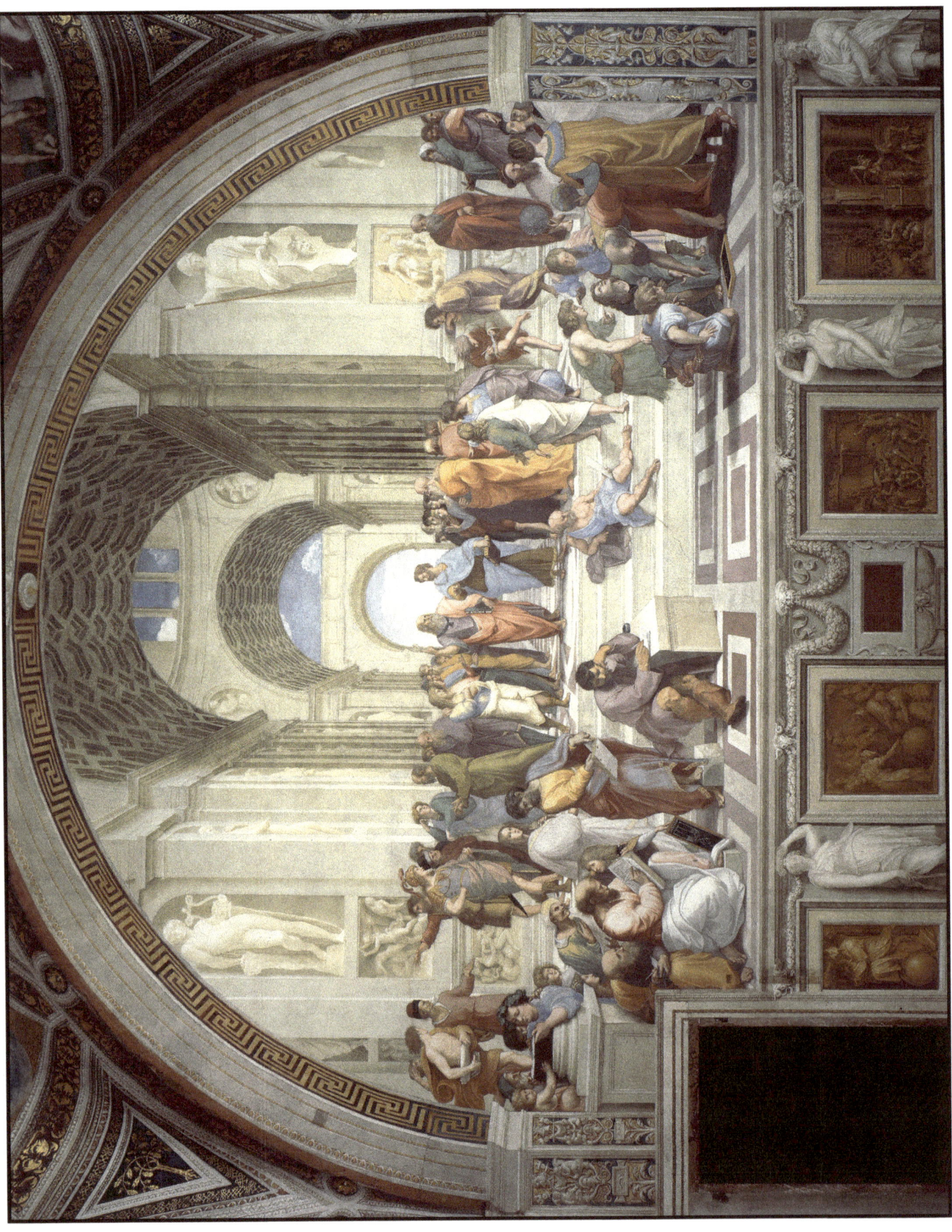

The School of Athens

Raphael

Date of Creation: 1509–1511.

Art Movement or Style: High Renaissance.

Medium and Technique: Fresco.

Dimensions of the Painting: Approximately 500 cm × 770 cm (200 in × 300 in).

Current Location: The Apostolic Palace in the Vatican City, specifically in the room known as the Stanza della Segnatura.

Historical and Cultural Context

The School of Athens was painted during the Italian Renaissance, a time of renewed interest in classical philosophy, literature, and art. Raphael was commissioned by Pope Julius II to decorate the rooms now known as the Raphael Rooms in the Vatican.

Subject Matter and Themes

The fresco represents philosophy and includes images of the greatest mathematicians, philosophers, and scientists from classical antiquity, gathered to share their ideas and learn from each other. Central figures are believed to be Aristotle and Plato. Themes include the pursuit of knowledge and the interrelation of truth and philosophy.

Artistic Significance

The School of Athens is considered one of Raphael's masterpieces and a perfect embodiment of the classical spirit of the Renaissance. Its composition, use of perspective, and depiction of various famous Greek philosophers has had a profound influence on Western art.

Critical Reception and Interpretations

The fresco was immediately recognized as a work of great importance. It has been interpreted in various ways, often seen as Raphael's commentary on the nature of wisdom and learning, reflecting the ideals of the Renaissance.

Visual Analysis

The fresco is known for its accurate use of perspective, creating a sense of three-dimensional space on a flat surface. The figures are arranged in a wide, open architecture, which serves to frame the action and draw the viewer into the scene. The gestures and poses of the figures reflect their intellectual engagement and contribute to the narrative of the gathering. Raphael's skill in depicting the human form, his use of color, and the clarity of his composition are all evident in this work.

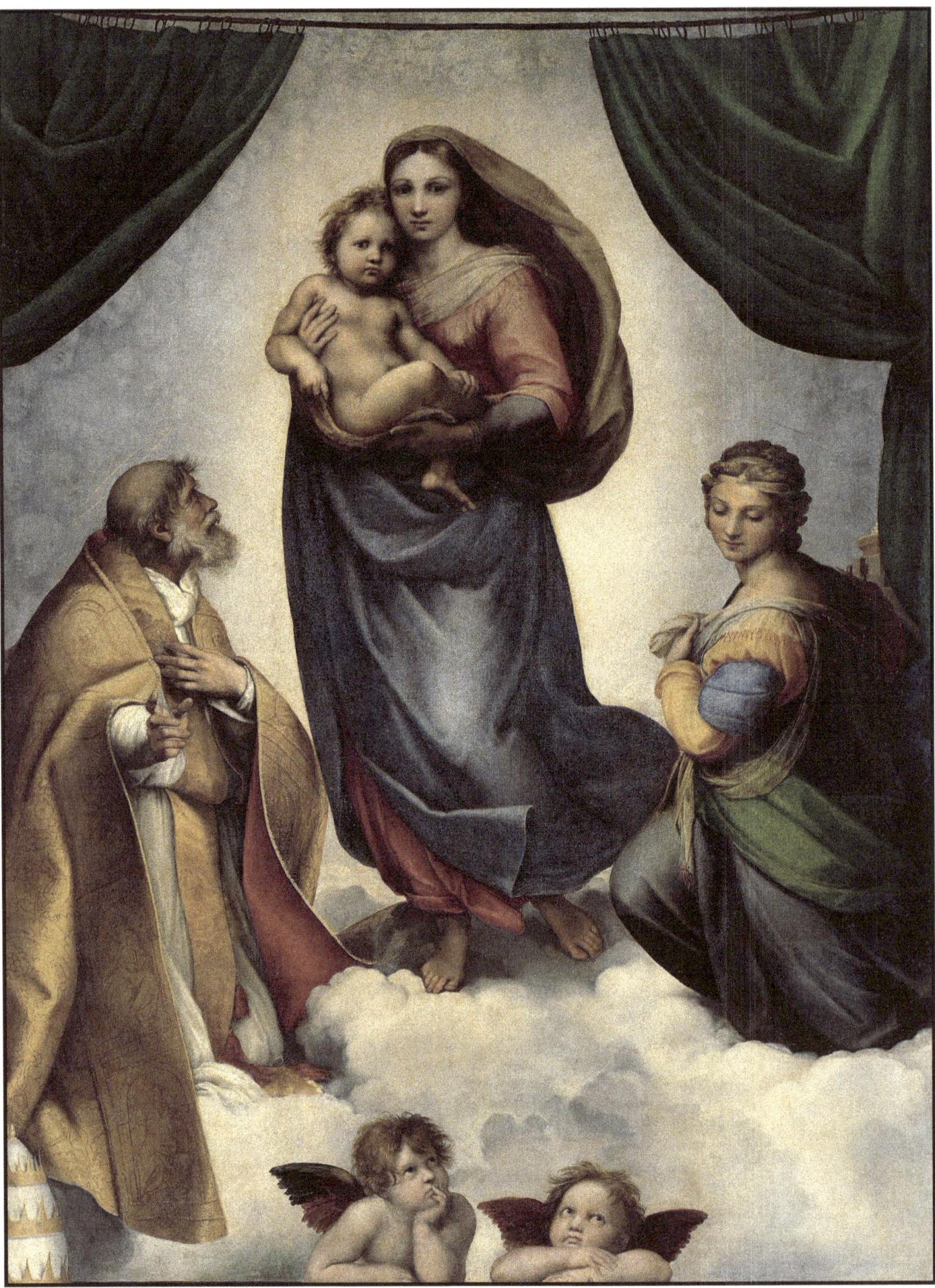

The Sistine Madonna

Raphael

Date of Creation: 1513–1514.

Art Movement or Style: High Renaissance.

Medium and Technique: Oil on canvas. Raphael is known for his precise compositions, clarity of form, and visual achievement of the Neoplatonic ideal of human grandeur.

Dimensions of the Painting: 265 cm × 196 cm (104 in × 77 in).

Current Location: The Gemäldegalerie Alte Meister (Old Masters Picture Gallery) in Dresden, Germany..

Historical and Cultural Context
Commissioned by Pope Julius II, the painting was originally intended for the Benedictine San Sisto Monastery in Piacenza, Italy. The Sistine Madonna was one of the last Madonnas painted by Raphael. The painting was created at a time when the High Renaissance was in full bloom, marked by a humanistic interest in classical ideals and the human form.

Subject Matter and Themes
The painting depicts the Virgin Mary holding the Christ Child, with Saint Sixtus and Saint Barbara. Below them are two cherubs, who have become iconic in their own right. Themes of the painting include the divine nature of the Madonna and Child, as well as the intercession of saints in the realm of the divine.

Artistic Significance
The Sistine Madonna is renowned for its grandeur and has been celebrated for the balance and harmony of its composition, as well as its emotional impact. It is considered one of Raphael's greatest masterpieces and an exemplar of Renaissance ideals of beauty and harmony.

Critical Reception and Interpretations
The Sistine Madonna was immediately recognized as a masterpiece of Renaissance art. It has been interpreted in various ways, with some focusing on its spiritual and religious qualities, and others on its artistic and compositional innovations.

Visual Analysis
The figures are set against a backdrop of curtains, which part to reveal a heavenly scene. The Madonna and Child are centrally placed and are flanked by the saints and angels. The use of sfumato creates a softness in the figures, and the light gives them a sculptural quality. The cherubs at the bottom are often noted for their thoughtful and introspective expressions, adding to the painting's emotional depth. The gaze of the Madonna engages the viewer, creating an intimate connection that is both sacred and personal.

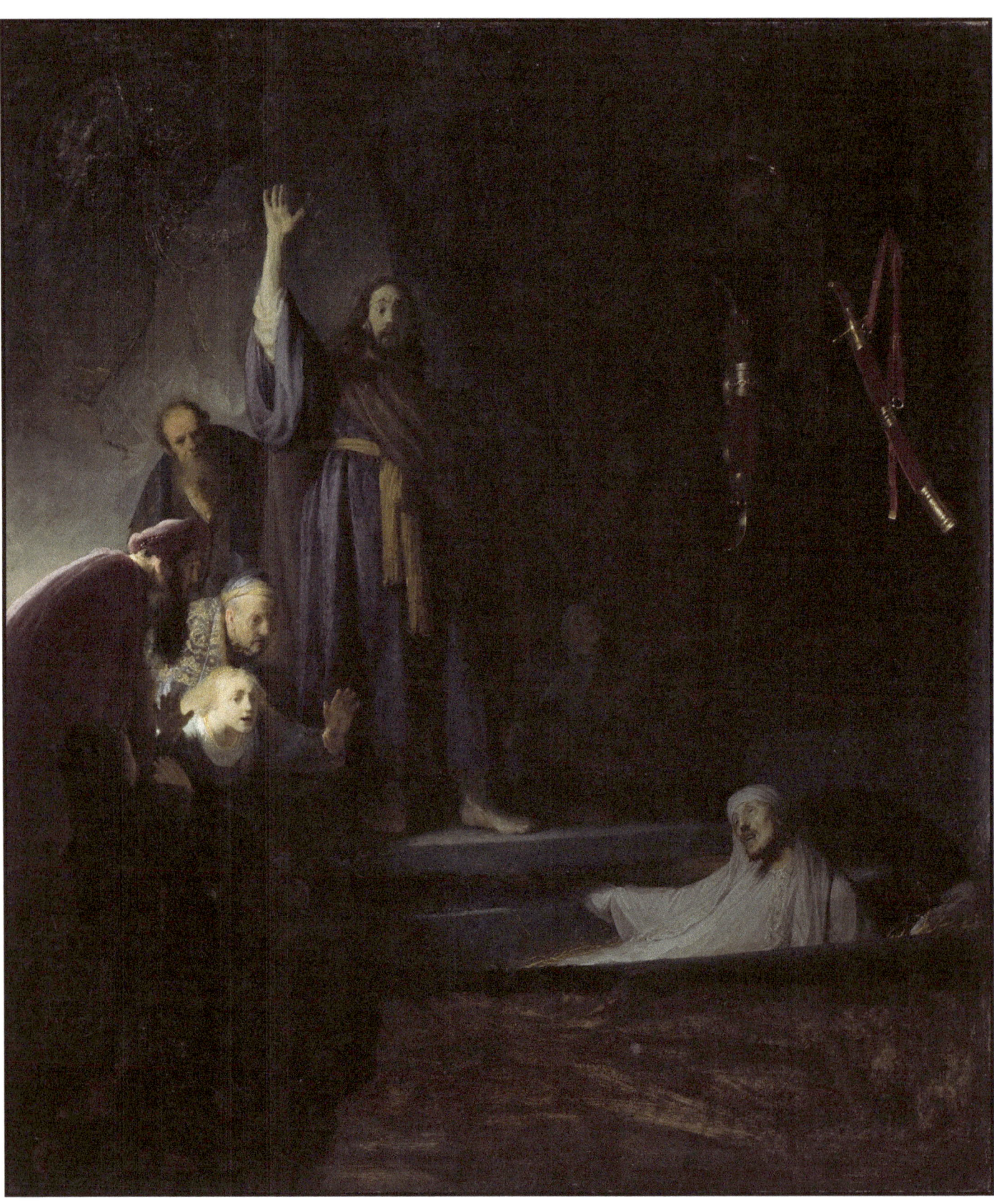

The Raising of Lazarus

Rembrandt Harmenszoon van Rijn

Date of Creation: Around 1630-1632

Art Movement or Style: Baroque

Medium and Technique: Oil on panel. Rembrandt is known for his masterful handling of light and shadow, and his expressive brushwork.

Dimensions of the Painting: Approximately 96 cm × 81 cm (37.8 in × 31.9 in).

Current Location: The Los Angeles County Museum of Art, Los Angeles, California, USA.

Historical and Cultural Context
Rembrandt painted *The Raising of Lazarus* early in his career, while he was still living in Leiden. It was during the Dutch Golden Age, a period of great wealth, trade expansion, and artistic output in the Netherlands.

Subject Matter and Themes
The painting depicts the biblical story of Jesus raising Lazarus from the dead, as told in the Gospel of John. Themes of divine power, faith, and the victory of life over death are central to the work.

Artistic Significance
This work is significant as an example of Rembrandt's early exploration of religious themes and his exceptional skill in using light to convey emotion and narrative. His ability to portray human emotion and the spiritual aspect of biblical stories was groundbreaking at the time.

Critical Reception and Interpretations
Rembrandt's treatment of biblical subjects was innovative, focusing on the emotional and human elements of these stories. *The Raising of Lazarus* in particular has been praised for its dramatic illumination and the intense expressions of its figures.

Visual Analysis
The painting is characterized by a strong contrast between light and dark (chiaroscuro), a hallmark of Rembrandt's work. The light emanates from Christ and illuminates the scene, highlighting Lazarus and the figures gathered around him. This use of light not only focuses the viewer's attention on the central action but also gives the scene a profound sense of depth and drama. The varied reactions of the figures, from amazement to awe, are rendered with great sensitivity and contribute to the narrative power of the painting.

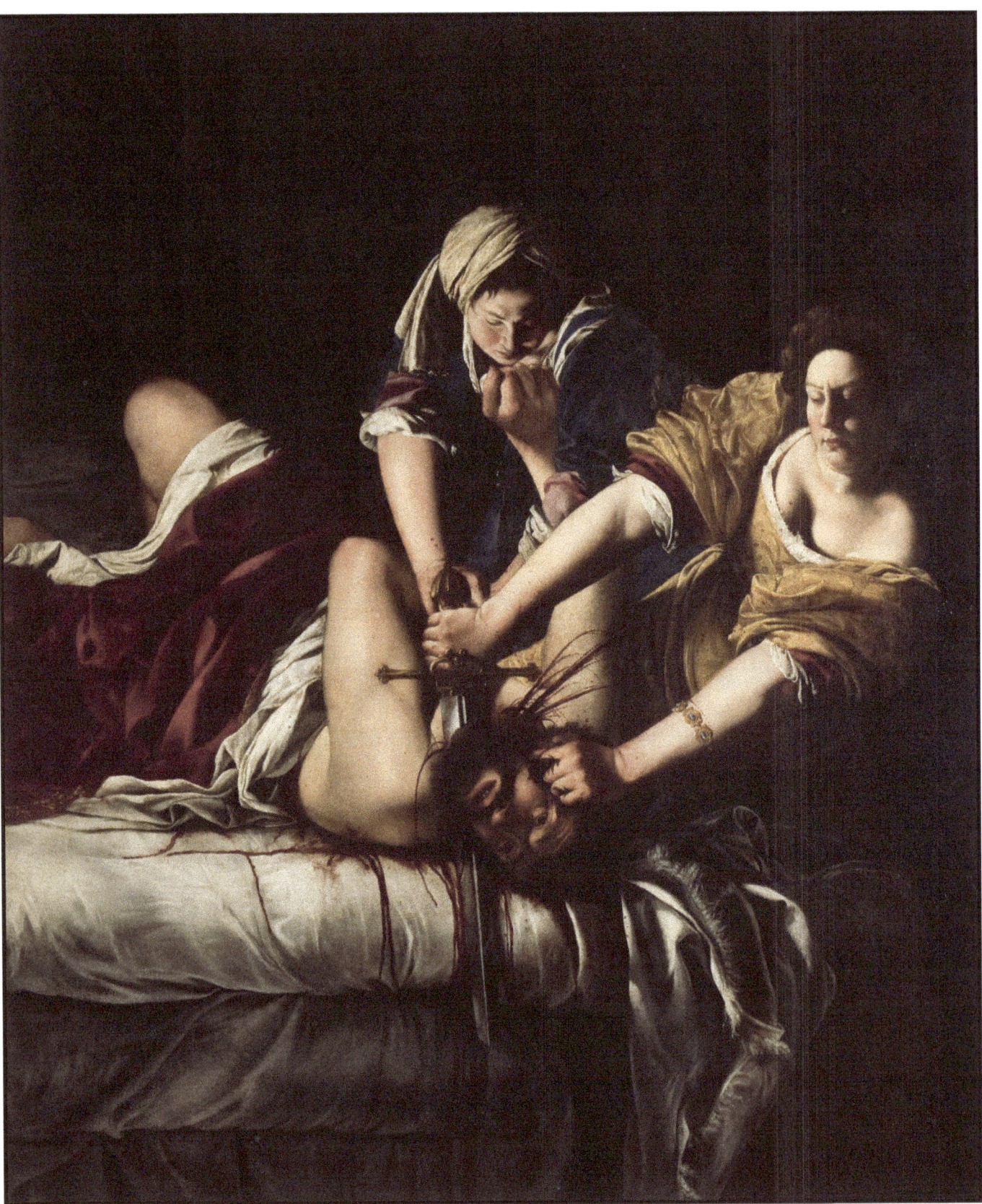

Judith Beheading Holofernes

Artemisia Gentileschi

Date of Creation: Circa 1614-1620.

Art Movement or Style: Baroque.

Medium and Technique: Oil on canvas.

Dimensions of the Painting: Approximately 199 cm × 162 cm (78 in × 63 in), although Gentileschi painted more than one version.

Current Location: The best-known version is in the Museo Nazionale di Capodimonte, Naples, Italy.

Historical and Cultural Context
Artemisia Gentileschi was one of the first well-known female painters and a follower of Caravaggio. This painting is a depiction of the biblical story of Judith, who seduced and then decapitated the Assyrian general Holofernes to save her city. Gentileschi's own experiences, including her survival of rape and the subsequent trial, inform the intense emotional gravity and violence of this work.

Subject Matter and Themes
The painting portrays Judith, a Jewish widow, and her maidservant beheading the Assyrian general Holofernes. Themes of power, justice, and retribution are prevalent, as well as the empowerment of women, which is often interpreted through the lens of Gentileschi's personal history.

Artistic Significance
The painting is notable for its dramatic use of chiaroscuro, a technique popularized by Caravaggio, which Gentileschi adapted to her own style, emphasizing physical strength and moral fortitude. It's a significant work that showcases the talent and perspective of a prominent female artist in a male-dominated field.

Critical Reception and Interpretations
Gentileschi's work was often overshadowed by her male contemporaries, but *Judith Beheading Holofernes* has been critically acclaimed for its vivid depiction of the scene and for its powerful, almost cathartic, representation of female agency. Interpretations of the work frequently acknowledge it as a statement on gender and power, and as a personal narrative of overcoming.

Visual Analysis
The painting is remarkable for its brutal realism and the emotional intensity of the figures. Judith's determination and Holofernes's horror are captured in their expressions and gestures. The dark background contrasts with the stark lighting on the figures, emphasizing the action and creating a sense of depth. The composition directs the viewer's attention to the central act of violence, portrayed with both technical skill and emotional depth.

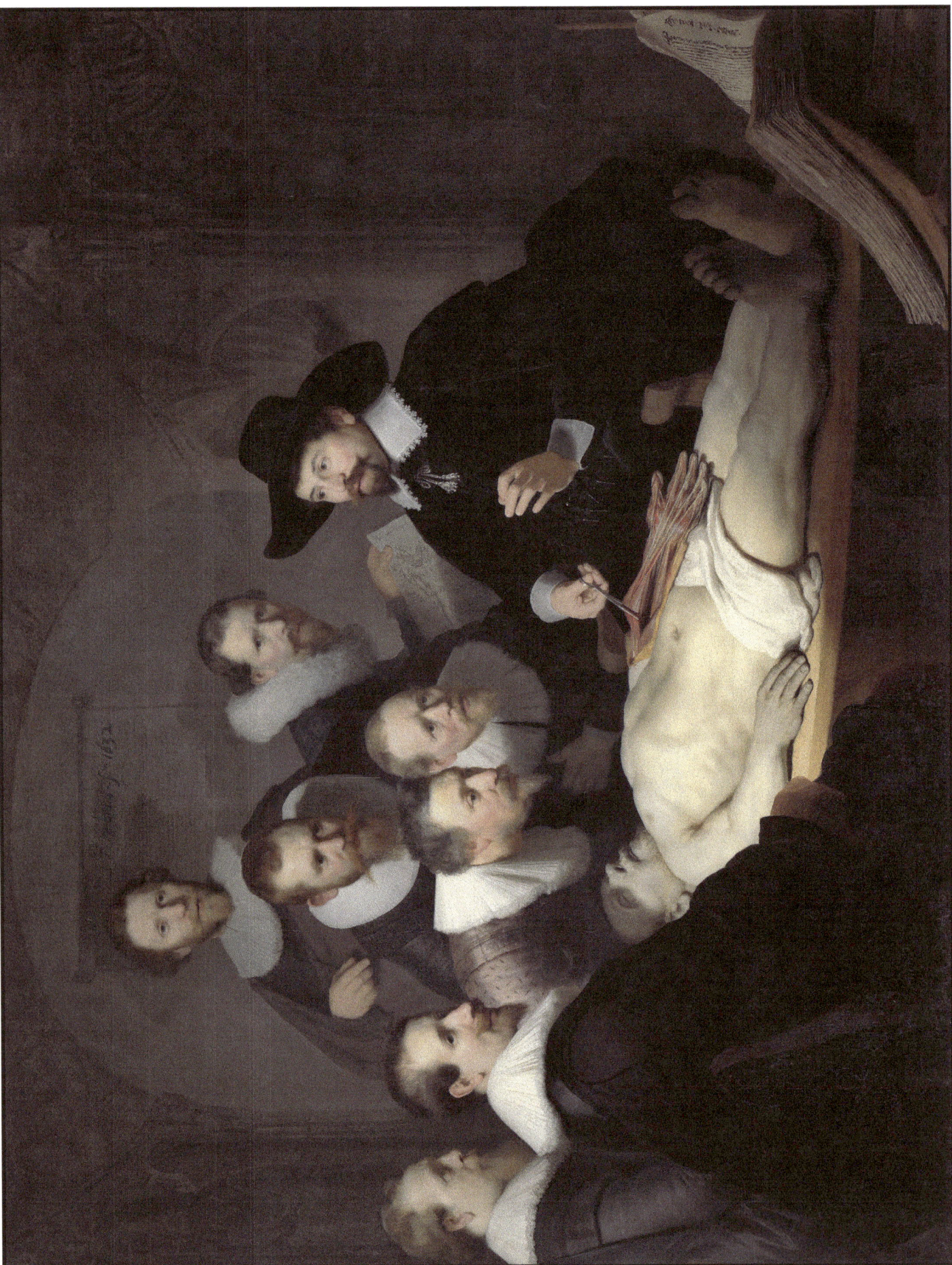

The Anatomy Lesson of Dr. Nicolaes Tulp

Rembrandt Harmenszoon van Rijn

Date of Creation: 1632.

Art Movement or Style: Baroque.

Medium and Technique: Oil on canvas.

Dimensions of the Painting: 169.5 cm × 216.5 cm (66.7 in × 85.2 in).

Current Location: The Mauritshuis museum in The Hague, Netherlands.

Historical and Cultural Context

The painting was commissioned by the Amsterdam Guild of Surgeons for their guild room. It depicts an actual event, the public dissection of a criminal conducted by Dr. Nicolaes Tulp, which was a common practice in the 17th century for both educational and entertainment purposes. Such events were of high social importance in Amsterdam and were attended by many curious spectators.

Subject Matter and Themes

The subject is a scientific demonstration, specifically an anatomy lesson by Dr. Tulp. Themes of the painting revolve around science, learning, and the exploration of the human body, as well as the idea of mortality.

Artistic Significance

This work is significant as it shows Rembrandt's skill in composition, use of light and shadow, and the depiction of different expressions and characters. It's a masterpiece of the Dutch Golden Age and highlights the shift in art towards realism and scientific inquiry.

Critical Reception and Interpretations

The painting is often interpreted as not just a depiction of an event, but also a comment on the progress of science and its place in society. It has been critically acclaimed for its originality and for the way Rembrandt captures the concentration of the figures.

Visual Analysis

The composition is arranged around the central figure of Dr. Tulp, whose hand is gesturing towards the opened body, drawing the viewer's attention to the dissection. The onlookers are portrayed with various expressions of curiosity and fascination. Rembrandt's use of chiaroscuro – the contrast of light and dark – focuses the viewer's eye on the action at the table, while the rest of the room fades into darkness, adding a dramatic effect to the scene.

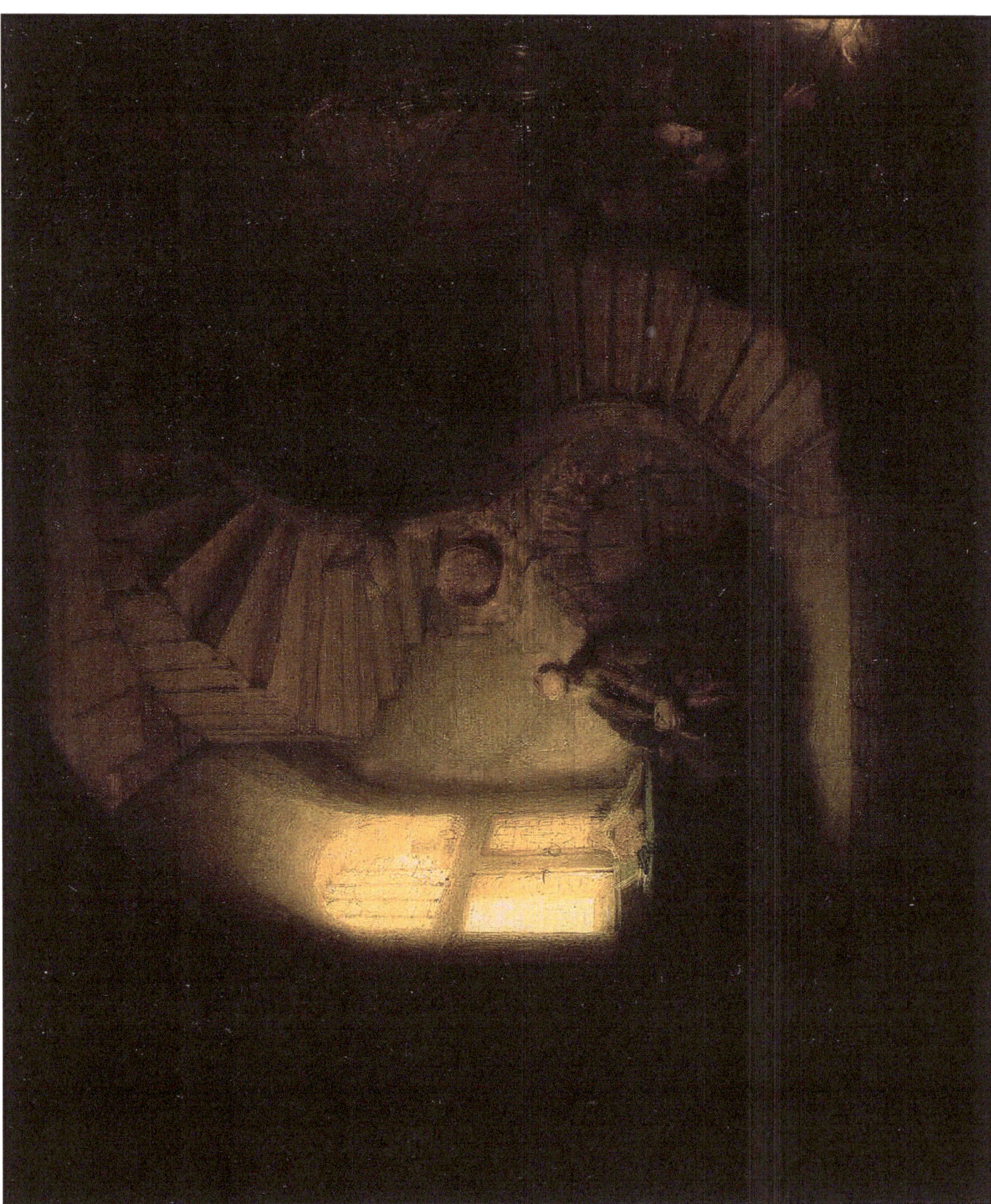

The Philosopher in Meditation

Rembrandt Harmenszoon van Rijn

Date of Creation: 1632.

Art Movement or Style: Baroque.

Medium and Technique: Oil on wood panel. The use of light coming from the window is an example of Rambrandt's mastery depicting light in his works..

Dimensions of the Painting: 28 cm × 34 cm (11 in × 13.4 in).

Current Location: The Louvre Museum in Paris, France.

Historical and Cultural Context
Rembrandt painted this work during the Dutch Golden Age, a period of great wealth, cultural achievement, and artistic production in the Netherlands. This was also a time when there was significant interest in science, philosophy, and the contemplation of the self.

Subject Matter and Themes
The painting depicts a solitary figure in a sunlit room with a winding staircase. It reflects themes of contemplation, wisdom, and perhaps the search for spiritual and philosophical truths. The figure is traditionally thought to be a philosopher due to the presence of books and the reflective pose.

Artistic Significance
Rembrandt's works are highly regarded for their emotional depth and realism, and this painting is a fine example of his ability to create a mood through the use of light and shadow. It is also significant as an example of his smaller, more intimate works.

Critical Reception and Interpretations
Rembrandt's paintings were well received in his time for their innovative approach to light and subject matter. *Philosopher in Meditation* has been subject to various interpretations, often focusing on its quiet and introspective quality and its representation of the contemplative life.

Visual Analysis:
The dramatic use of light and dark, with the warm sunlight streaming through the window, creates a striking contrast with the shadowy areas of the room. The circular staircase adds a geometric element and leads the viewer's eye into the depth of the space, while the figure is illuminated in such a way as to draw attention to his thoughtful pose. The composition and the use of light are carefully orchestrated to guide the viewer through the narrative of the painting.

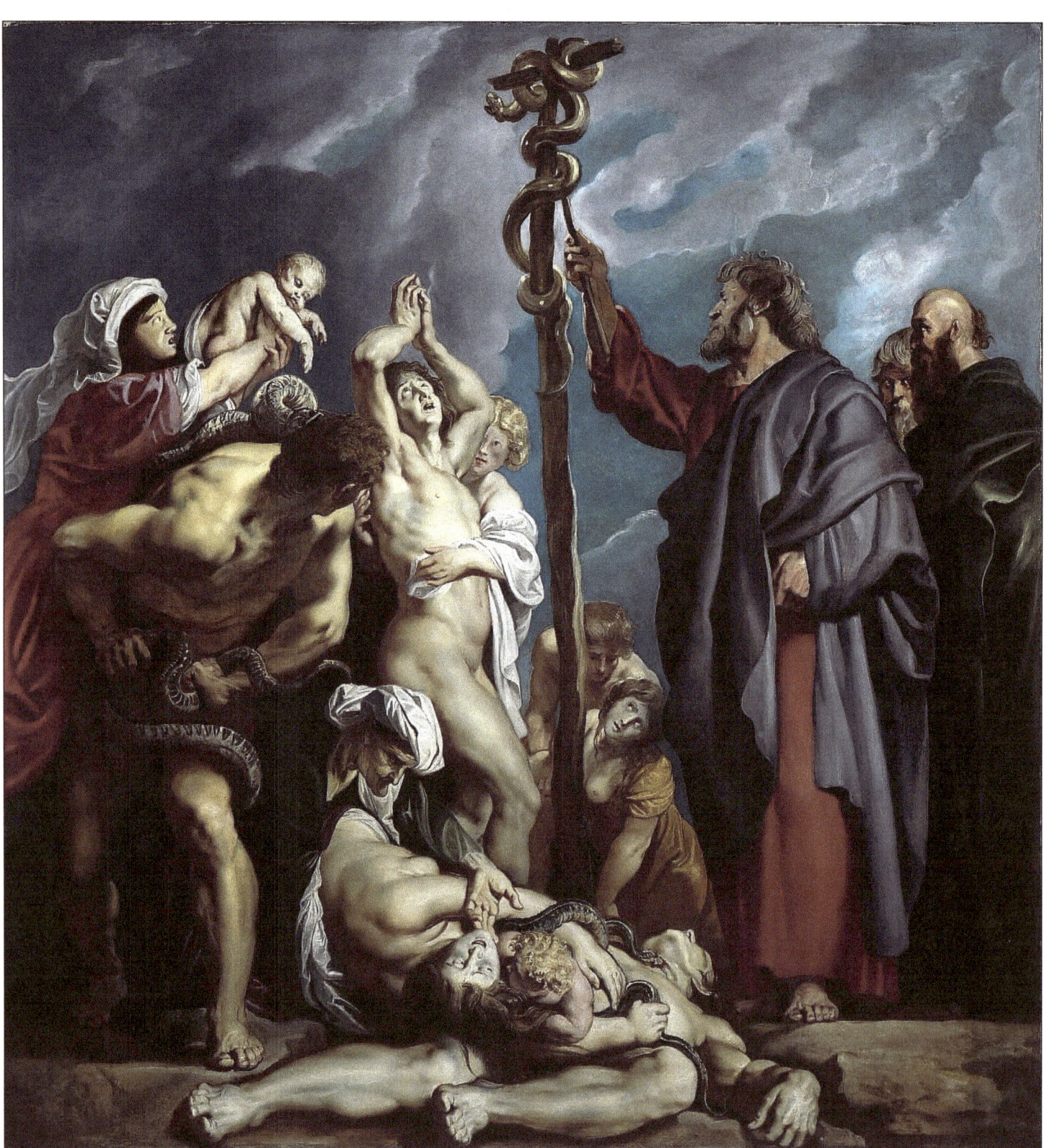

Moses and The Brazen Serpent

Peter Paul Rubens

Date of Creation: Between 1635 and 1640.

Art Movement or Style: Baroque.

Medium and Technique: Oil on canvas.

Dimensions of the Painting: 178 cm × 138 cm (70 in × 54 in).

Current Location: The Prado Museum, Madrid, Spain.

Historical and Cultural Context
The subject of the painting is from the Old Testament, Book of Numbers (21:4–9), where Moses is instructed to create a bronze serpent on a pole to cure the Israelites of snake bites. It reflects the religious fervor of the Counter-Reformation, during which the Catholic Church encouraged dramatic and emotional artwork that depicted biblical scenes.

Subject Matter and Themes
The painting depicts a biblical scene where the Israelites are being punished by venomous snakes. Moses, instructed by God, raises a bronze serpent on a pole, and those who gaze upon it are healed. Themes include salvation, divine intervention, and the power of faith.

Artistic Significance
Rubens' work is significant for its dynamic composition, dramatic use of light, and emotional intensity. It exemplifies the Baroque style, which is characterized by movement, vivid contrast, and a theatrical approach to painting.

Critical Reception and Interpretations
The work was likely commissioned as part of a series of paintings for a church, intended to teach and inspire the congregation. It has been praised for its powerful depiction of human suffering and divine mercy.

Visual Analysis
The painting is characterized by a strong diagonal composition, with the pole of the bronze serpent creating a vertical line that contrasts with the writhing bodies of the Israelites. Rubens uses light to highlight the central figures and the bronze serpent, guiding the viewer's gaze. The figures are painted with a strong sense of motion and emotion, which enhances the dramatic impact of the scene. The varied expressions of pain, hope, and relief on the faces of the Israelites convey the intensity of the narrative.

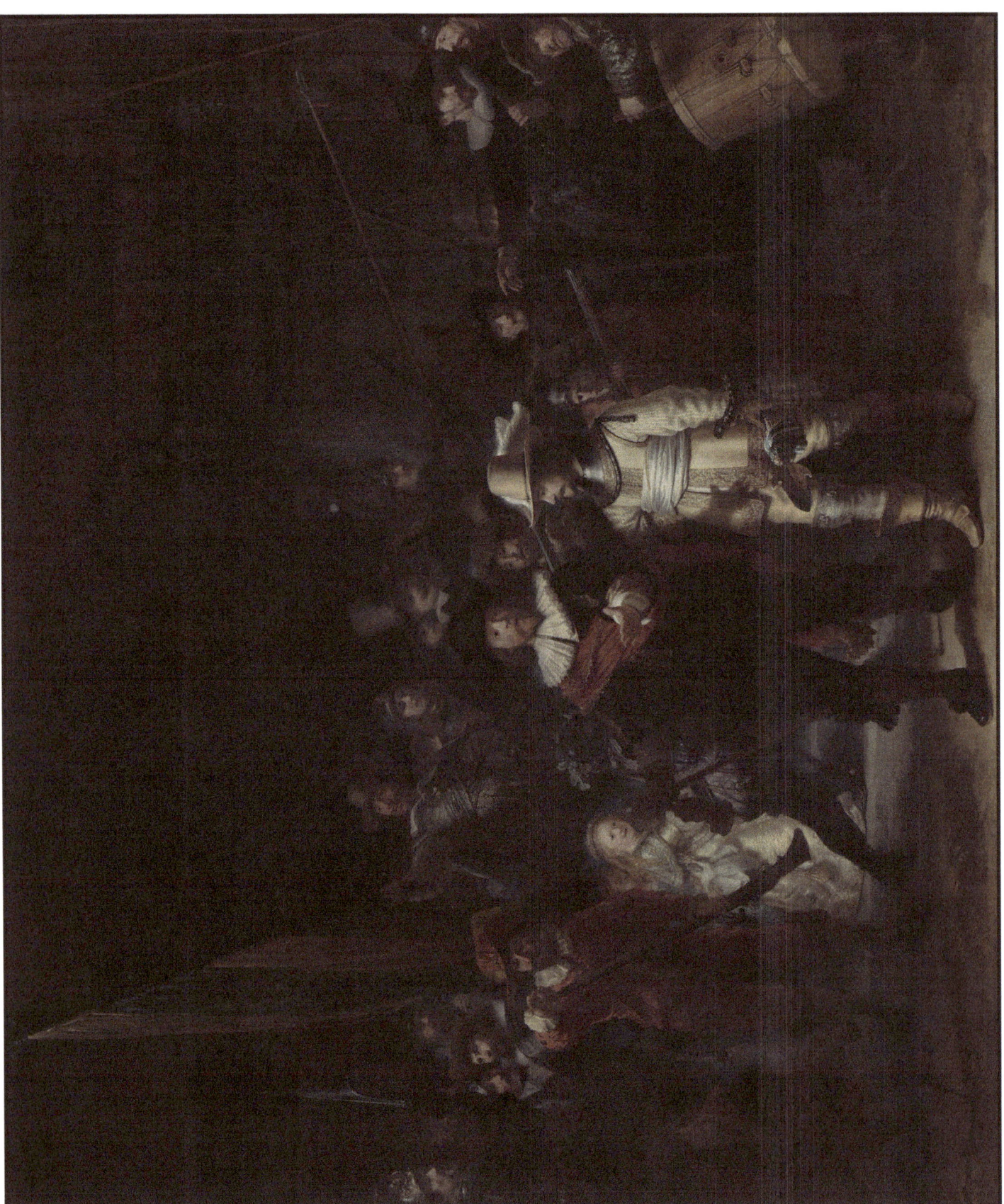

The Night Watch

Rembrandt Harmenszoon van Rijn

Date of Creation: 1642.

Art Movement or Style: Baroque.

Medium and Technique: Oil on canvas. The painting is known for its large scale and use of chiaroscuro - the dramatic use of light and shadow.

Dimensions of the Painting: Approximately 363 cm × 437 cm (143 in × 172 in), but it was later trimmed on all four sides.

Current Location: The Rijksmuseum in Amsterdam, Netherlands.

Historical and Cultural Context
The painting was commissioned by Captain Frans Banninck Cocq and seventeen members of his Kloveniers (civic militia guards). It depicts the company of militia as they are about to embark on a parade or a mission. This was during a time of great wealth and cultural achievement in the Netherlands.

Subject Matter and Themes
The Night Watch portrays a group of civic militia guards. It is notable for its size, the portrayal of motion in what would have traditionally been a static military group portrait, and the effective use of light and shadow to impart a sense of drama.

Artistic Significance
The Night Watch is one of Rembrandt's most famous works and a masterpiece of the Baroque period. It marked a departure from the traditional static militia portraits and is celebrated for its lively, and realistic portrayal of the guards.

Critical Reception and Interpretations
The painting was groundbreaking in its dynamic composition and its treatment of light and texture. It received mixed reactions initially because it broke so many conventions of traditional group portraiture. Interpretations have focused on its representation of civic pride and the complexity of its symbolism and narrative.

Visual Analysis
The Night Watch is a study in contrast and movement. The central figures of Captain Frans Banninck Cocq and Lieutenant Willem van Ruytenburch are illuminated, drawing the viewer's attention. The varied expressions and postures of the figures create a sense of immediacy and anticipation. Rembrandt's use of light not only highlights certain elements of the painting but also creates depth and volume, adding to the dramatic effect. The composition directs the viewer's eye throughout the painting, making it a dynamic and engaging work.

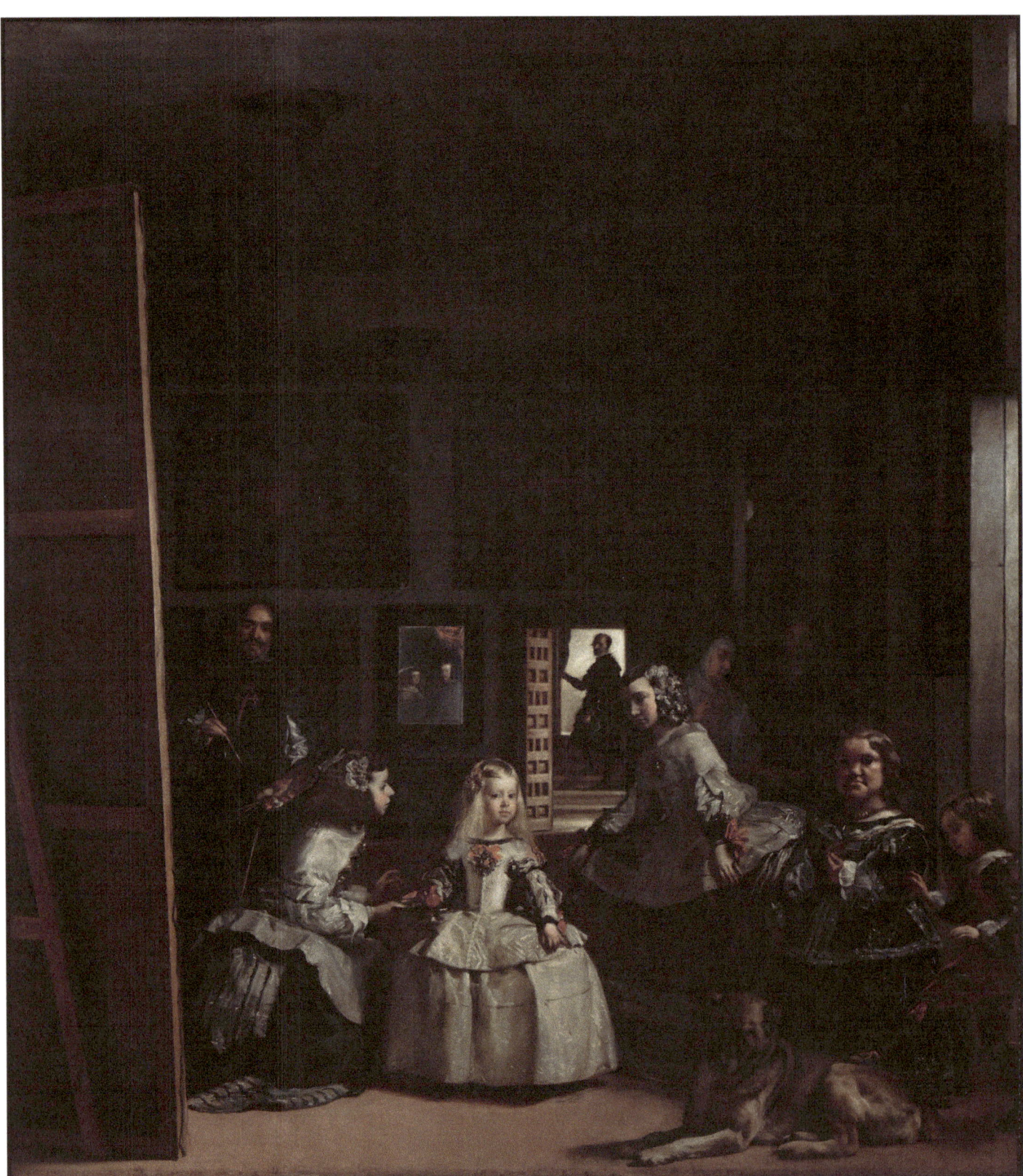

Las Meninas

Diego Velázquez

Date of Creation: 1656

Art Movement or Style: Baroque

Medium and Technique: Oil on canvas.

Dimensions of the Painting: 318 cm × 276 cm (125.2 in × 108.7 in).

Current Location: The Museo Nacional del Prado in Madrid, Spain.

Historical and Cultural Context

Las Meninas was painted during the reign of King Philip IV of Spain. It's a complex and enigmatic composition that raises questions about reality and illusion, and it portrays the young Infanta Margarita Teresa surrounded by her entourage of maids of honor, a dwarf, a dog, a mirror that reflects the King and Queen of Spain, and Velázquez himself. The painting captures a moment of daily life in the royal palace and is renowned for its use of perspective and light.

Subject Matter and Themes

The subject matter is a royal portrait featuring courtiers and the artist himself. Themes include the roles of the viewer and the artist and the nature of representation.

Artistic Significance

Las Meninas is celebrated for its complex and illusionistic depiction of life in the Spanish court, its masterful use of perspective and lighting, and its sophisticated commentary on the act of painting.

Critical Reception and Interpretations

Since its creation, *Las Meninas* has been analyzed and interpreted in countless ways. It has been read as a portrait, a self-portrait, a commentary on the Spanish monarchy, and an exploration of the nature of visual perception.

Visual Analysis

The painting is notable for its precise composition, the contrast of light and shadow, and the various gazes of the figures, which involve the viewer directly into the scene. Velázquez uses a naturalistic style to depict the figures, and the spatial arrangement of the room and the figures within it is complex, with each element carefully placed to create a balanced composition. The mirror at the back of the room adds a layer of depth and mystery, reflecting the image of the king and queen and challenging the viewer's perception.

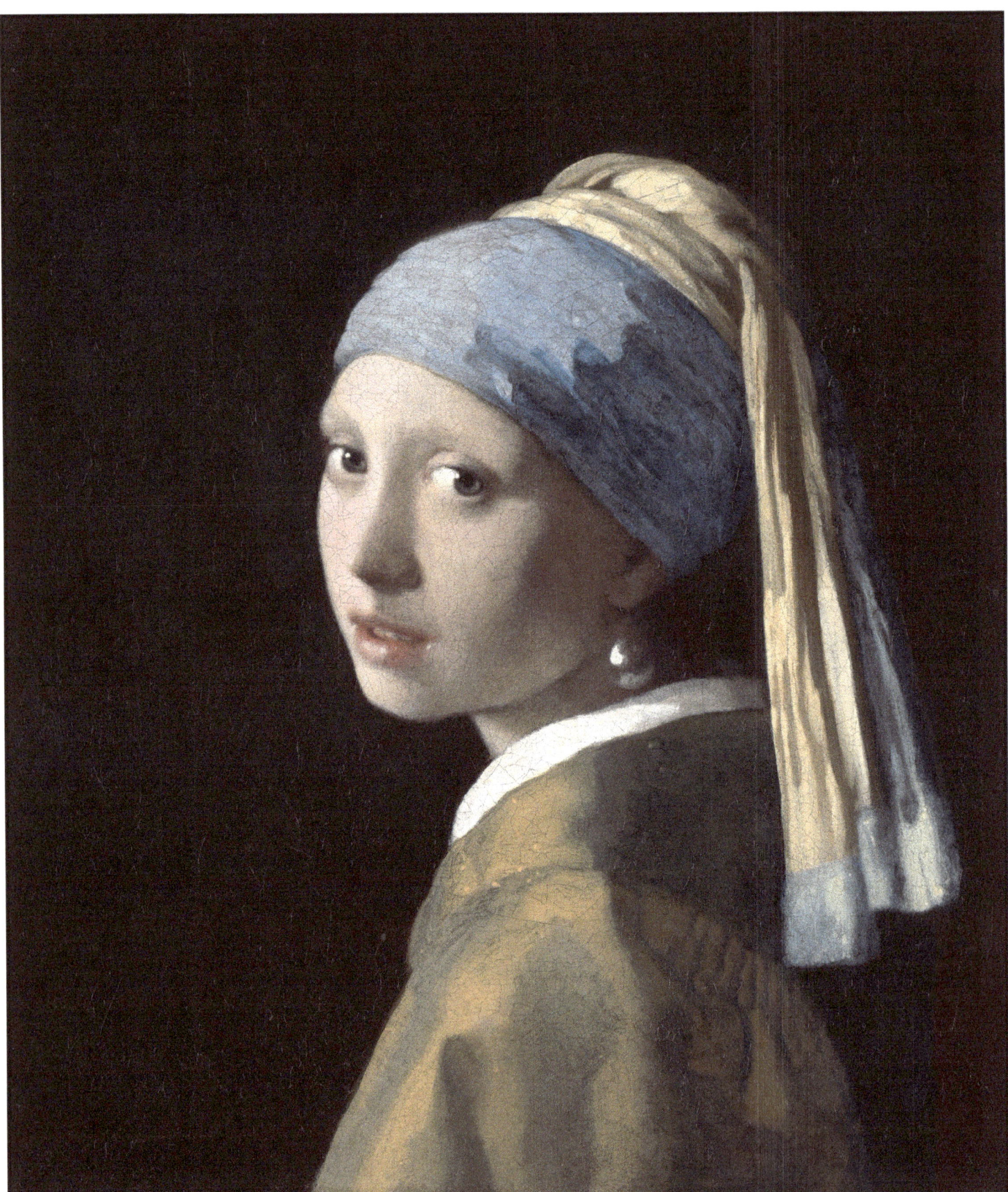

Girl with a Pearl Earring

Johannes Vermeer

Date of Creation: Circa 1665

Art Movement or Style: Baroque

Medium and Technique: Oil on canvas.

Dimensions of the Painting: 44.5 cm × 39 cm (17.5 in × 15 in).

Current Location: The Mauritshuis museum in The Hague, Netherlands.

Historical and Cultural Context

The painting is set against the backdrop of the Dutch Golden Age, a period of great wealth and cultural achievement in the Netherlands. The subject is thought to be a tronie, a study of a head meant to represent a certain character or type rather than an individual portrait.

Subject Matter and Themes

The painting features a young woman in exotic dress, an oriental turban, and an improbably large pearl earring. The theme revolves around beauty, innocence, and possibly curiosity, as the subject's gaze seems to capture a fleeting moment of engagement with the viewer.

Artistic Significance

"Girl with a Pearl Earring" is considered one of Vermeer's masterpieces and a prime example of his skill in using light and color to create softness and intimacy. It's sometimes referred to as the "Mona Lisa of the North."

Critical Reception and Interpretations

Over the years, the painting has been subject to various interpretations, with some seeing it as a portrait of exoticism and others as a depiction of a universal human expression. It has captured public imagination and has been the subject of books, films, and widespread scholarly attention.

Visual Analysis

The painting is known for its subtle use of light, particularly how it illuminates the girl's face and the pearl earring. Vermeer's technique creates a sense of realism and depth, with the soft focus suggesting movement and life. The dark background contrasts with the soft tones of the subject's skin and clothes, highlighting her figure and the earring.

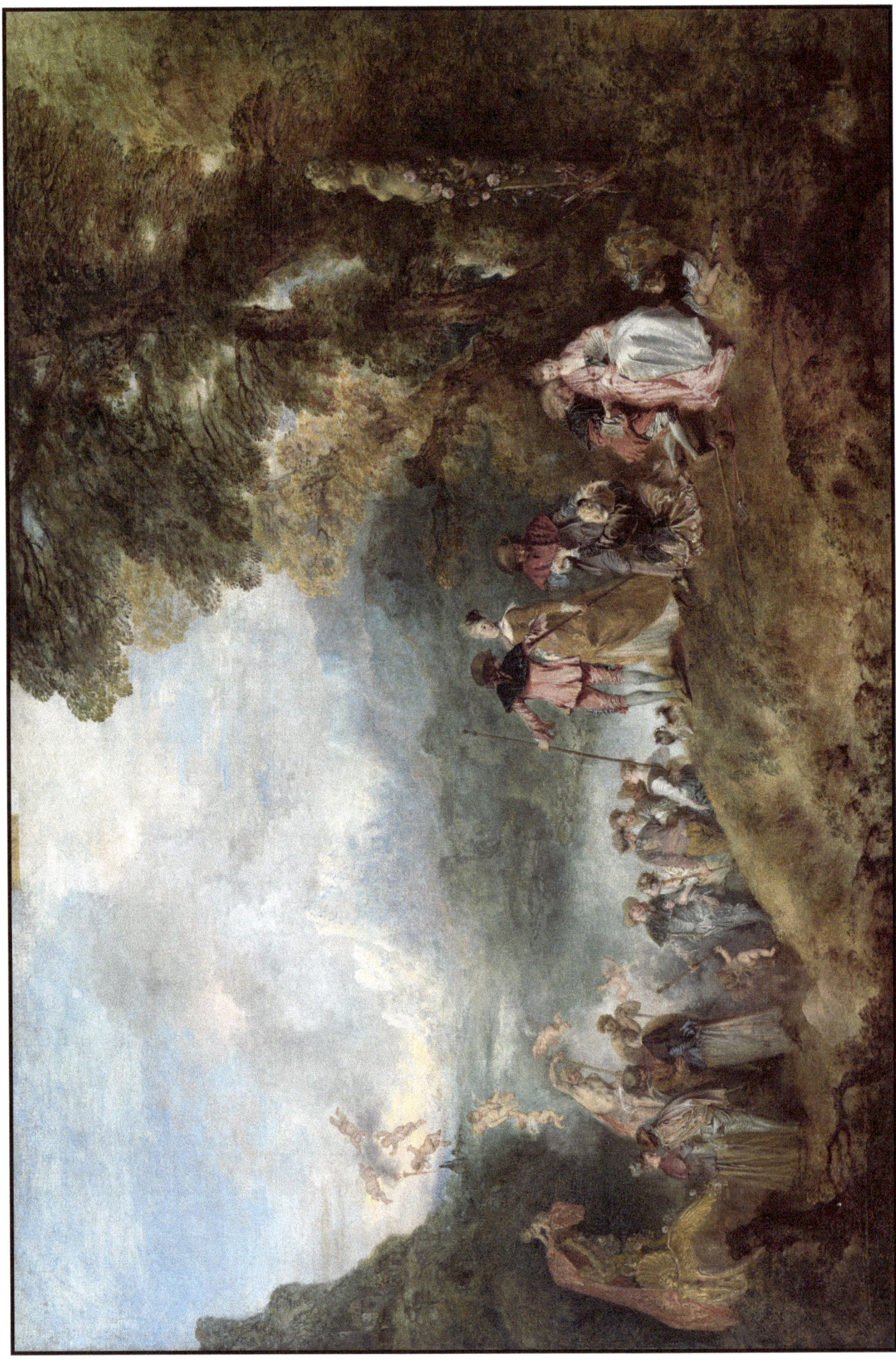

The Embarkation for Cythera

Jean-Antoine Watteau

Date of Creation: Circa 1717.

Art Movement or Style: Rococo.

Medium and Technique: Oil on canvas.

Dimensions of the Painting: 129 cm × 194 cm (51 in × 76 in).

Current Location: The Louvre Museum in Paris, France.

Historical and Cultural Context
Watteau painted this during the Rococo period, a time characterized by lightness, elegance, and an emphasis on frivolous, pastoral, and romantic themes. The painting was Watteau's reception piece for the Royal Academy of Painting and Sculpture in Paris.

Subject Matter and Themes
The subject of the painting is a mythical journey to the island of Cythera, the birthplace of Venus, the goddess of love. It reflects themes of love, romance, and idyllic pleasure.

Artistic Significance
The Embarkation for Cythera is considered a masterpiece of the Rococo era and is one of Watteau's most famous works. It is significant for its dreamlike quality and for its influence on the decorative arts and the genre of fête galante.

Critical Reception and Interpretations
The painting was well received for its poetic interpretation of an idyllic journey and is often interpreted as an allegory of love. Critics have praised its delicate color palette and the ephemeral quality of its light.

Visual Analysis
Watteau's use of soft brushwork and a pastel color palette contributes to the dreamy atmosphere. The composition is asymmetrical, with grouped figures that lead the viewer's eye through the painting in a diagonal movement, from the foreground to the ship in the distance. The figures are dressed in contemporary rather than classical attire, which, along with the lush landscape, enhances the fantastical and escapist quality of the scene. The painting is imbued with a sense of transience, capturing a fleeting moment of pleasure and beauty.

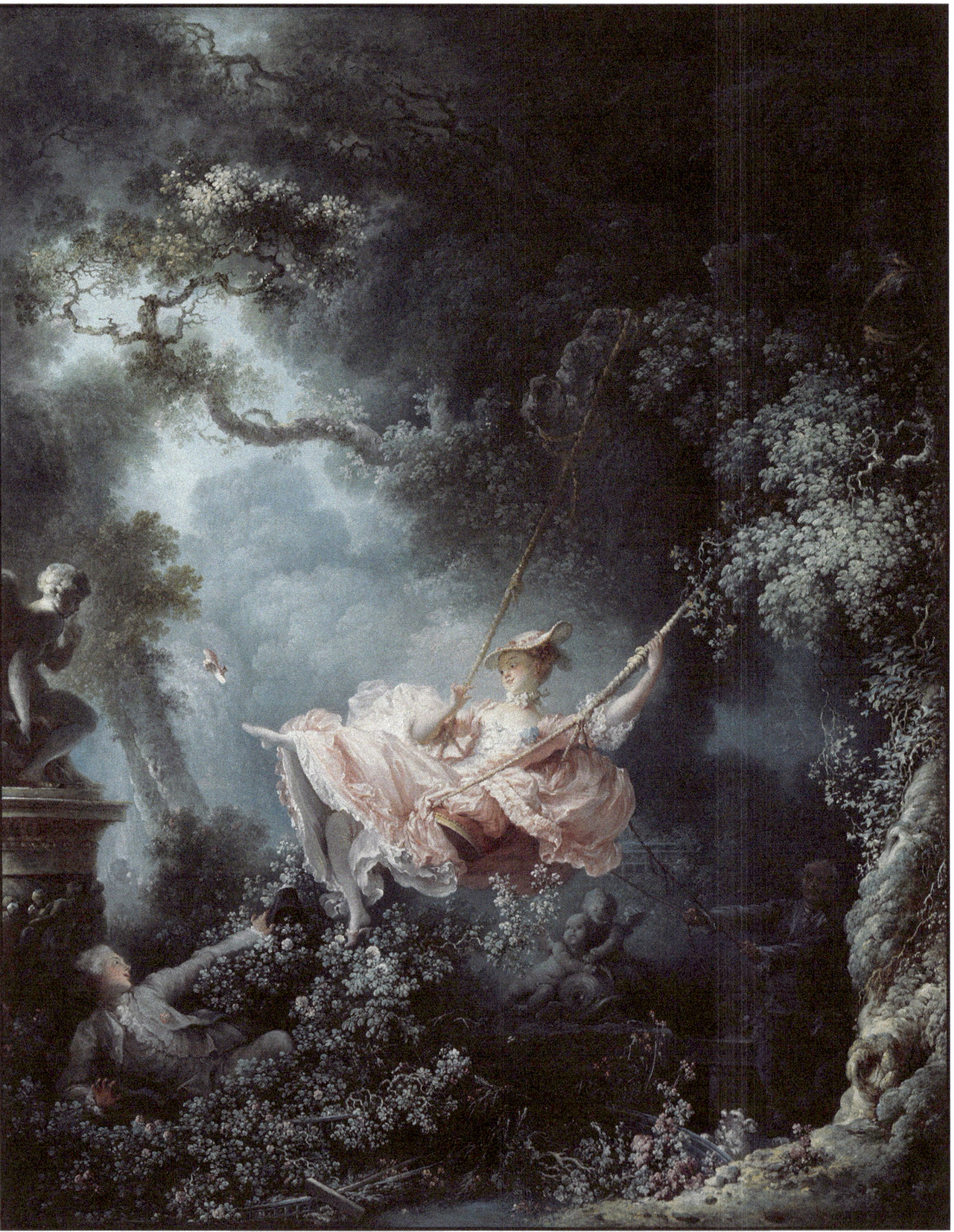

The Swing

Jean-Honoré Fragonard

Date of Creation: 1767.

Art Movement or Style: Rococo.

Medium and Technique: Oil on canvas. Painting is characterized by soft, pastel tones and playful, light-hearted themes.

Dimensions of the Painting: 81 cm × 64.2 cm (31.9 in × 25.3 in).

Current Location: The Wallace Collection, London, England.

Historical and Cultural Context

The Swing was painted during the Rococo period, a time associated with the aristocracy's indulgence in the arts, characterized by ornate decoration, pastel colors, and subjects of love and playfulness. It reflects the frivolity and the hedonistic spirit of the French court before the French Revolution.

Subject Matter and Themes

The Swing depicts a young woman on a swing, being pushed by an older man, while a younger man (hidden in the bushes) watches her from a vantage point that allows him to see up her skirt. Themes of romance, flirtation, and eroticism are prevalent in this painting.

Artistic Significance

The Swing is considered one of the quintessential works of the Rococo era and is celebrated for its light-hearted and erotic subject matter, its vibrant composition, and its exemplary use of color and light. Fragonard's work is significant for its contribution to the Rococo style, and it's often cited for its influence on later artists.

Critical Reception and Interpretations

The painting was well received in its time for its playful subject and masterful execution. It has been interpreted as a representation of the frivolity and the fleeting pleasures of the Rococo age.

Visual Analysis

The painting is characterized by its dynamic composition, with the diagonal line of the swing creating movement within the scene. The lush greenery, soft lighting, and the use of pastel colors contribute to the dreamlike quality of the painting. The flirtatious nature of the scene is enhanced by the young woman's carefree pose and the hidden voyeur, adding a sense of intrigue. The detailed rendering of the figures and the landscape, along with the light that filters through the trees, creates a scene that is both intimate and theatrical.

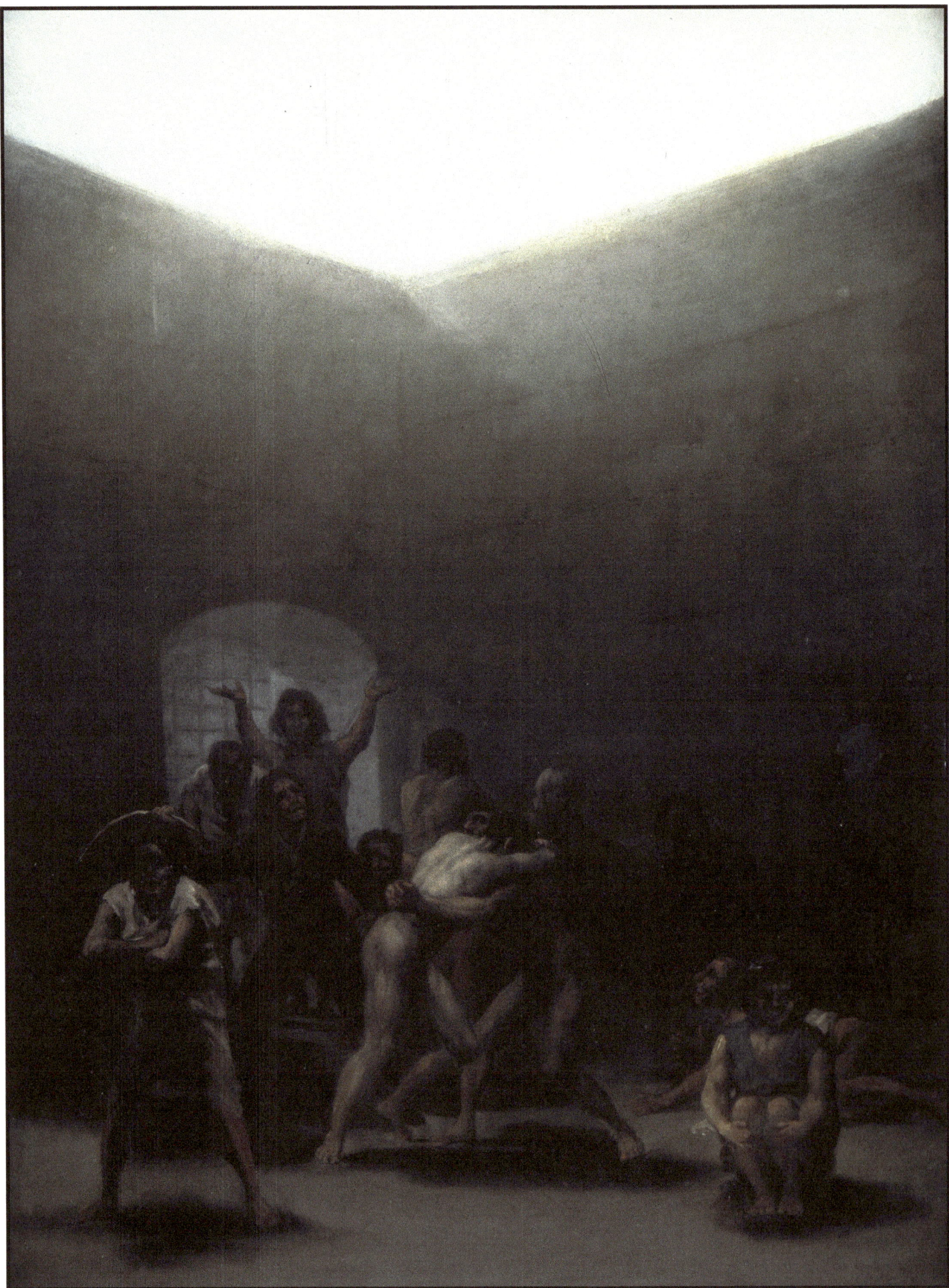

Yard with Lunatics (Corral de locos)

Francisco Goya

Date of Creation: Circa 1793–1794.

Art Movement or Style: Romanticism.

Medium and Technique: Oil on tinplate. Goya is known for his expressive brushwork and bold handling of paint.

Dimensions of the Painting: Approximately 43.8 cm × 32.7 cm (17.24 in × 12.87 in).

Current Location: The Meadows Museum, SMU, Dallas, Texas, United States.

Historical and Cultural Context
Goya created this work after a severe illness that left him deaf. This period marked a change in his artistic style, becoming darker and more concerned with themes of madness, the unconscious, and the grotesque.

Subject Matter and Themes
The painting depicts inmates in an asylum, engaging in violent or listless behavior. It reflects the period's attitudes towards mental illness and the inhumane conditions often found in asylums. Themes include human suffering, isolation, and the dark side of the human psyche.

Artistic Significance
Yard with Lunatics is an early example of Goya's dark, introspective works that prefigure his later "Black Paintings". It is significant for its unflinching portrayal of the human condition and is considered a precursor to modern expressionism.

Critical Reception and Interpretations
In Goya's time, the painting would have been seen as a social commentary on the treatment of the mentally ill. It has been subject to various interpretations, often revolving around the themes of the irrationality of the human mind and the cruelty inherent in society.

Visual Analysis
The composition is closed and claustrophobic, with the figures hemmed in by high walls. The lack of a clear light source and the murky atmosphere add to the sense of entrapment and despair. The figures are rendered with a sense of movement and emotional intensity, which serves to convey a sense of their inner turmoil. The limited color palette and the use of shadow contribute to the oppressive atmosphere of the scene.

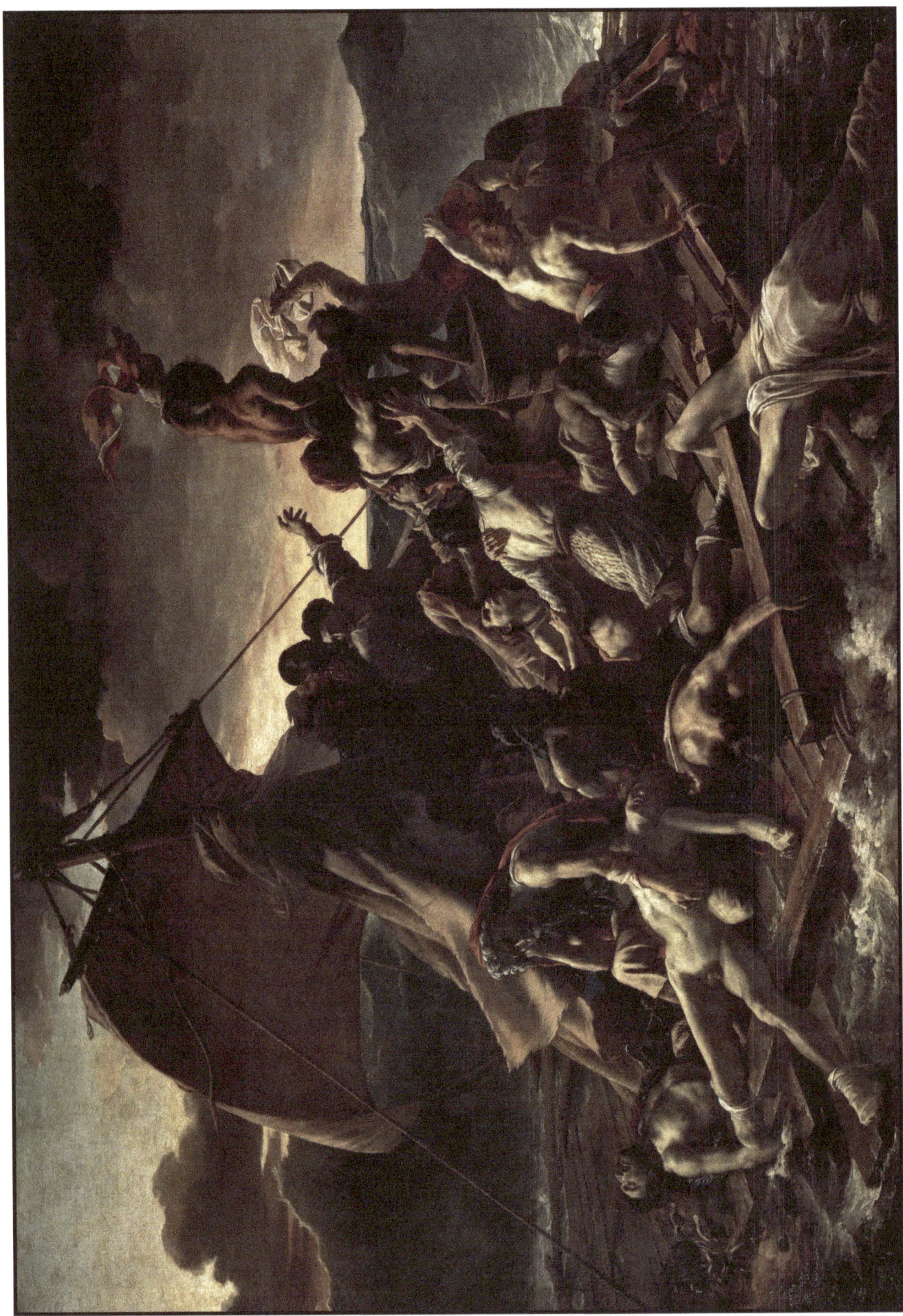

The Raft of the Medusa

Théodore Géricault

Date of Creation: 1818–1819

Art Movement or Style: Romanticism.

Medium and Technique: Oil on canvas. The painting is characterized by its dramatic and emotive qualities, often emphasizing the dynamic and the sublime.

Dimensions of the Painting: 491 cm × 716 cm (193.3 in × 282.3 in).

Current Location: The Louvre Museum in Paris, France.

Historical and Cultural Context
The painting was inspired by the tragedy of the Medusa, a French naval frigate that ran aground off the coast of Mauritania in 1816. The event became an international scandal due to the incompetence shown by the French captain, who was a political appointee. Many of the ship's passengers were left to die on a makeshift raft.

Subject Matter and Themes
The painting depicts the aftermath of the wreck of the Medusa. The central themes are human suffering, heroism in the face of despair, and the struggle for survival. It also carries political undertones, as the disaster was partly blamed on the incompetence of the French monarchy's restoration government.

Artistic Significance
The Raft of the Medusa is considered an iconic work of French Romanticism and is one of Géricault's most important works. It represents a break from the traditional themes of the time and is noted for its raw emotion and stark portrayal of human desperation.

Critical Reception and Interpretations
Upon its exhibition, the painting caused a sensation and was both praised and condemned for its daring subject matter and its unflinching depiction of suffering and death. It has been interpreted as an indictment of the government and as a metaphor for human endurance.

Visual Analysis
The painting is remarkable for its use of light, which illuminates the figures from the left, creating stark contrasts and highlighting the expressions of agony and hope on the survivors' faces. The composition forms a diagonal from the lower left with dead and dying figures, leading up to the animated figures at the top right, frantically signaling to a ship on the horizon. The tumultuous sea and stormy skies add to the dramatic intensity of the scene. The physicality and emotion of the figures are rendered with intense realism, drawing the viewer into the narrative.

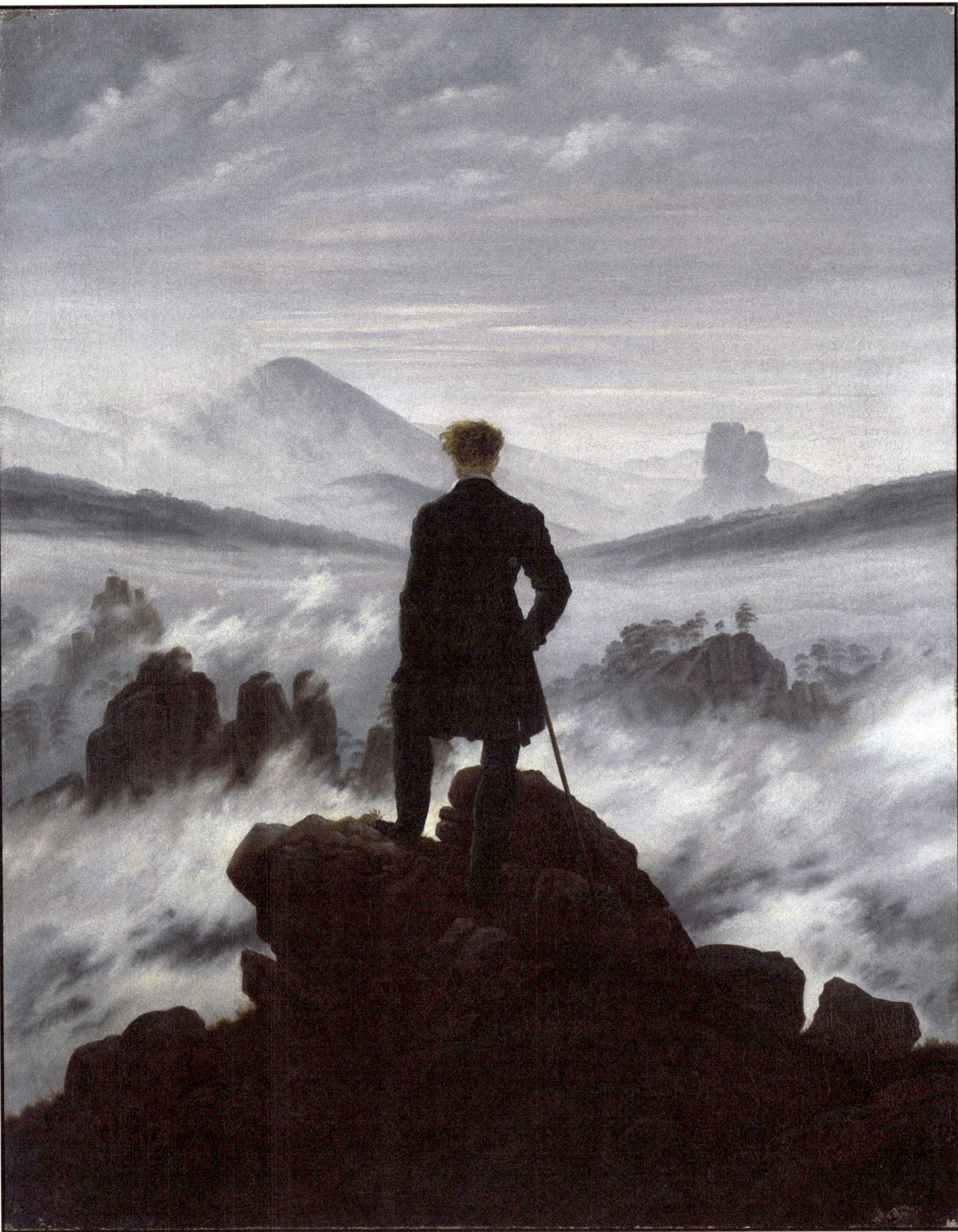

Wanderer Above the Sea of Fog

Caspar David Friedrich

Date of Creation: Circa 1818.

Art Movement or Style: Romanticism.

Medium and Technique: Oil on canvas. Friedrich is known for his allegorical landscapes, which typically feature contemplative figures silhouetted against night skies, morning mists, barren trees, or Gothic ruins.

Dimensions of the Painting: 94.8 cm × 74.8 cm (37.3 in × 29.4 in).

Current Location: The Kunsthalle Hamburg, in Hamburg, Germany.

Historical and Cultural Context
The work was created during a period where there was a growing appreciation for the sublime in nature — that is, an appreciation for the awe-inspiring and the majestic that is beyond human comprehension. It reflects the Romantic interest in the individual's experience of the natural world.

Subject Matter and Themes
The painting shows a solitary figure standing atop a mountain, gazing out over a misty landscape. It represents the Romantic theme of the sublime, depicting the grandeur and beauty of nature, and the individual's contemplation of it. It also explores themes of exploration, the unknown, and the individual's relationship with the natural world.

Artistic Significance
Wanderer Above the Sea of Fog is one of Friedrich's most notable works and is a defining image of the Romantic era. It encapsulates key Romantic ideals, such as the emotional response to nature and the notion that the natural world is a source of spiritual renewal.

Critical Reception and Interpretations
Friedrich's work was not fully appreciated during his lifetime, but *Wanderer Above the Sea of Fog* has come to be celebrated for its evocative portrayal of the sublime in nature. It has been interpreted as a metaphor for the introspective search for meaning in the face of the vastness of nature and the world.

Visual Analysis
The figure's back is turned to the viewer, which invites the audience to share in the experience of the sublime view. The mist and rugged terrain create a sense of the unknown, with the figure acting as an intermediary between the viewer and the landscape. The use of light and shadow, along with the mist, gives the painting a mysterious quality. The figure's stance and the craggy peaks reaching out of the fog convey both the majesty and the danger inherent in nature.

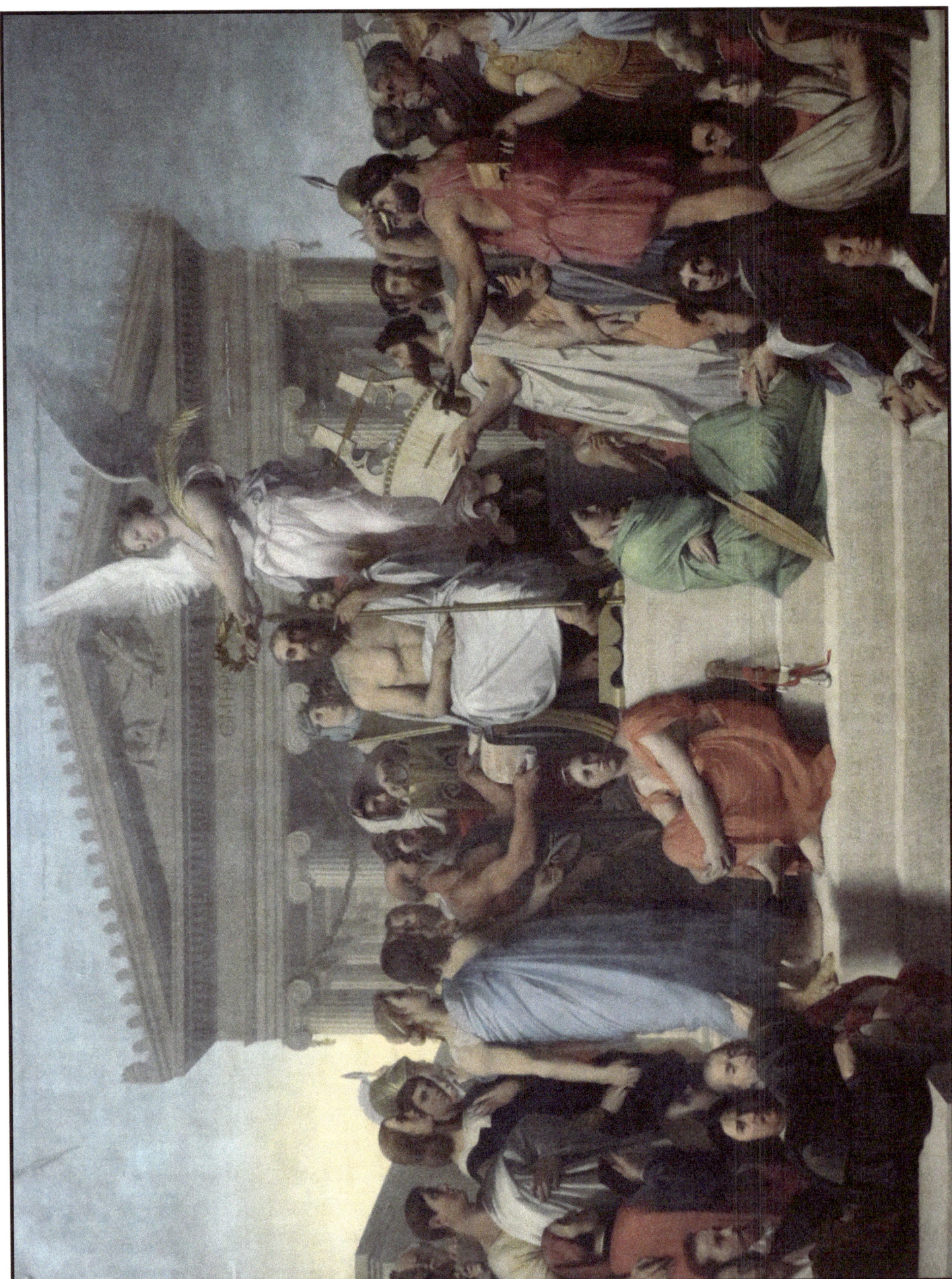

The Apotheosis of Homer

Jean-Auguste-Dominique Ingres

Date of Creation: Circa 1827.

Art Movement or Style: Neoclassicism.

Medium and Technique: Oil on canvas.

Dimensions of the Painting: 386 cm × 512 cm (152 in × 202 in).

Current Location: The Louvre Museum in Paris, France.

Historical and Cultural Context
The painting was a commission by Charles X to decorate the ceiling of the Louvre Museum. It honors the Greek poet Homer and reflects the Neoclassical interest in classical antiquity. It depicts an assembly of great artists and thinkers of the past paying homage to Homer, who is being crowned by the personification of the Iliad and the Odyssey.

Subject Matter and Themes
The subject is the glorification of the poet Homer, who is central in the composition. The themes include the celebration of classical wisdom, the arts, and the transcendental nature of true genius.

Artistic Significance
The Apotheosis of Homer is considered a masterpiece of Neoclassicism, showcasing Ingres's precision and clarity in form and his reverence for classical tradition. It reflects the values of the time, where great importance was placed on the ideas of the Enlightenment and the cultural achievements of classical antiquity.

Critical Reception and Interpretations
The painting was well received in its time and continues to be celebrated for its grandeur and composition. It has been interpreted as a statement on the enduring nature of artistic and intellectual achievements across time.

Visual Analysis
The painting is structured with Homer at the center, symbolically elevated above the other figures, suggesting his importance and eternal legacy. The assembly of figures around him includes both mythological characters and historical intellectuals, each carefully posed in a manner reflecting their character and significance. The clear, crisp lines and balanced composition are typical of the Neoclassical style, and the use of light serves to highlight Homer and the allegorical figures crowning him.

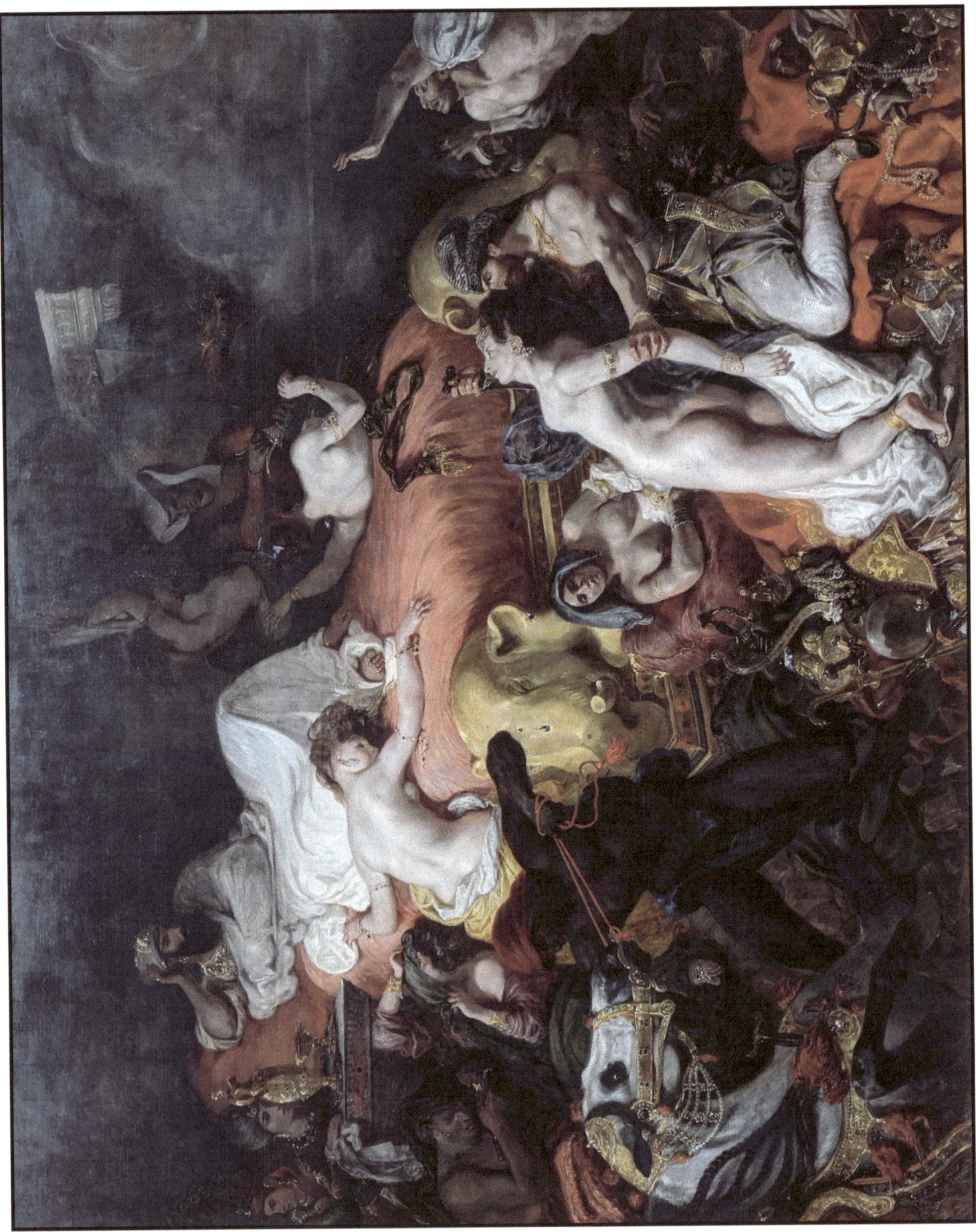

The Death of Sardanapalus

Eugène Delacroix

Date of Creation: Circa 1827.

Art Movement or Style: Romanticism.

Medium and Technique: Oil on canvas.

Dimensions of the Painting: 392 cm × 496 cm (154 in × 195 in).

Current Location: The Louvre Museum in Paris, France.

Historical and Cultural Context

Delacroix's painting is based on the play *Sardanapalus* by Lord Byron, which itself was inspired by the historical account of the Assyrian king's last hours. In the 19th century, there was a fascination with the exotic and the dramatic, which this painting epitomizes.

Subject Matter and Themes

The subject is the legendary last king of Assyria, Sardanapalus, who, facing defeat, orders the destruction of his possessions, including his slaves and concubines. Themes include the transience of life and power, the excesses of decadence, and the destructive nature of despotic rule.

Artistic Significance

The painting is significant as a masterpiece of Romantic art, demonstrating the movement's characteristic emphasis on drama, emotion, and color. Delacroix's work is known for its dynamic compositions and vibrant use of paint, which influenced future generations of artists.

Critical Reception and Interpretations

Upon its unveiling, the painting elicited mixed reactions due to its controversial subject matter and bold execution. It has been interpreted as a statement on the futility of violence and the fall of empires, as well as an exploration of the human capacity for self-destruction.

Visual Analysis

The painting is notable for its chaotic composition, with figures in various states of distress and the rich, vibrant colors emphasizing the drama of the scene. The central figure of Sardanapalus is depicted with a languid pose, contrasting with the violent actions around him. Delacroix's use of light and shadow enhances the theatrical and tragic atmosphere of the scene. The sprawling composition, replete with details of opulence and destruction, creates an overwhelming sense of finality and doom.

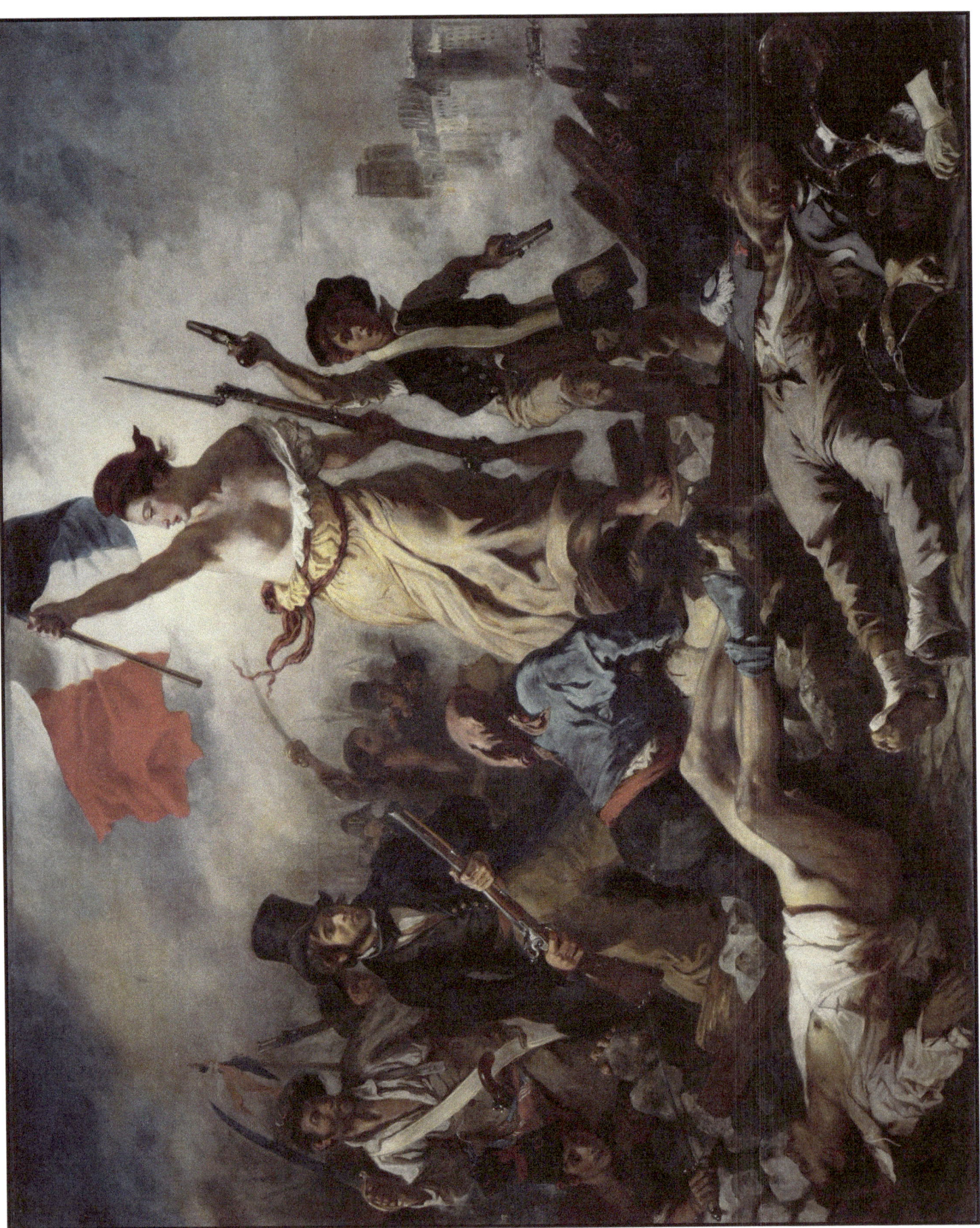

Liberty Leading the People

Eugène Delacroix

Date of Creation: Circa 1830.

Art Movement or Style: Romanticism.

Medium and Technique: Oil on canvas.

Dimensions of the Painting: 260 cm × 325 cm (102.4 in × 128.0 in).

Current Location: The Louvre Museum in Paris, France.

Historical and Cultural Context

The painting commemorates the July Revolution of 1830 in France, which toppled King Charles X. Delacroix has depicted Liberty as both a real and allegorical figure leading the people forward over the bodies of the fallen, holding the flag of the French Revolution - the tricolor flag which is still France's flag today.

Subject Matter and Themes

The subject is a mixture of contemporary history and allegory, capturing the spirit of the revolution. Themes include liberty, the struggle for freedom, and the power of the people.

Artistic Significance

Liberty Leading the People is considered one of the defining works of Romanticism, capturing the emotion and fervor of the revolutionary spirit. It is also significant for its influence on later art and political imagery.

Critical Reception and Interpretations

The painting has been a symbol of republican values and revolutionary fervor. It received mixed reactions for its political content but was eventually bought by the French government.

Visual Analysis

The work is characterized by its dramatic composition, the movement of the figures, and the use of light to highlight the central figure of Liberty. The color palette is both realistic and symbolic, with the red, white, and blue of the French flag standing out against the more muted tones of the background and the figures. The faces of the people reflect a range of emotions, from determination to anguish, adding to the painting's emotional impact.

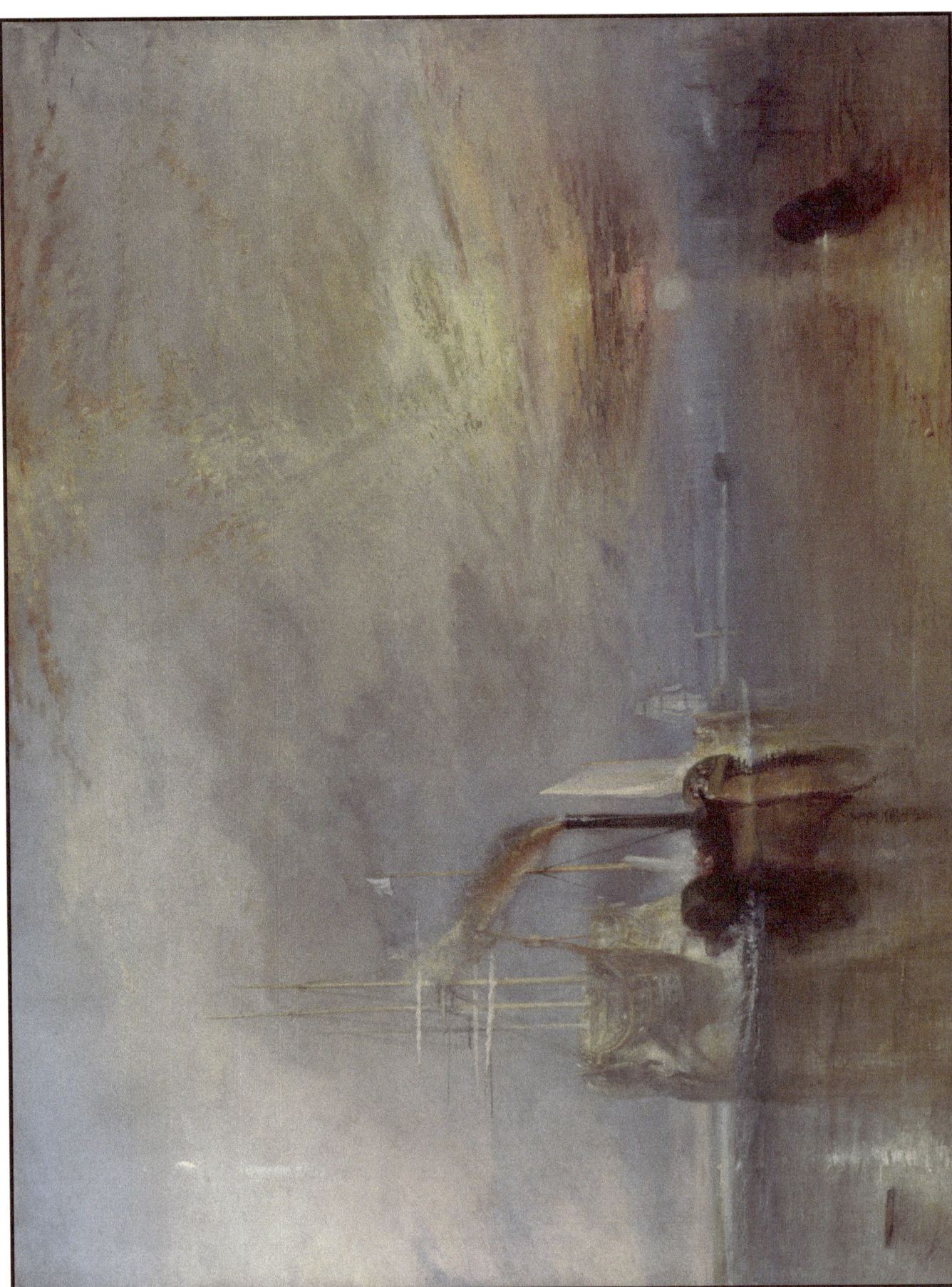

The Fighting Temeraire Tugged to Her Last Berth to be Broken Up , 1938

Joseph Mallord William Turner

Date of Creation: 1839.

Art Movement or Style: Romanticism.

Medium and Technique: Oil on canvas.

Dimensions of the Painting: 90.7 cm × 121.6 cm (35.7 in × 47.9 in).

Current Location: The National Gallery's collection in London, United Kingdom

Historical and Cultural Context

The HMS Temeraire was a famous warship that played a distinguished role in the Battle of Trafalgar. Turner's painting captures the ship's final journey to the breaker's yard, symbolizing the end of an era with the advent of steam-powered vessels.

Subject Matter and Themes

The painting depicts the majestic warship being towed by a steam-powered tugboat. It is often interpreted as a meditation on the passage of time and the transition from the age of sail to the industrial age.

Artistic Significance

The Fighting Temeraire is one of Turner's most celebrated works, exemplifying his mastery of light and atmospheric effect. It showcases his innovative technique and his ability to evoke emotion and narrative through landscape.

Critical Reception and Interpretations

The painting was lauded for its poignant beauty and its complex interplay of progress and loss. It has been seen as a powerful statement about the costs of industrialization and change.

Visual Analysis

Turner's use of light and color is particularly noteworthy in this painting. The setting sun casts a warm glow over the scene, reflecting off the water and the ship's masts, contrasting with the cool tones of the surrounding sky and the sea. The steam tugboat, darker and less detailed, symbolizes the new industrial era, while the grandeur of the Temeraire is both celebrated and mourned. The painting is characterized by Turner's loose brushwork, which gives the work a sense of movement and fluidity.

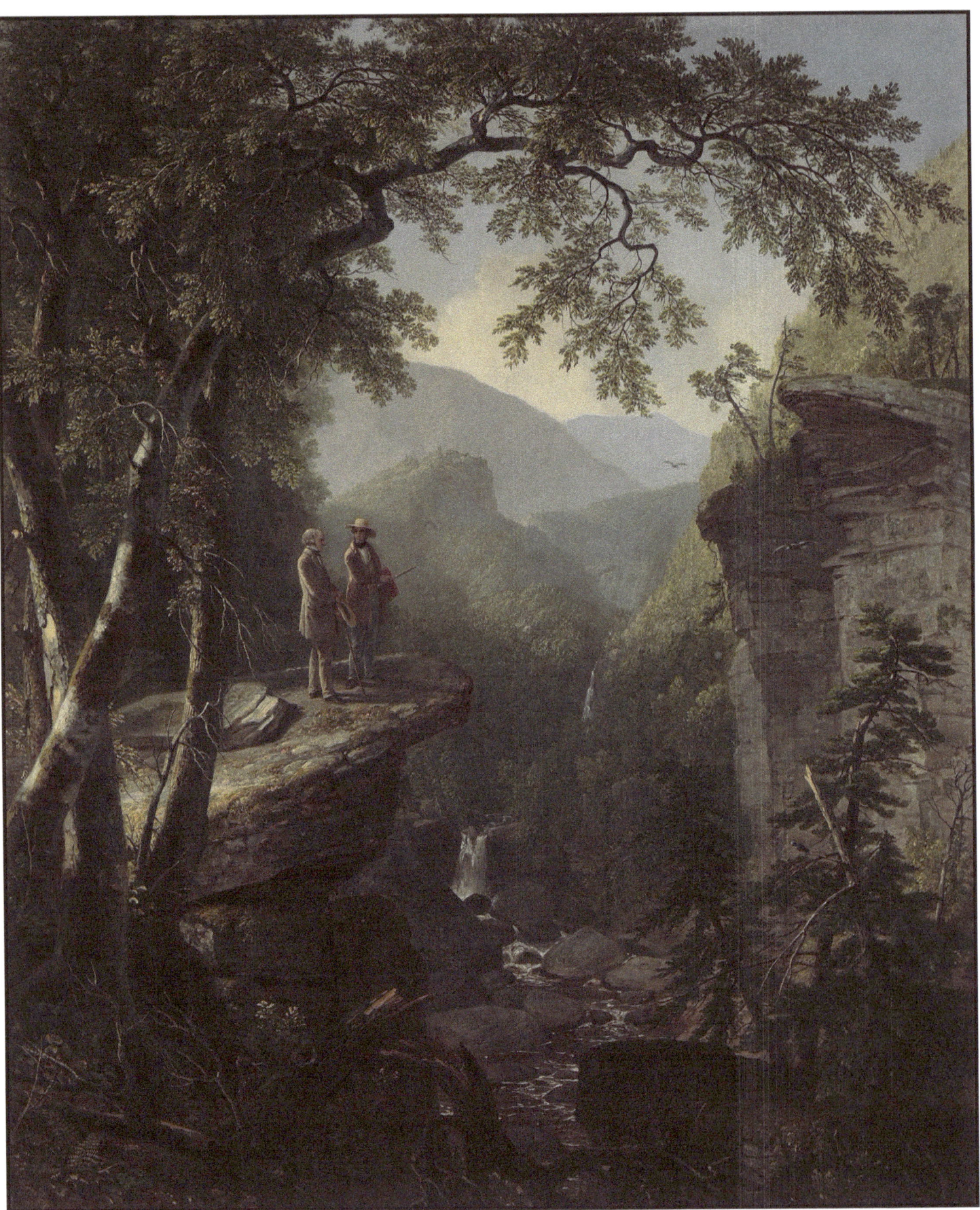

Kindred Spirits

Asher B. Durand

Date of Creation: 1849.

Art Movement or Style: Hudson River School

Medium and Technique: Oil on canvas.

Dimensions of the Painting: 44 in × 36 in (110 cm × 91 cm).

Current Location: The Crystal Bridges Museum of American Art in Bentonville, Arkansas, USA.

Historical and Cultural Context
Kindred Spirits was painted in honor of Thomas Cole, the founder of the Hudson River School, following his death in 1848. The painting reflects the American Romantic landscape movement and embodies the themes of wilderness, the sublime in nature, and the American identity.

Subject Matter and Themes
The painting depicts Thomas Cole and his friend, the poet William Cullen Bryant, in a vast American wilderness. It reflects the themes of companionship, the appreciation of nature, and the idea of the landscape as a divine creation.

Artistic Significance
Kindred Spirits is one of Durand's most famous works and is considered an iconic piece of American art. It symbolizes the ethos of the Hudson River School, which celebrated the beauty and spirituality of the American landscape.

Critical Reception and Interpretations
The painting was well-received for its detail, composition, and emotional depth. It has been interpreted as a spiritual and philosophical reflection on humanity's relationship with nature, as well as a eulogy to Thomas Cole.

Visual Analysis
The painting is marked by its detailed portrayal of the natural world, with lush vegetation, rugged terrain, and a distant waterfall. The figures of Cole and Bryant are dwarfed by the grandeur of the landscape, emphasizing the Romantic ideal of the sublime—the awe-inspiring power and beauty of nature. The use of light and shadow creates a serene yet dynamic environment, inviting contemplation and reverence for the natural world.

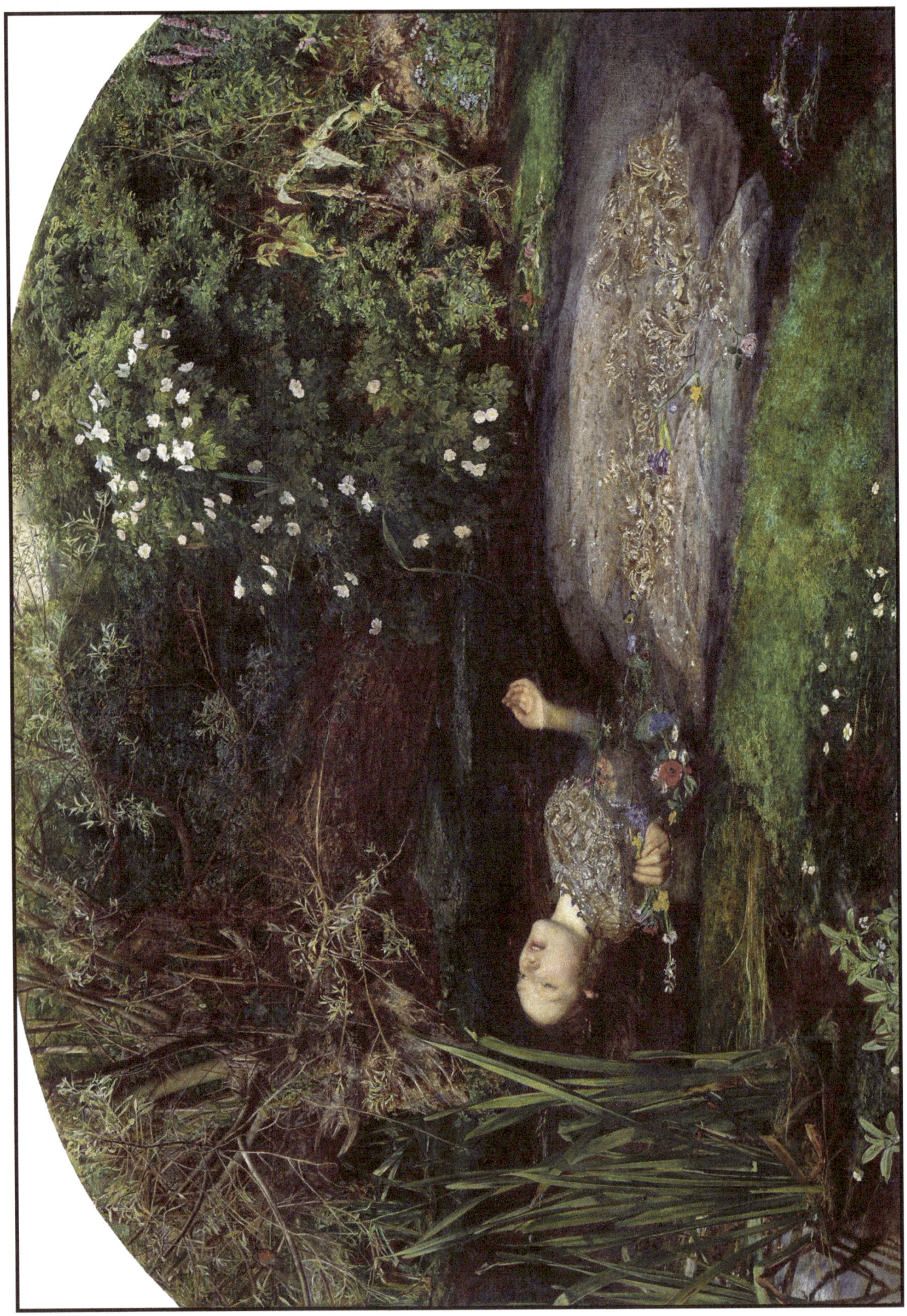

Ophelia

John Everett Millais

Date of Creation: 1851–1852.

Art Movement or Style: Pre-Raphaelite Brotherhood

Medium and Technique: Oil on canvas.

Dimensions of the Painting: 76.2 cm × 111.8 cm (30.0 in × 44.0 in).

Current Location: The Tate Britain gallery in London, England.

Historical and Cultural Context

Ophelia was painted during the Victorian era, a period which often romanticized death and held a deep fascination with Shakespearean themes. The Pre-Raphaelite Brotherhood, to which Millais belonged, was known for its vivid colors, attention to detail, and complex compositions, often with themes of romance, beauty, and nature.

Subject Matter and Themes

The painting depicts Ophelia, a character from Shakespeare's *Hamlet*, in the moments before her death as she floats in a stream, surrounded by nature. Themes include nature, beauty, tragedy, and the romanticized portrayal of death.

Artistic Significance

Ophelia is considered one of the iconic works of the Pre-Raphaelite movement and is celebrated for its beauty and its faithful rendition of natural details, which Millais painted from life.

Critical Reception and Interpretations

Since its creation, *Ophelia* has been subject to various interpretations. It has been seen as a depiction of tragic beauty and as a commentary on the role of women in society and in literature, reflecting the Victorian fascination with death and the idealization of female suffering.

Visual Analysis

The painting is notable for its rich detail and lush colors, creating a lifelike and immersive scene. Millais meticulously painted the flora and fauna around Ophelia, each plant chosen for its symbolic reference to Shakespeare's play. Ophelia herself is rendered with a poignant beauty, capturing both her serenity and the sadness of her fate. The water in which she floats reflects the sky, adding a sense of depth and tranquility to the scene.

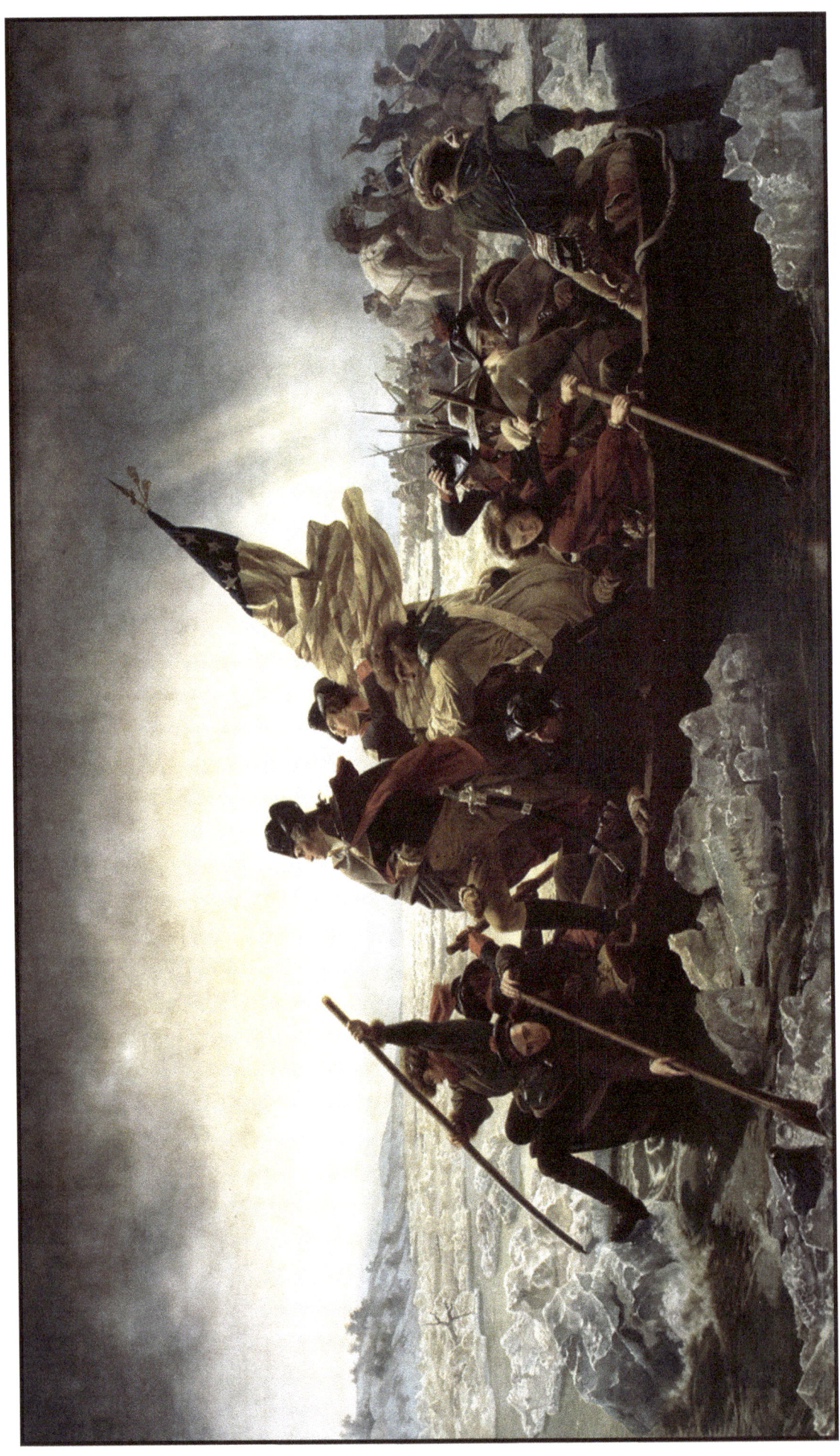

Washington Crossing the Delaware

Emanuel Leutze

Date of Creation: 1851

Art Movement or Style: Romanticism.

.

Medium and Technique: Oil on canvas. Leutze used dramatic lighting and strong gestures to convey the heroism and determination of the scene.

Dimensions of the Painting: 378.5 cm × 647.7 cm (149 in × 255 1/8 in).

Current Location: The Metropolitan Museum of Art in New York, New York, USA.

Historical and Cultural Context

Leutze painted this iconic image in the mid-19th century, a time when the United States was looking back at its Revolutionary War history with a sense of nationalism and pride. It was painted in Düsseldorf, Germany, and was intended to encourage Europe's liberal reformers through the example of the American Revolution.

Subject Matter and Themes

The painting depicts General George Washington's famous crossing of the Delaware River during the American Revolutionary War on the night of December 25–26, 1776. Themes include courage, leadership, and the fight for freedom.

Artistic Significance

Washington Crossing the Delaware is one of the most famous American history paintings and is emblematic of the Romantic period's style. It has been reproduced countless times and remains a significant piece of American patriotic iconography.

Critical Reception and Interpretations

The painting was well received for its grand scale and its emotional portrayal of a pivotal moment in American history. It has been interpreted as a symbol of American perseverance and heroism.

Visual Analysis

The painting is noted for its dramatic use of light, which focuses on Washington standing firmly at the helm. The ice-filled water and the struggling figures manning the boats create a sense of the struggle and the epic nature of the event. The composition, with the flag billowing and the boats pointing toward victory on the horizon, adds to the narrative of overcoming adversity. The figures are idealized and heroic, which was typical of the Romantic style and aimed to inspire and uplift the viewer.

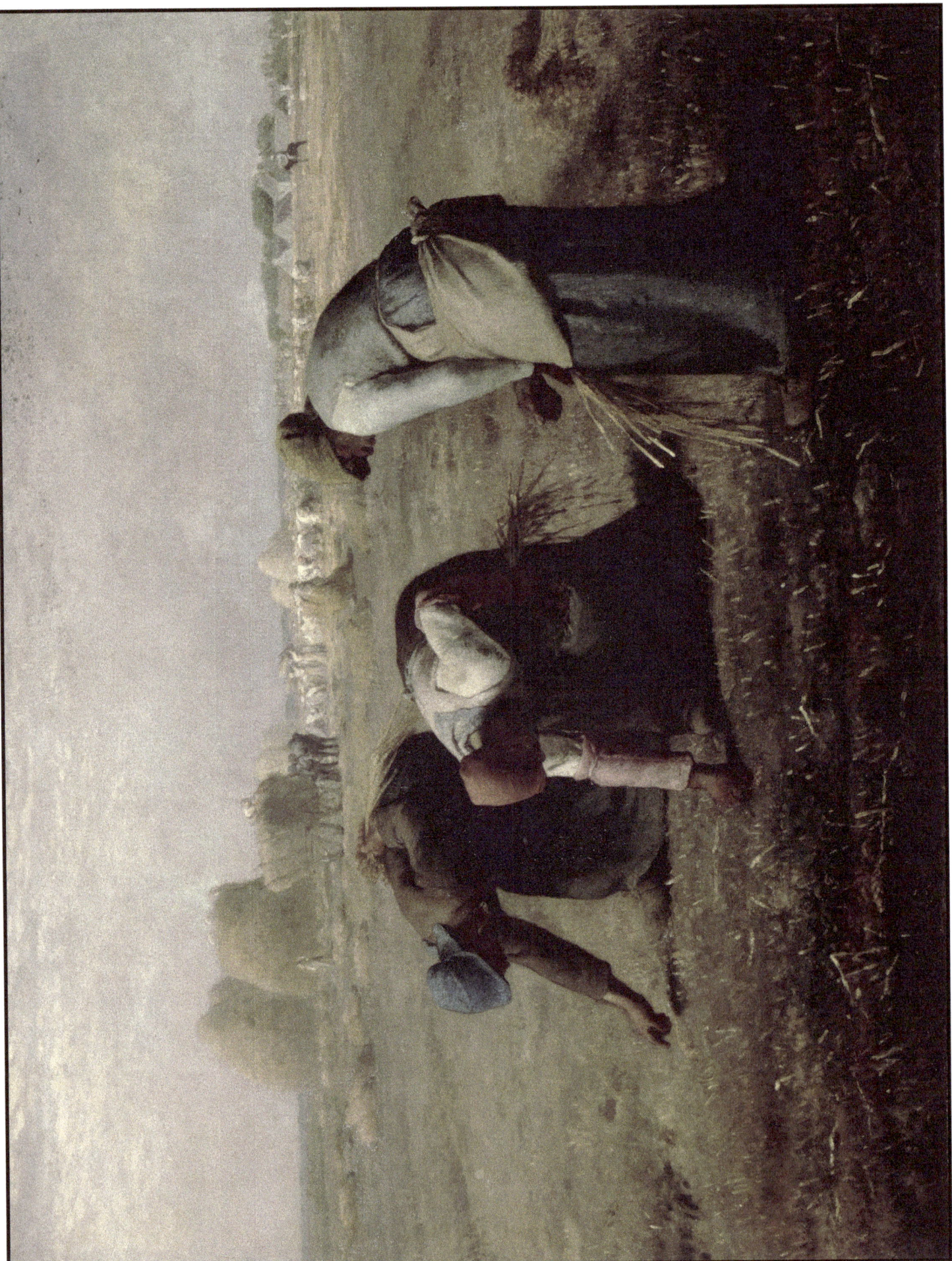

The Gleaners

Jean-François Millet

Date of Creation: 1857.

Art Movement or Style: Realism.

Medium and Technique: Oil on canvas.

Dimensions of the Painting: 83.8 cm × 111.8 cm (33 in × 44 in).

Current Location: The Musée d'Orsay, Paris, France.

Historical and Cultural Context
The Gleaners depicts three peasant women gleaning a field of stray grains of wheat after the harvest. Millet's work is set against the backdrop of the rural economic difficulties of 19th-century France, which were often ignored by the urban elites. The painting was created during the July Monarchy, a period that led up to the French Revolution of 1848, and reflects the social realities and hardships faced by the peasant class.

Subject Matter and Themes
The painting's subject matter is the act of gleaning, an ancient right of poor women to pick up the remains of the harvest. The themes include the dignity of labor, the inequities between social classes, and the rural hardship.

Artistic Significance
The Gleaners is significant for its realistic portrayal of rural life and its sympathetic look at the lives of the poor, which was in contrast to the Romantic or historical subjects that were popular at the time. It is one of Millet's most famous works and contributed to the development of Realism as an important art movement.

Critical Reception and Interpretations
The Gleaners was not well received by the French upper classes at the time of its creation; it was perceived as a glorification of the lower classes and a challenge to the social order. Over time, however, the painting has been recognized as a powerful social document and a masterful artistic creation.

Visual Analysis
The Gleaners is characterized by its subdued earth tones, which evoke the colors of the fields and the peasant attire. The composition draws attention to the back-breaking work of the gleaners, as they are stooped over in the foreground. The distance between the gleaners in the foreground and the harvesters in the background highlights the social divide. The use of light and shadow, as well as the attention to detail in the depiction of the women's clothing and gestures, contribute to the realism of the work.

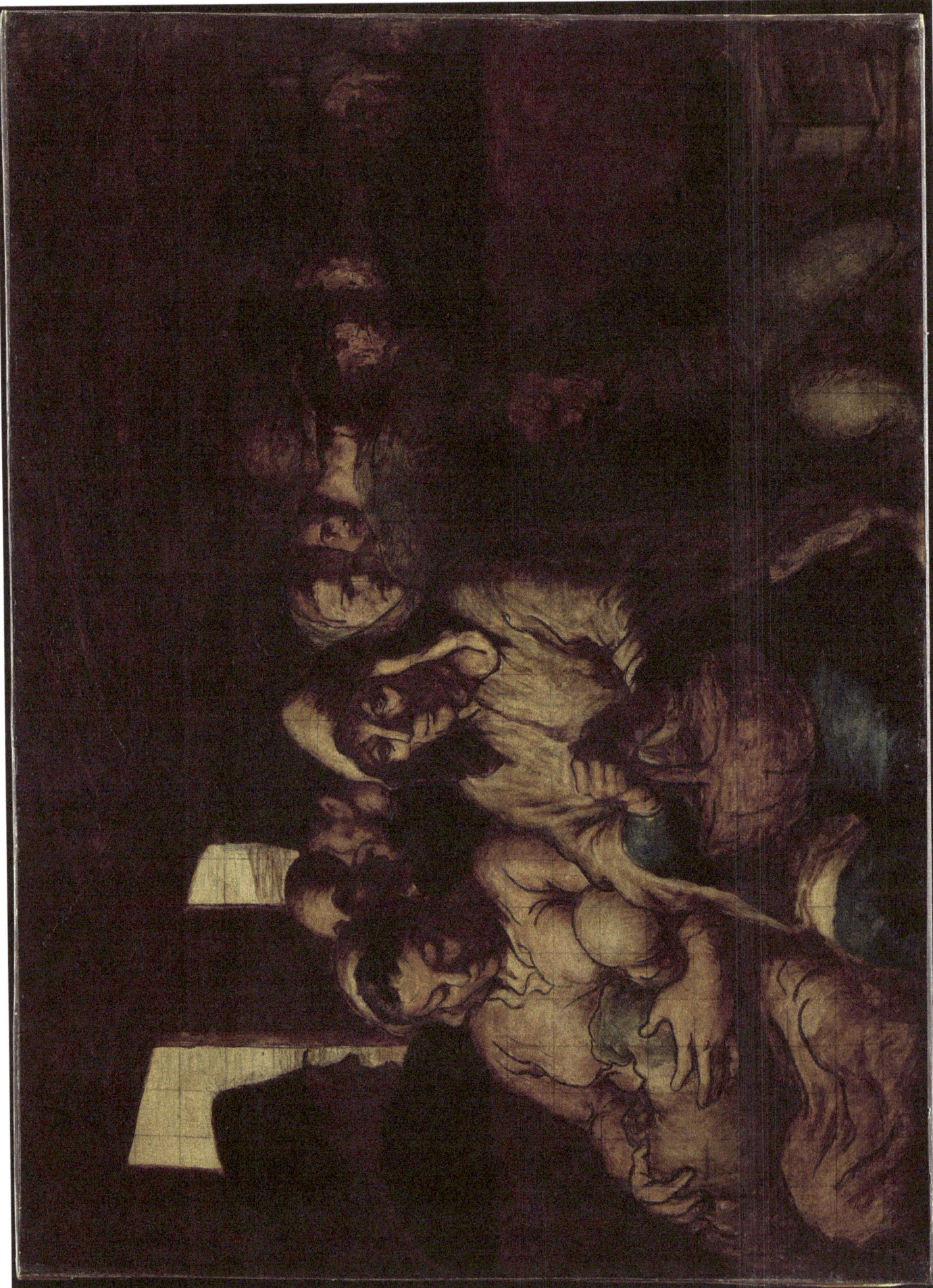

The Third-Class Carriage

Honoré Daumier

Date of Creation: Circa 1862–1864

Art Movement or Style: Realism.

Medium and Technique: Oil on canvas. Daumier used loose brushwork characteristic of the Realist movement, aiming to depict the subjects with honesty and without idealization.

Dimensions of the Painting: 83.8 cm × 111.8 cm (33 in × 44 in).

Current Location: The Metropolitan Museum of Art in New York, New York, USA.

Historical and Cultural Context

Daumier was a French artist known for his social commentary on 19th-century French society. *The Third-Class Carriage* reflects the realities of urban life during the Industrial Revolution when railway travel became more common and class distinctions were pronounced.

Subject Matter and Themes

The painting shows passengers in a third-class railway carriage. Daumier highlights the varied social conditions of the time, focusing on the working class. Themes include the human condition, social realism, and the impact of industrialization on society.

Artistic Significance

The Third-Class Carriage is one of Daumier's most famous works and is considered a significant contribution to the Realist art movement. It is notable for its empathetic portrayal of ordinary people and the dignified representation of the working class.

Critical Reception and Interpretations

Daumier's work was initially appreciated more for its political and social content than its artistic value. Over time, however, his artistry has been recognized, and *The Third-Class Carriage* is now seen as a profound statement on the human experience and the stark realities of 19th-century life.

Visual Analysis

The composition is compact, with the figures crowded together, emphasizing the cramped conditions of third-class travel. The use of light and shadow creates a sense of volume and depth, with the figures almost sculpturally rendered. There is a muted color palette, which adds to the somber mood of the scene. Daumier's work captures a moment in time with a quiet dignity, focusing on the expressions and postures of the passengers, which convey a range of emotions and experiences.

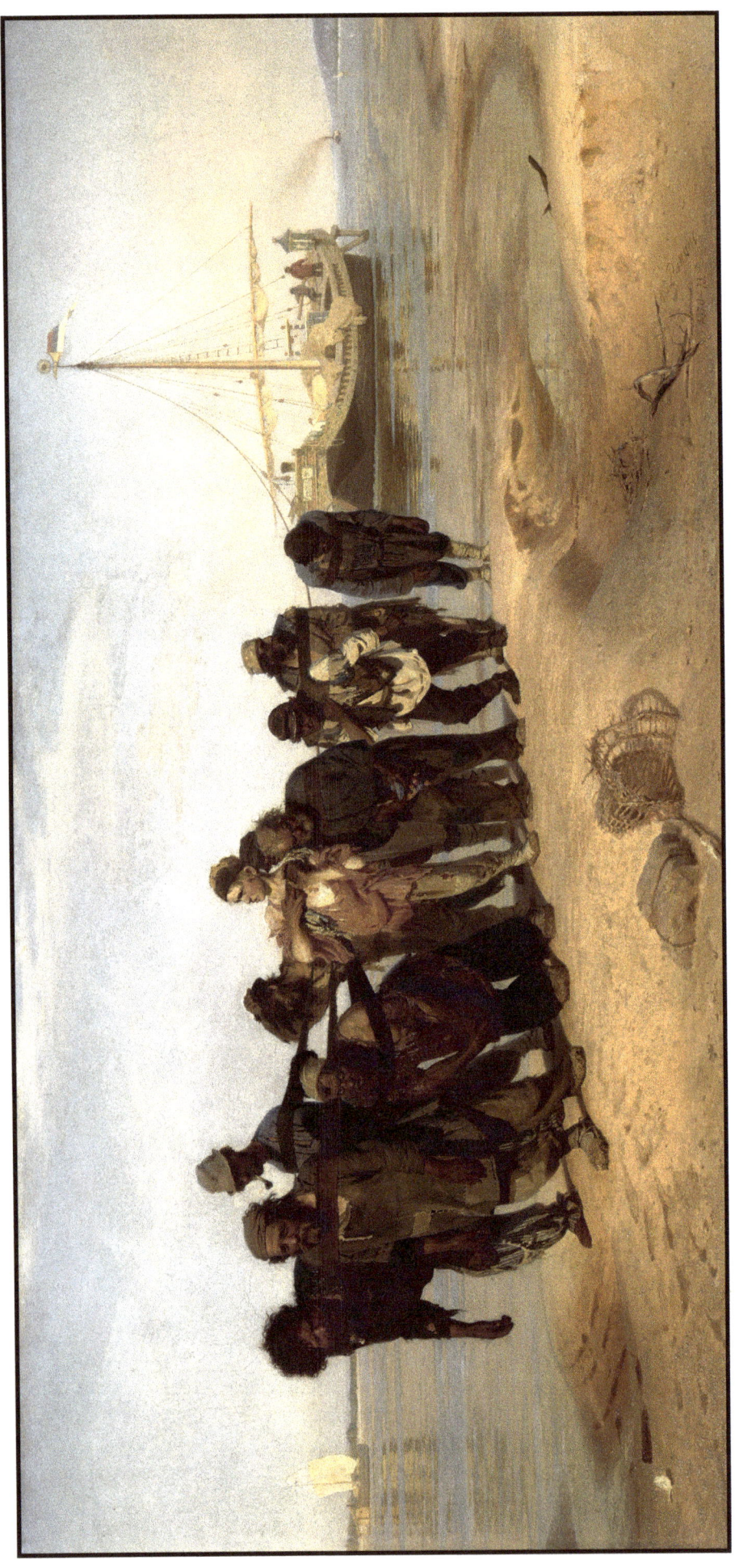

The Barge Haulers on the Volga

Ilya Repin

Date of Creation: 1870-1873

Art Movement or Style: Realism.

Medium and Technique: Oil on canvas.

Dimensions of the Painting: 131.5 cm × 281 cm (51.8 in × 110.6 in).

Current Location: The Russian Museum in Saint Petersburg, Russia.

Historical and Cultural Context
Repin created this work after a trip to the Volga River, where he witnessed the harsh conditions of barge haulers. This scene reflects the social and economic realities of Russia during the 19th century, particularly the hardships faced by the lower classes and the issue of serfdom.

Subject Matter and Themes
The painting depicts a group of burlaks, or barge haulers, dragging a large boat up the Volga River. Themes include the struggle against oppression, the dignity of labor, and the inequality and human suffering present within Russian society at the time.

Artistic Significance
The Barge Haulers on the Volga is considered one of Repin's greatest works and a notable example of Russian Realist painting. It's praised for its portrayal of the human spirit and physical realism.

Critical Reception and Interpretations
At the time of its creation, the painting was both praised for its artistic merit and critiqued for its social commentary. It's been interpreted as a poignant social critique, a glorification of the working man, and an emblem of human resilience and suffering.

Visual Analysis
The composition of the painting is dynamic, with the diagonal line of the barge haulers creating a sense of movement and tension. The figures are individualized, each showing a different response to their labor. Repin's use of light and color accentuates the physical strain and the heat of the sun. The figure in the center appears to be breaking from the line, possibly symbolizing the potential for resistance and change. The Volga River and the distant sailboat provide a stark contrast to the toil of the barge haulers, suggesting the vastness of Russia and the smallness of the individual within it.

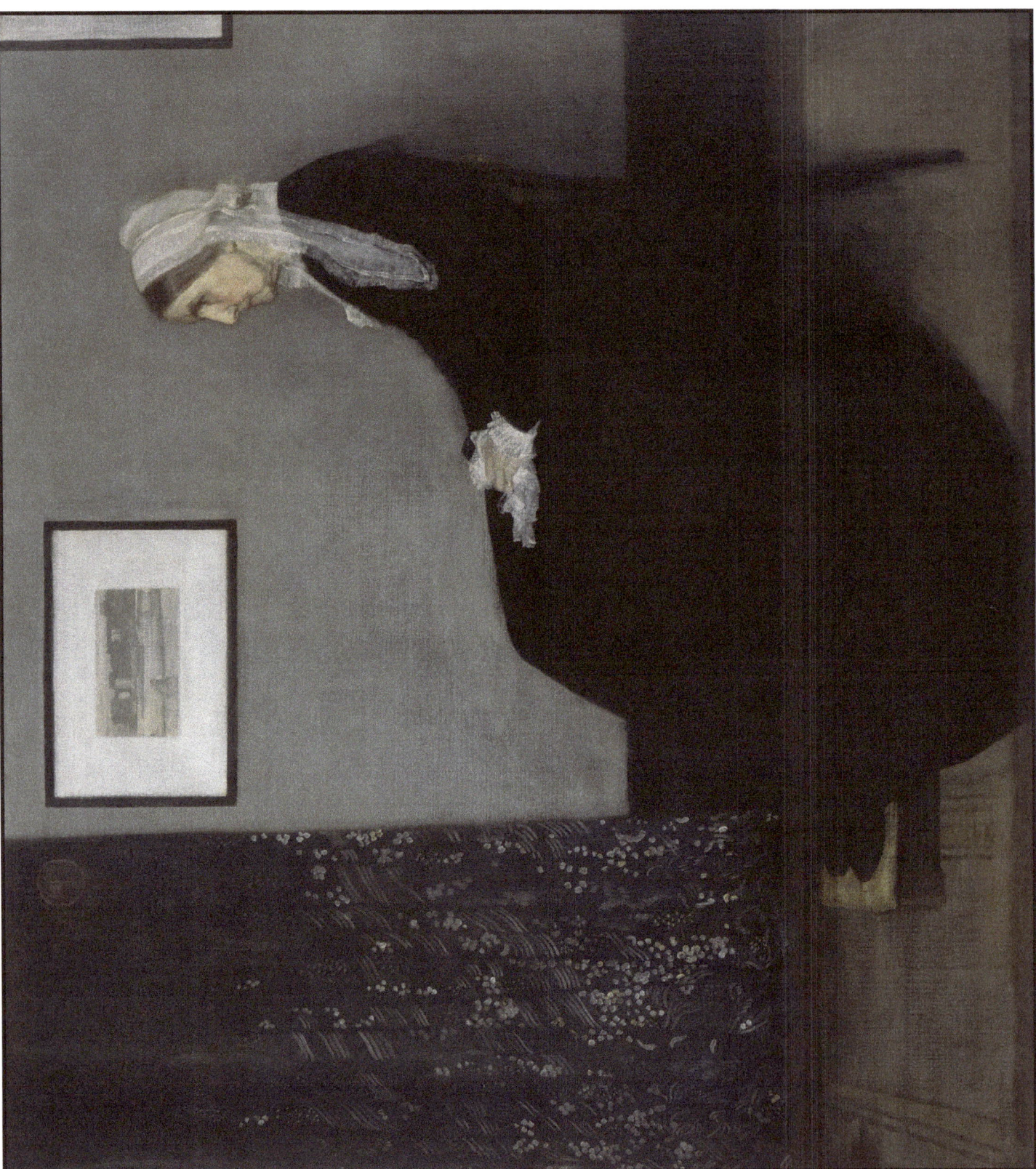

Whistler's Mother (Arrangement in Grey and Black No. 1)

James McNeill Whistler

Date of Creation: 1871

Art Movement or Style: American Realism

Medium and Technique: Oil on canvas. Whistler's technique emphasized the harmony of the composition and subtle tonal variations over the narrative and subject detail.

Dimensions of the Painting: 144.3 cm × 162.4 cm (56.81 in × 63.98 in).

Current Location: The Musée d'Orsay in Paris, France.

Historical and Cultural Context
Painted during the Victorian era, the work is a fine example of Whistler's belief in 'art for art's sake'. It reflects the period's complex attitudes towards representations of motherhood and family values, as well as the increasing emphasis on form and design in the Aesthetic Movement.

Subject Matter and Themes
The subject of the painting is the artist's mother, Anna McNeill Whistler, captured in a moment of repose, reflecting Whistler's interest in the arrangement of color and form. Themes include the dignity of old age, the beauty in everyday life, and a focus on composition and tone over narrative.

Artistic Significance
This painting is one of Whistler's most famous works and is an iconic image within American art. It represents a shift from literal representation to a composition that focuses on color harmony and form, which was influential in the development of modern art.

Critical Reception and Interpretations
The painting was initially met with mixed reviews but has since become an emblematic image of motherhood and American art. It has been interpreted as both a personal and impersonal depiction; a portrait of the artist's mother and a study in form and color.

Visual Analysis
The painting is notable for its restricted color palette and the strong verticals and horizontals that create a sense of stability and calm. The figure's rigid, frontal position contrasts with the softness of her face, and the various textures, from the curtain to the dress, are rendered with great care. The overall composition has a geometric simplicity that focuses attention on the form and mood of the subject, rather than on a narrative.

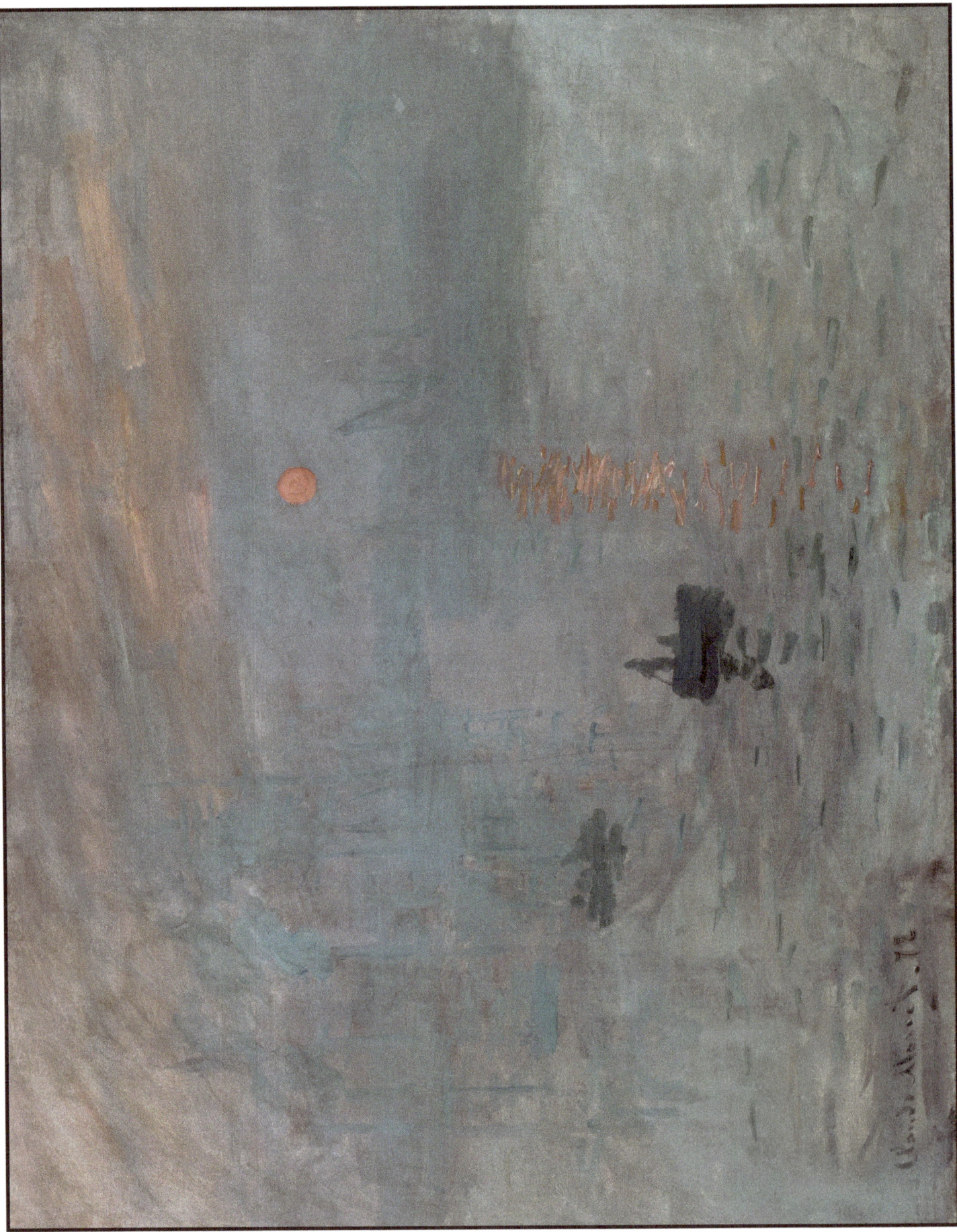

Impression, Sunrise

Claude Monet

Date of Creation: 1872

Art Movement or Style: Impressionism

Medium and Technique: Oil on canvas.

Dimensions of the Painting: 48 cm × 63 cm (18.9 in × 24.8 in).

Current Location: The Musée Marmottan Monet, Paris, France.

Historical and Cultural Context
Impression, Sunrise was painted in 1872 and depicts the port of Le Havre in France. The painting is credited with inspiring the name of the Impressionist movement. It captures the atmosphere of the port with a focus on light and color rather than detail.

Subject Matter and Themes
The painting portrays the harbor of Le Havre at sunrise, with the focus on light reflections and the silhouettes of ships and other structures. Themes include the interplay of light on water, the industrialization of France, and the fleeting moments of daily life.

Artistic Significance
Impression, Sunrise is one of Monet's most notable works and is significant for being emblematic of the Impressionist movement. Its innovative approach to depicting light and color was revolutionary at the time and had a significant impact on the direction of modern art.

Critical Reception and Interpretations
Initially, the painting received mixed reviews, with some critics deriding its loose brushwork and unfinished appearance. However, it has since been recognized as a work of great importance and has been interpreted as a response to the modernization of society and the transient nature of life.

Visual Analysis
The painting is characterized by its loose brushwork, use of color, and emphasis on light. Monet uses quick brushstrokes to capture the essence of the sunrise and its reflection on the water. The sun, though a simple smudge of color, is the focal point and is reflected in the water, creating a path of light that draws the viewer's eye into the depth of the composition.

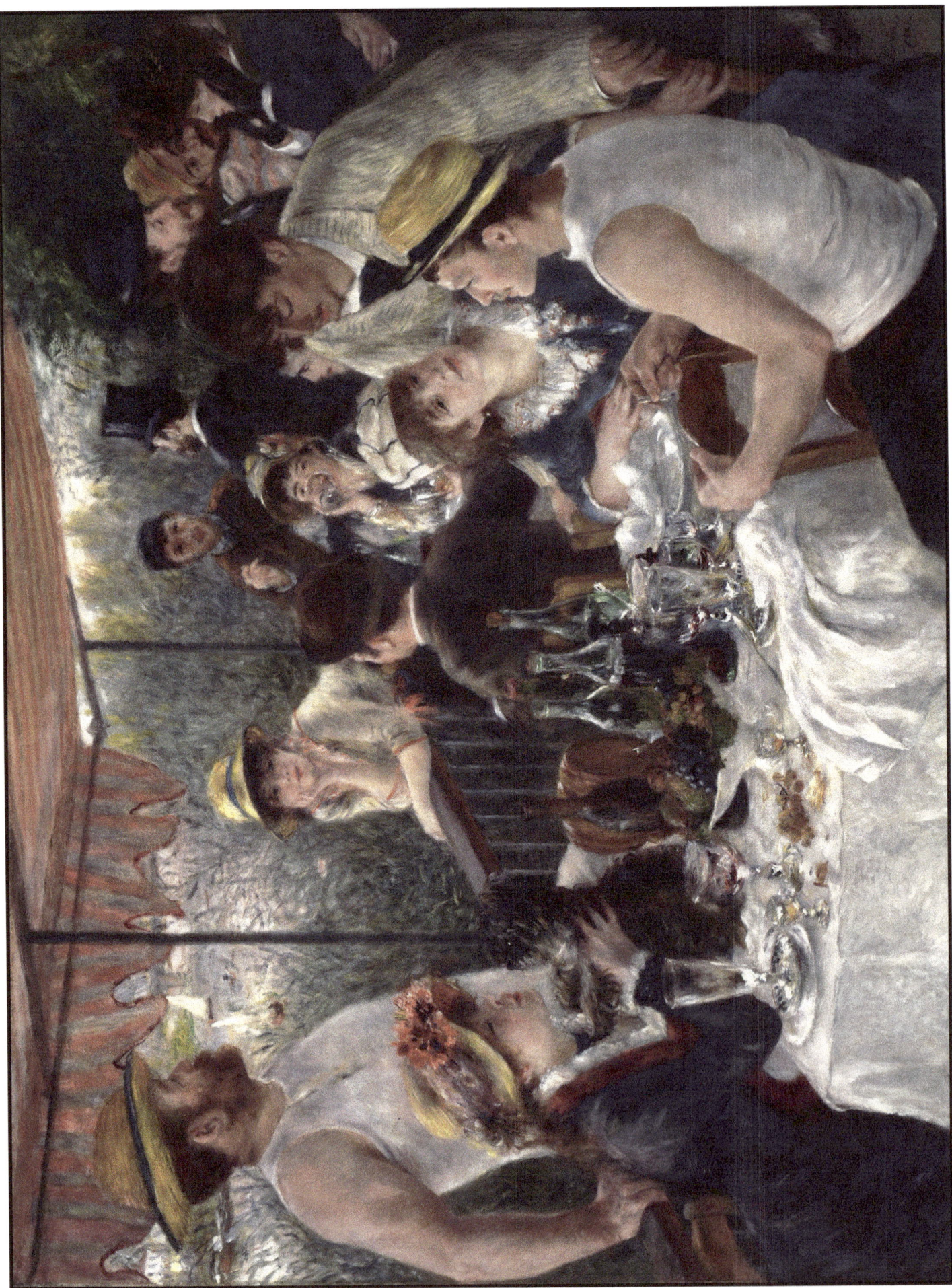

Luncheon of the Boating Party

Pierre-Auguste Renoir

Date of Creation: 1880-81.

Art Movement or Style: Impressionism

Medium and Technique: Oil on canvas. The painting is characterized by loose brushwork and an emphasis on the depiction of light and its changing qualities.

Dimensions of the Painting: 130 cm × 175 cm (51.2 in × 69.3 in).

Current Location: The Phillips Collection in Washington, D.C., USA.

Historical and Cultural Context
Painted toward the end of the Impressionist movement, *Luncheon of the Boating Party* reflects the social and leisurely activities of the Parisian middle class at the end of the 19th century. The setting is the balcony of the Maison Fournaise, a restaurant along the Seine River in Chatou, France, which was a popular spot for boating.

Subject Matter and Themes
The painting captures a group of Renoir's friends relaxing on a balcony by the Seine. It includes a variety of figures from different social backgrounds, reflecting the modern and democratic spirit of the time. Themes of leisure, the joy of life, companionship, and the blurring of social boundaries are all present in the work.

Artistic Significance
Luncheon of the Boating Party is considered one of Renoir's masterpieces and an excellent example of Impressionism. It showcases his skill in using light and color to capture a moment in time, and it is noted for its vibrant atmosphere and the complex composition of its figures.

Critical Reception and Interpretations
The painting was well received for its vibrant representation of contemporary life. Critics have praised its composition and Renoir's ability to capture the character of his subjects. It has been interpreted as an idealized vision of social harmony.

Visual Analysis
The painting is notable for its luminous palette, lively depiction of figures, and the sense of movement conveyed by the brushwork. The arrangement of the figures creates a dynamic yet balanced composition. Light filters through the trees and canopy, casting patterns on the figures and table, contributing to the overall impression of a fleeting moment captured in time. The interplay of gazes and interactions between the characters invites the viewer into the scene, making it feel alive and engaging.

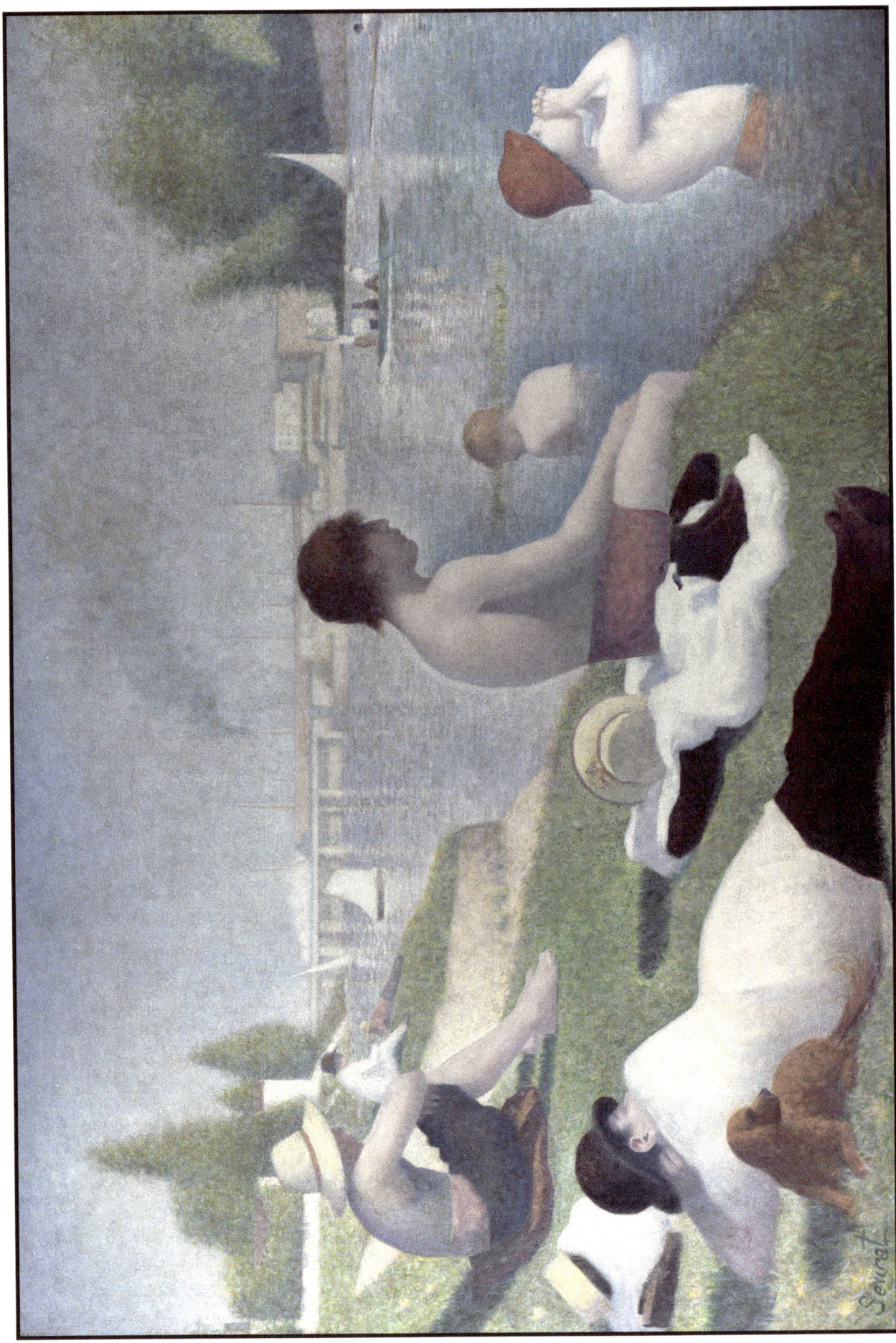

Bathers at Asnières

Georges Seurat

Date of Creation: 1884.

Art Movement or Style: Pointillism, part of the larger Neo-Impressionism movement

Medium and Technique: Oil on canvas. It is noted for its use of small, distinct dots of color applied in patterns to form an image, known as pointillism.

Dimensions of the Painting: 201 cm × 300 cm (79 in × 118 in).

Current Location: The National Gallery in London, England.

Historical and Cultural Context

Seurat painted *Bathers at Asnières* during a time when Paris was undergoing rapid transformation and modernization. The painting reflects the leisure activities of the Parisian suburban middle class, a relatively new social group at the time, and the industrial landscape emerging in the background.

Subject Matter and Themes

The painting depicts young men bathing and relaxing by the Seine River in the industrial suburb of Asnières. It explores themes of leisure, the modern life of Parisians, and the impact of industrialization.

Artistic Significance

Bathers at Asnières is one of Seurat's early masterpieces and is significant for its early use of pointillism. It marked a departure from the more fluid and spontaneous brushwork of Impressionism, showing a structured, studied approach to painting light and color.

Critical Reception and Interpretations

At the time of its creation, *Bathers at Asnières* was not well received by the art establishment and was rejected by the Paris Salon. However, it has since been recognized as a pivotal work that contributed to the development of modern art.

Visual Analysis

The painting is characterized by its bright, unmixed colors applied in dots, which allows the viewer's eye to blend the colors from a distance and creates a luminous effect. The composition is balanced, with a focus on the figures in the foreground against the industrial backdrop.

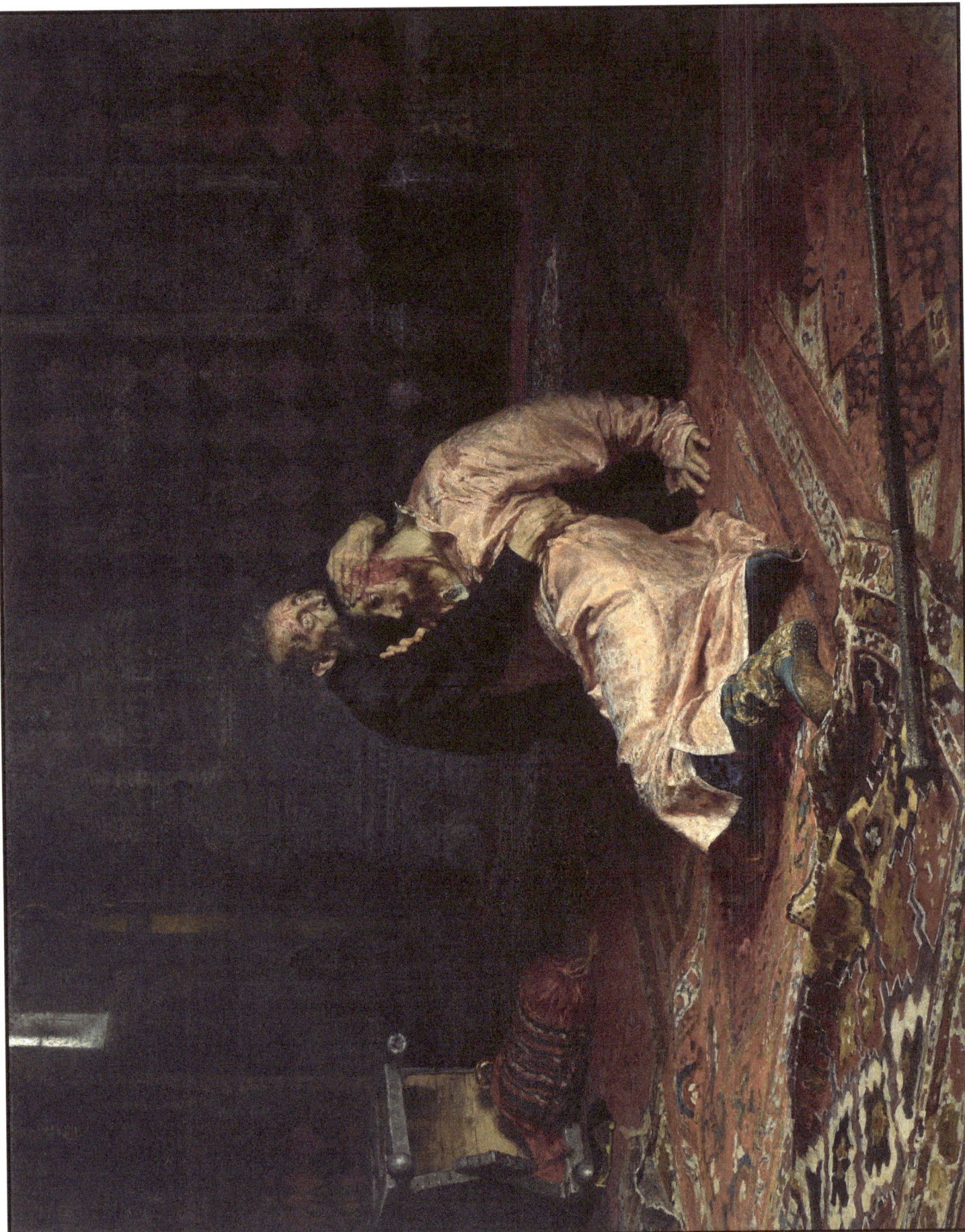

Ivan the Terrible and His Son Ivan

Ilya Repin

Date of Creation: 1883-1885.

Art Movement or Style: Realism

Medium and Technique: Oil on canvas.

Dimensions of the Painting: 199.5 cm × 254 cm (78.5 in × 100 in)

Current Location: The State Tretyakov Gallery, Moscow, Russia.

Historical and Cultural Context
The painting depicts a historical scene from November 16, 1581, where Ivan the Terrible grievously wounded his son, Ivan Ivanovich, in a fit of rage. The event is a subject of historical speculation, but Repin's painting has played a significant role in embedding this moment in Russian cultural memory.

Subject Matter and Themes
The painting portrays the immediate aftermath of the tsar's violent act, with Ivan the Terrible cradling his dying son. Themes include the consequences of unchecked power, the tragedy of family conflict, and the human capacity for both violence and remorse.

Artistic Significance
Repin's work is renowned for its emotional depth and psychological complexity. This painting, in particular, is noted for its dramatic portrayal of the subjects and the stark depiction of remorse and despair. It is one of Repin's most famous and is considered a masterpiece of Russian art.

Critical Reception and Interpretations
The painting was controversial at the time of its creation due to its graphic depiction of violence and its portrayal of a notorious historical figure. It has been interpreted as a critique of autocratic rule, a reflection on human tragedy, and an examination of the burden of leadership.

Visual Analysis
The painting is characterized by its intense realism and dramatic use of lighting, which focuses on the pale, anguished face of Ivan and the lifeless head of his son. Repin's mastery of texture is evident in the depiction of the fabrics and blood, adding to the realism of the scene. The dark, subdued palette accentuates the somber mood of the painting.

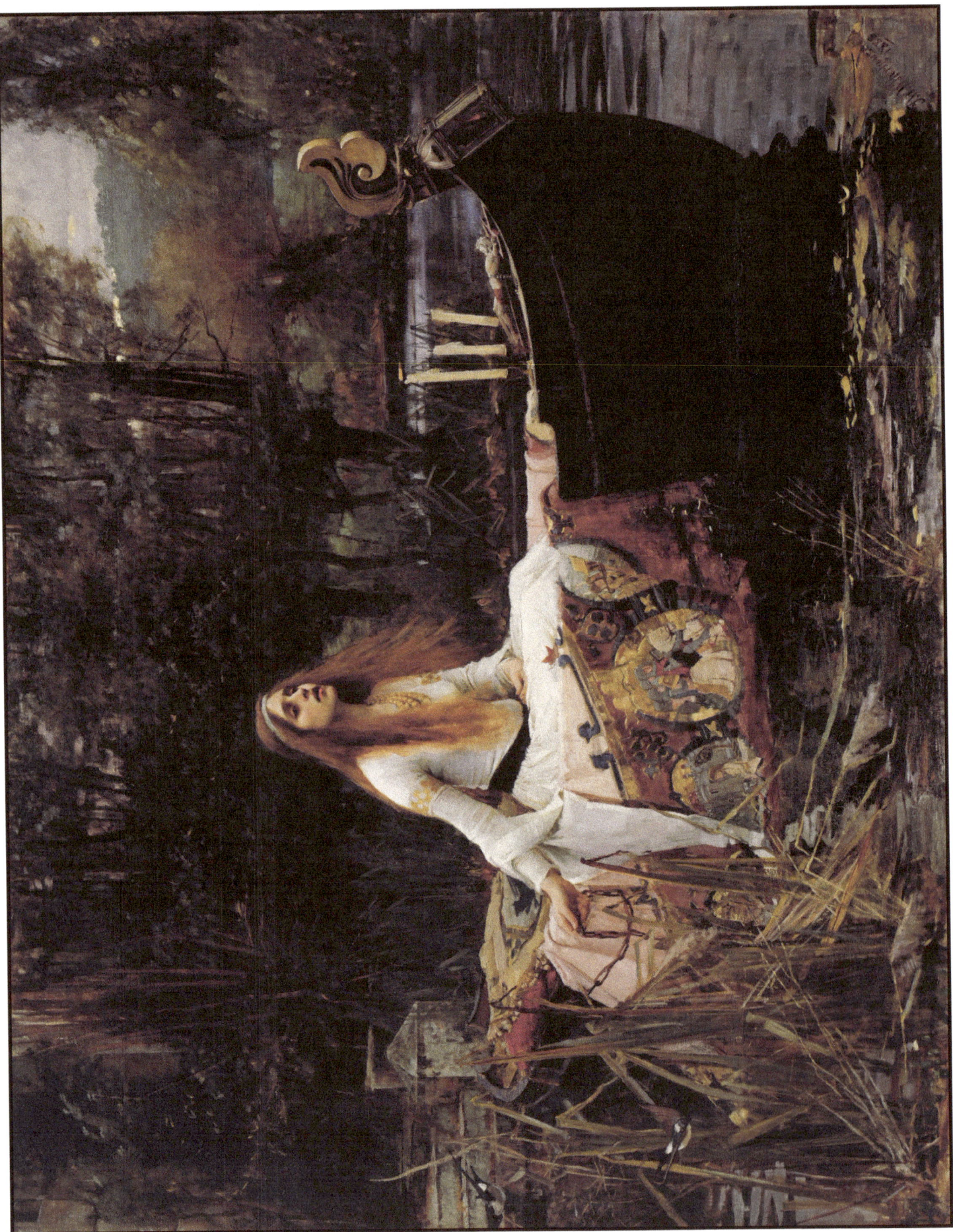

The Lady of Shalott

John William Waterhouse

Date of Creation: 1888.

Art Movement or Style: Pre-Raphaelite Brotherhood.

Medium and Technique: Oil on canvas.

Dimensions of the Painting: 183 cm × 230 cm (72 in × 91 in)

Current Location: The Tate, London, England.

Historical and Cultural Context

The painting illustrates a scene from Alfred, Lord Tennyson's 1832 poem of the same name, which tells the story of a woman who is cursed to weave a magic web without looking directly at the outside world. Waterhouse's depiction comes from the part of the poem when the Lady sees Sir Lancelot and decides to look out of her window, bringing about her tragic fate.

Subject Matter and Themes

The Lady of Shalott is depicted in a boat, having left her tower in which she was confined, floating down to Camelot. Themes of the painting include the conflict between art and life, the role of the artist, the dichotomy of isolation and desire for the worldly experiences, and the tragic beauty of the unattainable.

Artistic Significance

The painting is one of Waterhouse's most famous works and is an excellent example of Pre-Raphaelite art, known for its intricate detail, vivid colors, and emphasis on themes from mythology and literature.

Critical Reception and Interpretations

At the time, Waterhouse's work was well-received for its beauty and romantic style. Modern interpretations often view the painting through the lens of feminist critique, examining the role and agency of the Lady as an artist and as a woman.

Visual Analysis

In this work, Waterhouse uses rich, vibrant colors and meticulous attention to detail to create a lush, romantic setting. The Lady's forlorn expression and the way her body is positioned suggest a tragic resignation. The inclusion of symbolic elements, such as the tapestry and the chains from which her boat is moored, add layers of meaning to the work. The naturalistic elements, reflective water, and the atmospheric perspective give the painting a sense of depth and realism.

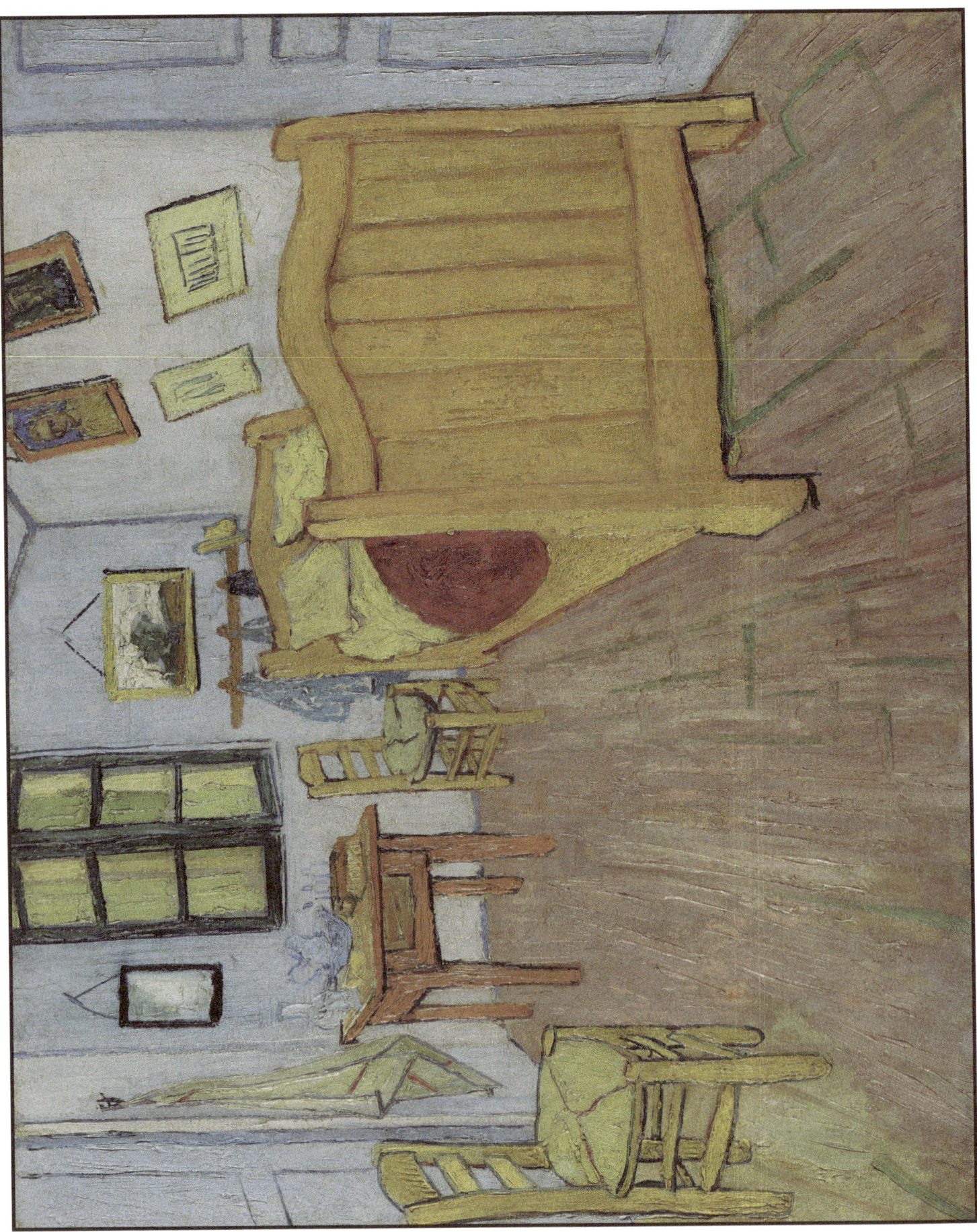

The Bedroom

Vincent van Gogh

Date of Creation: 1888.

Art Movement or Style: Post-Impressionism.

Medium and Technique: Oil on canvas.

Dimensions of the Painting: 72 cm × 90 cm (28.3 in × 35.4 in).

Current Location: There are three authentic versions of **The Bedroom** by van Gogh, and they are located in the Van Gogh Museum in Amsterdam, the Art Institute of Chicago, and the Musée d'Orsay in Paris.

Historical and Cultural Context
Van Gogh painted this work while he was living in the Yellow House in Arles, France. The painting shows his bedroom in the house, and it is one of his most famous works. It reflects the artist's interest in color and his desire to convey calm and rest through his art.

Subject Matter and Themes
The subject is van Gogh's own bedroom. The themes include the comfort of domesticity, the significance of home, and the use of color and perspective to evoke mood and emotion.

Artistic Significance
The painting is significant for its bold color, emphatic line, and distinctive compositional elements. Van Gogh's use of color was innovative for its time and contributed to the development of modern art.

Critical Reception and Interpretations
The painting has been widely acclaimed for its vibrant color scheme and emotional resonance. Interpretations of the work often discuss van Gogh's state of mind and the sense of solace he sought through the ordered simplicity of his bedroom.

Visual Analysis
The Bedroom is characterized by a bright and simplified use of color and form, which creates a peaceful and contemplative space. Van Gogh has used contrasting colors and straight lines to structure the composition, and the perspective is deliberately skewed to enhance the intimacy of the space. The furniture and the objects in the room are painted with solid blocks of color and outlined with thick contours, which adds to the sense of stability and tranquility.

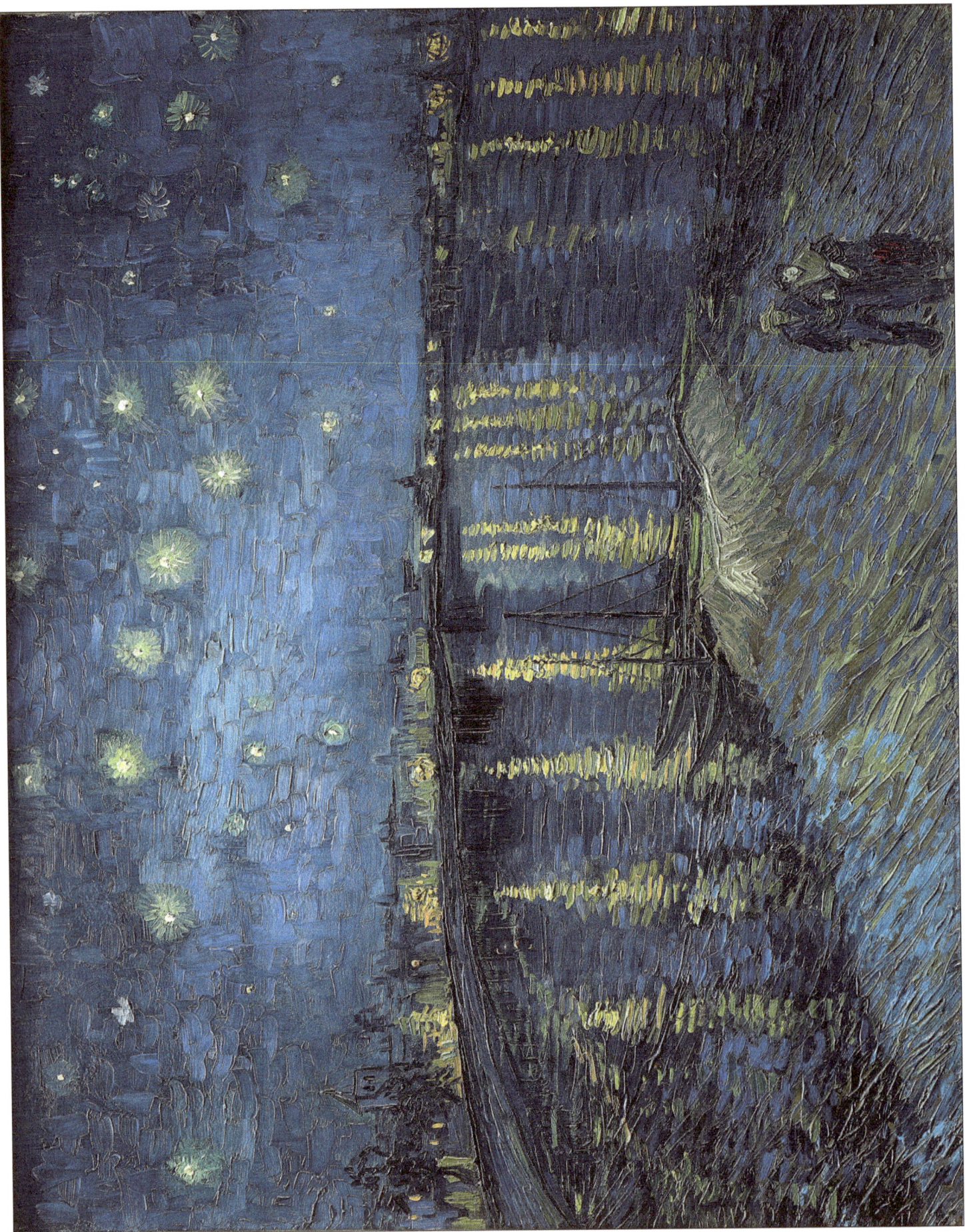

Starry Night Over the Rhône

Vincent van Gogh

Date of Creation: 1888.

Art Movement or Style: Post-Impressionism.

Medium and Technique: Oil on canvas.

Dimensions of the Painting: 72.5 cm × 92 cm (28.5 in × 36.2 in).

Current Location: The Musée d'Orsay in Paris, France.

Historical and Cultural Context

Van Gogh painted *Starry Night Over the Rhône* while he was living in Arles, France. It was a period of immense productivity for the artist, just before the decline of his mental health. The painting captures Van Gogh's fascination with the night sky and reflects his desire to depict the stars as they appeared in nature.

Subject Matter and Themes

The painting depicts the Rhône River at night. Themes in the painting include the contrast between the serene river and the vibrant night sky, the reflection of the city lights in the water, and the vastness of the universe.

Artistic Significance

Starry Night Over the Rhône is significant as it is a precursor to Van Gogh's later work *The Starry Night*. It demonstrates his innovative use of color and brushwork, as well as his ability to convey emotion through the landscape.

Critical Reception and Interpretations

The painting was not widely known during Van Gogh's lifetime, but it has since become one of his most admired works. Critics have praised the painting for its visionary qualities and its influence on later generations of artists.

Visual Analysis

The painting is characterized by its bold use of color, with deep blues and bright yellows. Van Gogh used swirling brushstrokes to create a dynamic sky, which contrasts with the calm river. The composition leads the viewer's eye around the painting, from the couple in the foreground to the stars above.

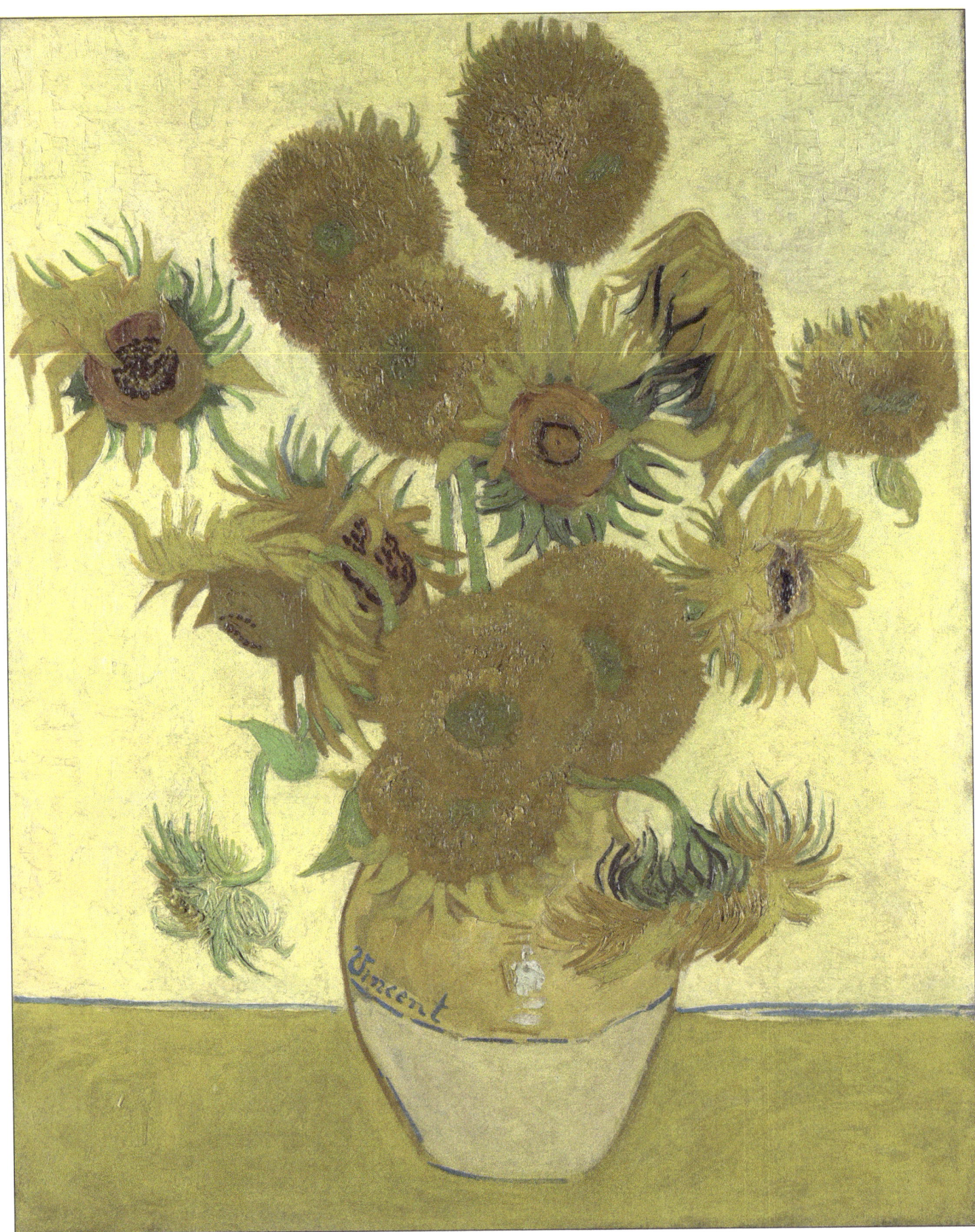

Sunflowers

Vincent van Gogh

Date of Creation: 1887-1889 (series of paintings).

Art Movement or Style: Post-Impressionism.

Medium and Technique: Oil on canvas.

Dimensions of the Painting: The dimensions vary because van Gogh painted several versions of Sunflowers. One of the most famous versions measures 95 cm × 73 cm (37.4 in × 28.7 in).

Current Location: There are several versions of "Sunflowers" and they are spread across various museums around the world. One of the most famous versions is located in the Van Gogh Museum in Amsterdam, the Netherlands.

Historical and Cultural Context
Van Gogh created the *Sunflowers* series during his time in Arles, France. They were intended to decorate the room of his friend Paul Gauguin in the house they briefly shared. The series reflects van Gogh's innovative use of color and his emotional response to the subject matter.

Subject Matter and Themes
The subject is a vase of blooming sunflowers. Themes include the cycle of life and death, the beauty of the everyday, and the passage of time, as some of the sunflowers are in full bloom while others are wilting.

Artistic Significance
The *Sunflowers* series is among van Gogh's most famous works and is renowned for its bold colors, dramatic textures, and the emotional intensity conveyed through a seemingly simple still life.

Critical Reception and Interpretations
The *Sunflowers* are celebrated for their vibrant color scheme that challenged the traditional, more muted still-life paintings of the time. They are often seen as symbolizing the artist's search for light and hope.

Visual Analysis
The *Sunflowers* paintings feature thick, expressive brushstrokes, a hallmark of van Gogh's style. The use of contrasting colors, such as the blue of the vase against the yellow of the flowers and background, creates a vivid image that seems to pulse with energy. The varying stages of the sunflowers' lifespans are depicted with empathetic detail, lending the work a sense of poignancy.

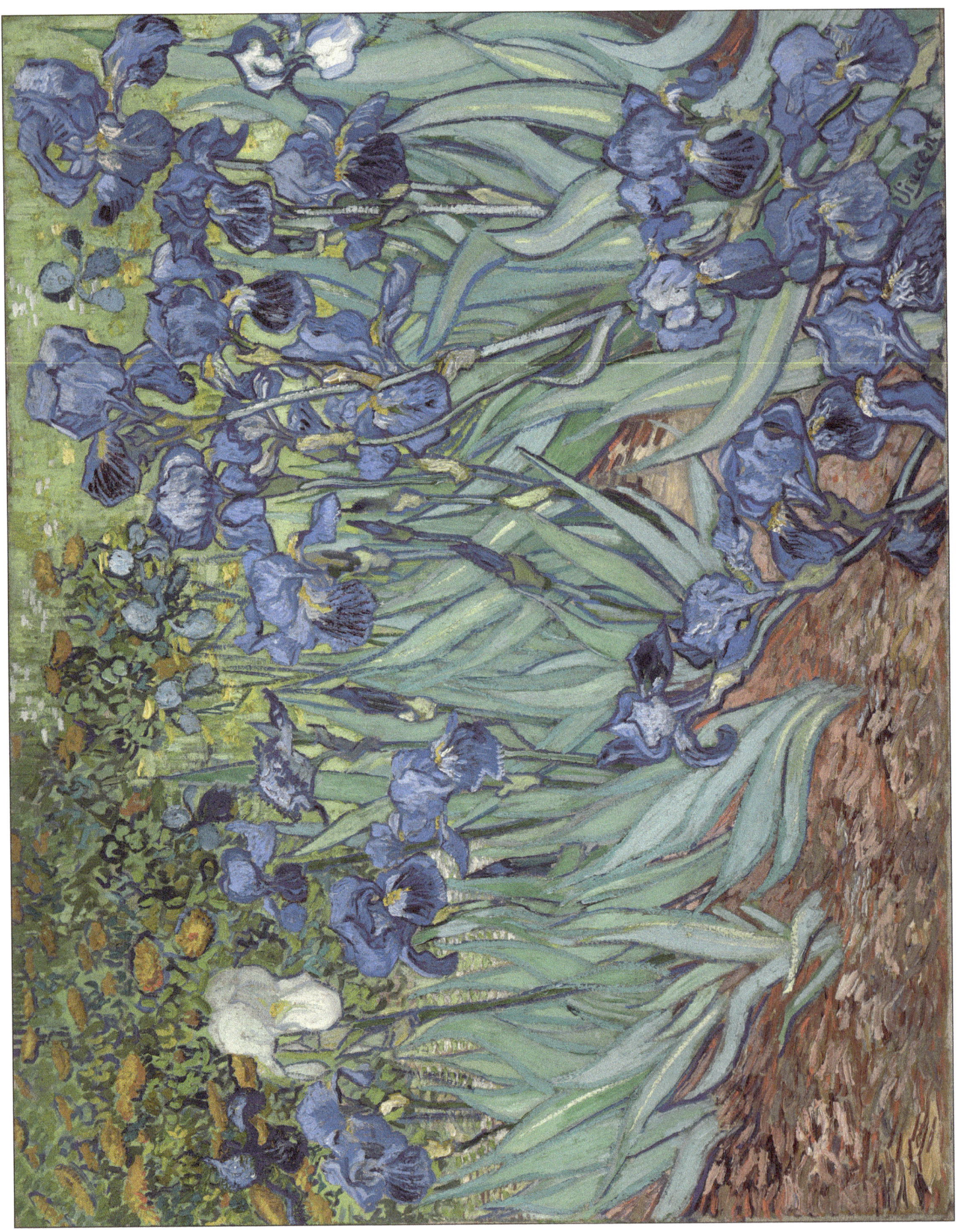

Irises

Vincent van Gogh

Date of Creation: 1889.

Art Movement or Style: Post-Impressionism.

Medium and Technique: Oil on canvas.

Dimensions of the Painting: 71 cm × 93 cm (28 in × 36.6 in)

Current Location: The Getty Center, Los Angeles, California, USA

Historical and Cultural Context

Irises was painted in 1889 during van Gogh's stay at the asylum of Saint Paul-de-Mausole in Saint-Rémy-de-Provence, France. Van Gogh had voluntarily admitted himself to the asylum and this work was done before his first attack of mental illness. The garden of the asylum became a source of inspiration for him.

Subject Matter and Themes

The painting depicts a garden of irises, with one white iris standing out among the blue and purple ones. Themes of the painting often point to growth, life, and the beauty of nature, as well as possibly reflecting the isolation and difference van Gogh may have felt in his life.

Artistic Significance

Irises is considered one of van Gogh's most important works and is one of the most expensive paintings ever sold. It represents a period of intense creativity for the artist that was also marked by turmoil and illness.

Critical Reception and Interpretations

Irises has been widely acclaimed for its vivid color, energetic brushwork, and emotional intensity. It has been interpreted as a reflection of van Gogh's state of mind, with the single white iris often thought to represent the artist himself.

Visual Analysis

The painting is notable for its bold and expressive use of line and color. Van Gogh's characteristic swirling brushstrokes imbue the scene with movement and life, while the contrasting colors and shapes create a dynamic and harmonious composition. The painting is filled with a sense of vitality and the thick application of paint adds a three-dimensional quality to the work.

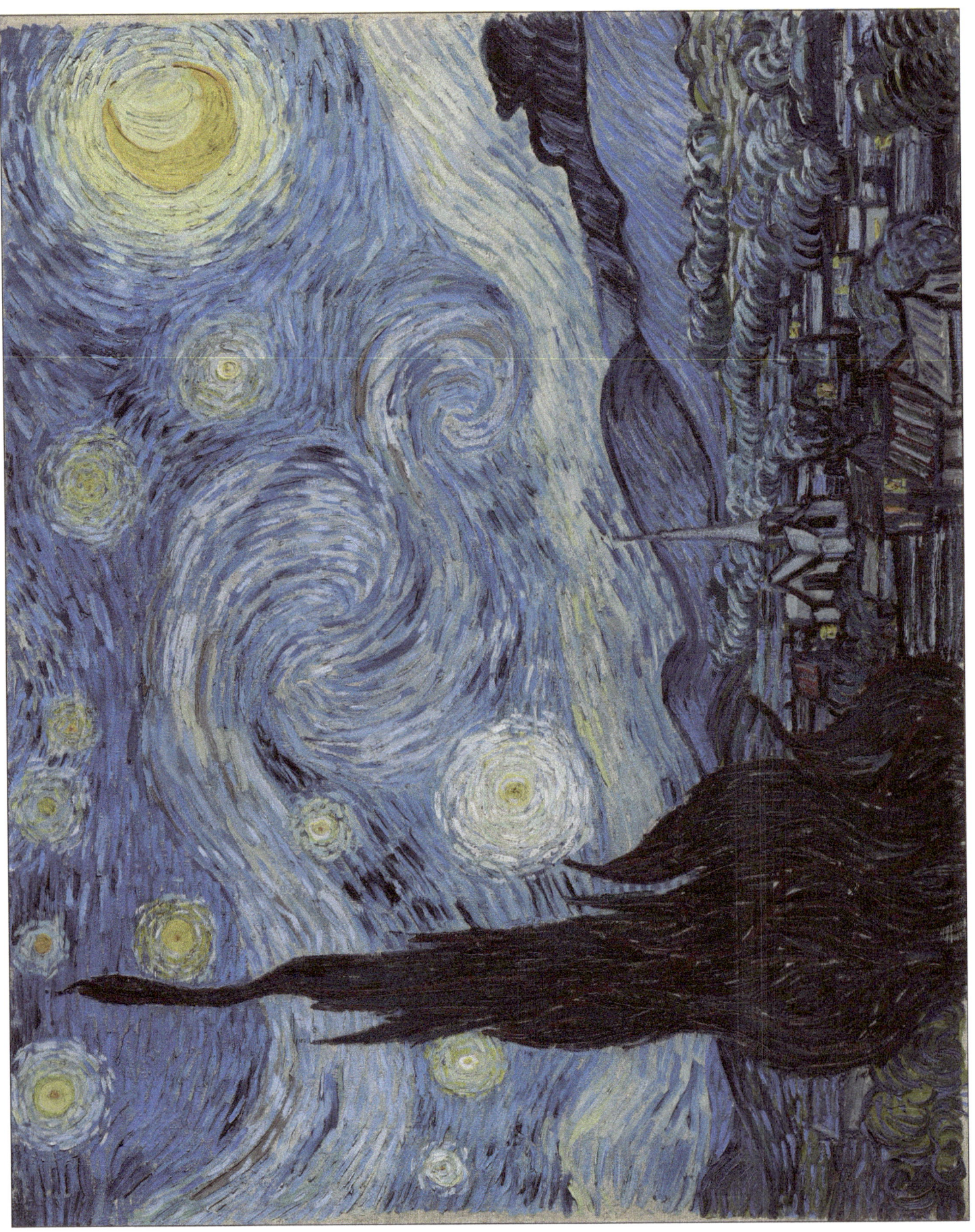

The Starry Night

Vincent van Gogh

Date of Creation: 1889.

Art Movement or Style: Post-Impressionism.

Medium and Technique: Oil on canvas. Van Gogh's technique is characterized by the application of thick brushstrokes, a vibrant color palette, and the emotional intensity conveyed through the swirling patterns of the stars and sky.

Dimensions of the Painting: 73.7 cm × 92.1 cm (29 in × 36.25 in).

Current Location: The Museum of Modern Art, New York., New York,. USA

Historical and Cultural Context
Van Gogh painted *The Starry Night* during his stay at the Saint-Paul-de-Mausole asylum in Saint-Rémy-de-Provence, France, following a breakdown that led to the severing of part of his left ear. Despite his troubled mental state, he continued to paint and produced some of his most famous work during this period.

Subject Matter and Themes
The painting depicts the view outside Van Gogh's sanatorium room window at night, although it was painted from memory during the day. Themes include the vastness of the universe and the interplay between life and death. The painting reflects Van Gogh's fascination with the nocturnal sky and his sense of isolation and quest for solace through the act of painting.

Artistic Significance
The Starry Night is one of Van Gogh's most famous works and is often regarded as his magnum opus. It is celebrated for its beauty, emotional depth, and the innovative technique that has inspired countless artists.

Critical Reception and Interpretations
The painting was not well known during Van Gogh's lifetime but has since become one of the most recognized and admired works in Western art. It has been interpreted in various ways, including as a representation of Van Gogh's turbulent psyche, a symbol of hope and creativity, and as an expression of his spiritual and existential struggles.

Visual Analysis
The Starry Night is noted for its swirling and flowing lines, the contrast between the bright, illuminating stars and the dark, foreboding sky. The cypress tree in the foreground connects the earth to the heavens, and the tranquil village below contrasts with the dynamic and animated sky. The painting's thick, impasto brushstrokes create a textured surface that adds to the painting's sense of turbulence and intensity. The use of color, with the dominating blues and yellows, creates a night scene that is more imaginative than realistic, imbued with emotion and energy.

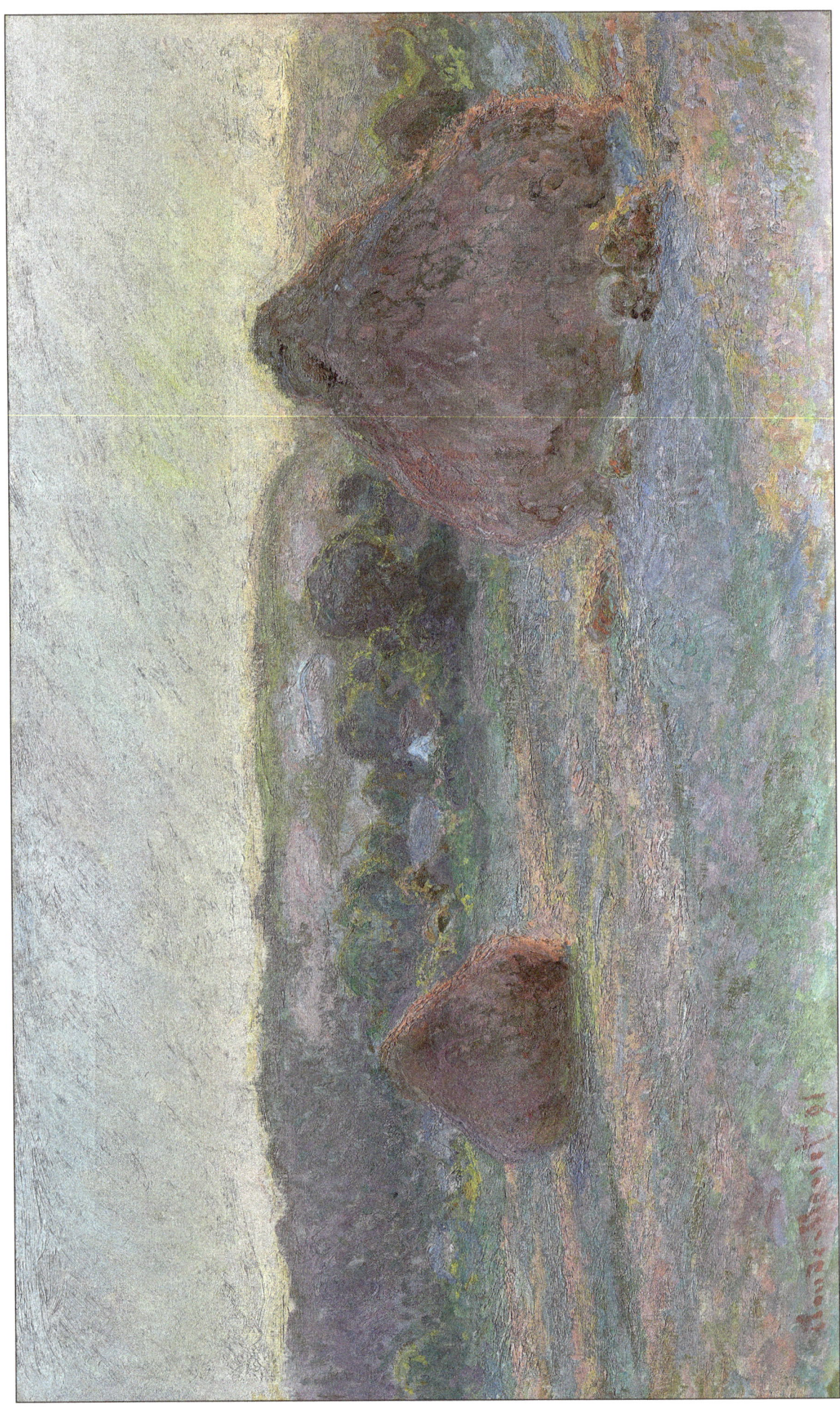

Haystacks (Series)

Claude Monet

Date of Creation: Between 1890 and 1891.

Art Movement or Style: Impressionism.

Medium and Technique: Oil on canvas.

Dimensions of the Painting: The dimensions vary as there are multiple paintings in the "Haystacks" series, but they generally measure around 65 cm × 100 cm (25.6 in × 39.4 in).

Current Location: The series is distributed across various museums and private collections worldwide.

Historical and Cultural Context

Monet's *Haystacks* series captures the essence of rural French life at the turn of the 20th century, reflecting both the landscape of the countryside and the changing seasons. The series is renowned for its thematic focus on the effects of light and time on a single subject.

Subject Matter and Themes

The subject is the haystacks in the fields near Monet's home in Giverny, France. Themes of the series include the transient nature of light, the changing seasons, and the passage of time as reflected in the agricultural cycle.

Artistic Significance

The *Haystacks* series is one of Monet's most famous and is significant for its role in the development of Impressionism. Monet's approach to capturing the same scene under different light conditions was groundbreaking and contributed to a deeper understanding of light in art.

Critical Reception and Interpretations

The series was well-received and praised for its innovative representation of light and atmosphere. It has been interpreted as a meditation on temporality and perception, inviting viewers to consider the subjective nature of reality.

Visual Analysis

Monet's *Haystacks* are characterized by their vibrant color palette, loose brushwork, and emphasis on light and shadow. The texture of the paint application itself is as much a part of the subject matter as the haystacks, illustrating Monet's interest in the surface interplay between color and light.

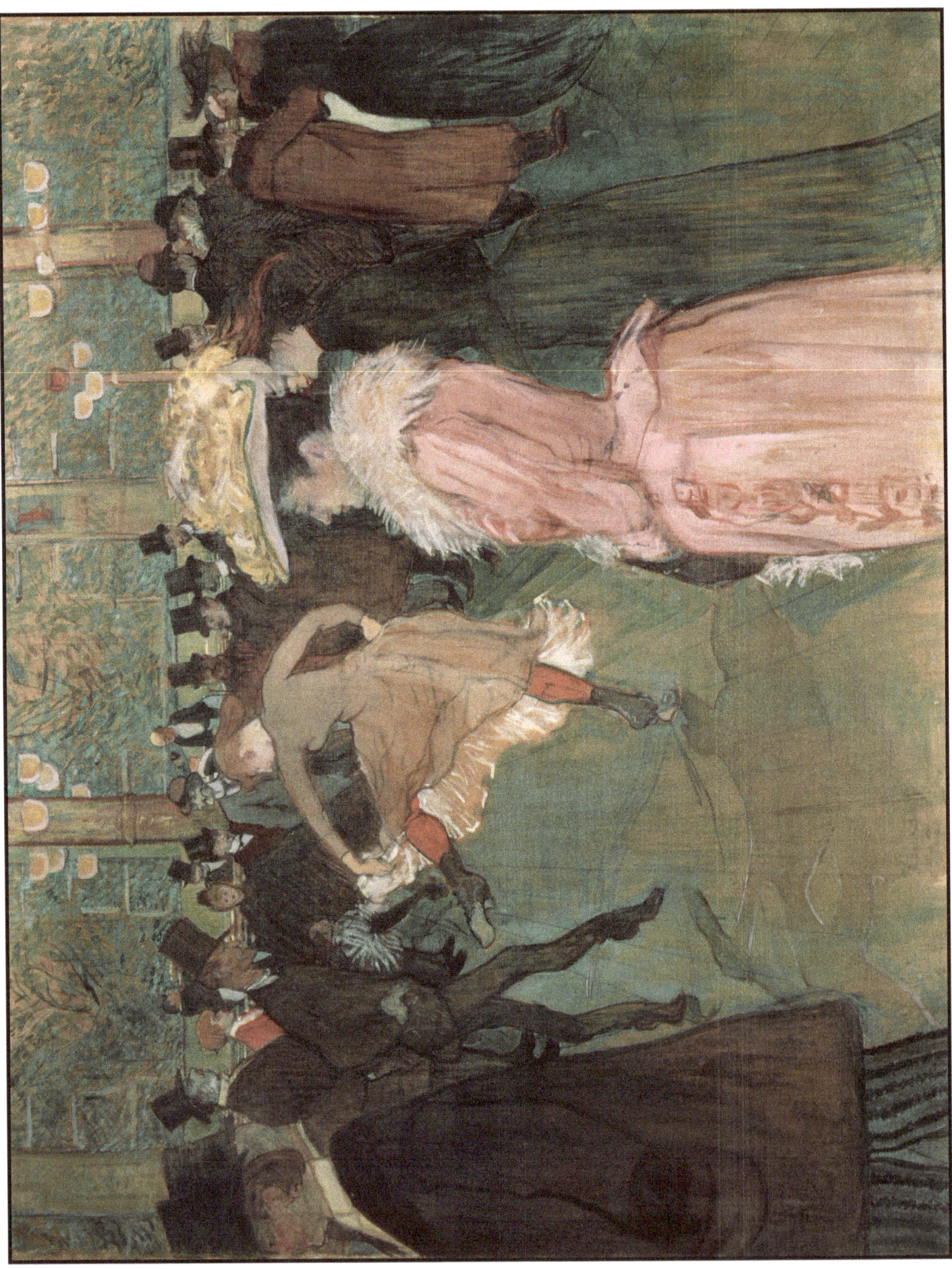

At the Moulin Rouge

Henri de Toulouse-Lautrec

Date of Creation: 1890

Art Movement or Style: Post-Impressionism

Medium and Technique: Oil on canvas.

Dimensions of the Painting: Approximately 123 cm × 140 cm (48 in × 55 in).

Current Location: The Art Institute of Chicago, Illinois, USA.

Historical and Cultural Context
Toulouse-Lautrec's work is often associated with the bohemian lifestyle of late 19th-century Paris, especially the nightlife of areas like Montmartre, where he lived and worked. This painting captures the vibrant atmosphere of the Moulin Rouge, a popular nightclub.

Subject Matter and Themes
The painting depicts the lively scene of the Moulin Rouge, a place known for its eclectic patrons from the world of art, culture, and the demimonde. It features a mix of characters, possibly including the artist himself, and captures the nightlife and the social interactions of the period.

Artistic Significance
Toulouse-Lautrec was noted for his ability to capture the essence of Parisian nightlife and his innovative use of color and form. His work influenced the development of modern art and provided a visual record of the social life of his era.

Critical Reception and Interpretations
Toulouse-Lautrec's work was not fully appreciated during his lifetime but gained recognition posthumously. This painting is seen as an important example of his ability to capture movement and the vibrant quality of the Parisian nightlife.

Visual Analysis
The painting is characterized by its bold use of color, light, and the sense of movement conveyed by the swirling dancers and bustling crowd. The perspective is slightly elevated, giving viewers the sense of being part of the scene. The composition is carefully structured, with figures at the edges framing the central action

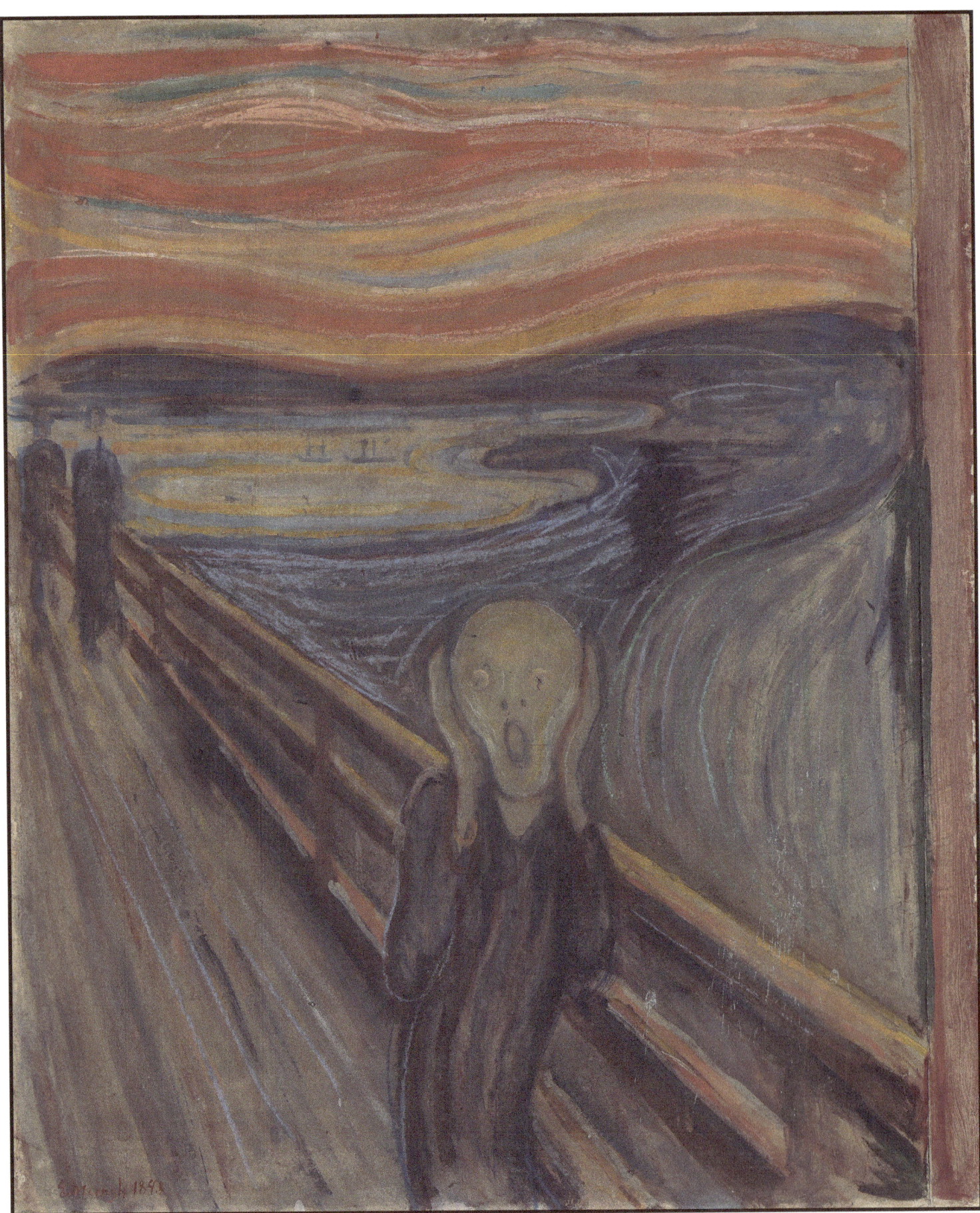

The Scream

Edvard Munch

Date of Creation: 1893

Art Movement or Style: Expressionism

Medium and Technique: *The Scream* has several versions created with a variety of mediums, including oil, tempera, pastel, and crayon on cardboard.

Dimensions of the Painting: The dimensions of the tempera on cardboard version are 91 cm × 73.5 cm (36 in × 28.9 in).

Current Location: There are several versions of *The Scream*. One of the most famous tempera on cardboard versions is located in the National Gallery in Oslo, Norway.

Historical and Cultural Context
The Scream was created during a period of personal anguish for Munch. It represents Munch's attempt to explore themes of life, death, and the human psyche. It was part of his series "The Frieze of Life," which delved into psychological themes and was reflective of the artist's own mental state.

Subject Matter and Themes
The painting portrays an agonized figure against a blood-red sky, which has been interpreted as representing the individual's existential crisis and the universal anxiety of the human condition.

Artistic Significance
The Scream is one of the most iconic images in the history of art and is a symbol of existential angst and the loss of innocence in the modern world. It is one of the earliest works that can be associated with the Expressionist movement.

Critical Reception and Interpretations
The painting has been widely analyzed and interpreted as an expression of modern anxiety. It has received critical acclaim for its innovative composition and its capacity to evoke emotional response from viewers.

Visual Analysis
The Scream is characterized by its bold colors, dramatic lines, and the use of perspective that draws the viewer into the emotional center of the painting. The swirling sky creates a sense of movement and chaos, while the lone figure's open mouth and wide eyes directly engage the viewer in its silent scream. The painting's palette of vibrant reds and yellows contrasts with the dark figure, emphasizing the intensity of the scene.

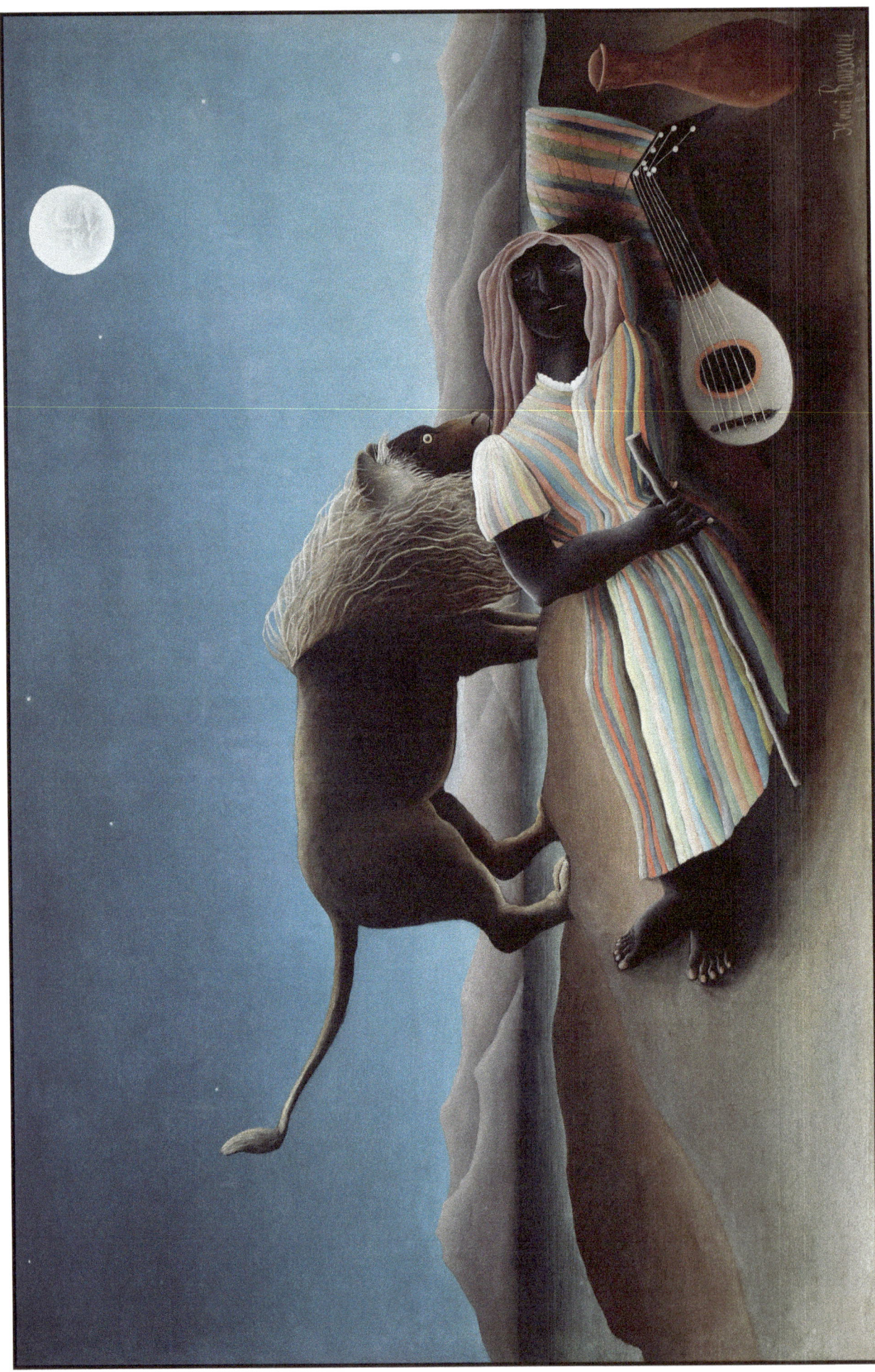

The Sleeping Gypsy

Henri Rousseau

Date of Creation: 1897

Art Movement or Style: Post-Impressionism, Naïve art, or Primitivism

Medium and Technique: Oil on canvas.

Dimensions of the Painting: 129.5 cm × 200.7 cm (51 in × 79 in).

Current Location: The Museum of Modern Art in New York City.

Historical and Cultural Context
Henri Rousseau was a self-taught painter who worked during the late 19th century, a period when the art world in Paris was dominated by the Impressionists and the beginnings of modernism. Rousseau was known for his 'naïve' or 'primitive' style, which was outside the mainstream and not fully appreciated during his lifetime.

Subject Matter and Themes
The painting depicts a solitary figure of a sleeping gypsy woman, lying in the desert with a lion peering over her. It is a mysterious and dreamlike image that has been interpreted as a meditation on the human condition, the relationship between civilization and nature, and the power of dreams.

Artistic Significance
The Sleeping Gypsy is one of Rousseau's most famous works and is celebrated for its poetic, dreamlike quality and its highly individualistic style. Rousseau's work has been influential in the development of modernism, particularly for his imaginative approach to subject matter and his bold, simplistic style.

Critical Reception and Interpretations
Rousseau's work was often met with skepticism and ridicule by contemporary critics, but it was later celebrated by the avant-garde for its expressive and innovative qualities. *The Sleeping Gypsy* has intrigued viewers and critics alike with its enigmatic theme and its surreal atmosphere.

Visual Analysis
The painting is characterized by a flatness of form and a lack of perspective, typical of Rousseau's style. The vibrant colors and clear outlines give the image a striking and graphic quality. The use of stark contrasts, with the brightly lit figure and animal against the dark blue background, creates a sense of stillness and intensity. The moon and the stars add to the surreal and timeless quality of the scene. The lion's ambiguous interaction with the sleeping figure—whether protective or threatening—adds to the painting's mystique.

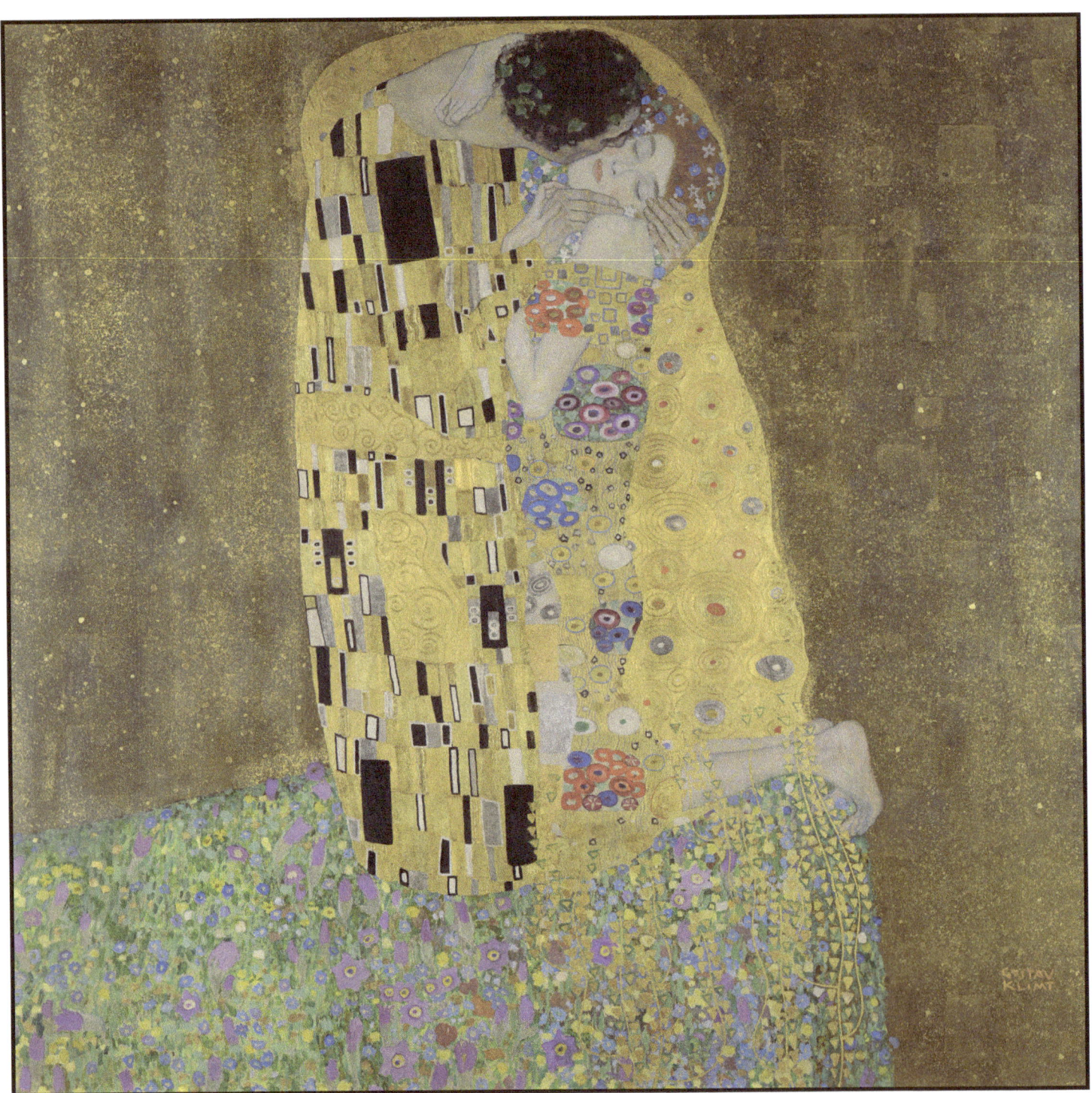

The Kiss (Lovers)

Gustav Klimt

Date of Creation: 1907-1908

Art Movement or Style: The Kiss is associated with the Art Nouveau movement and is considered a masterpiece of the early modern period. It also fits within the Vienna Secession movement, of which Klimt was a founding member.

Medium and Technique: Oil on canvas. The painting is renowned for its use of oil paint and applied layers of gold leaf, which give it a unique texture and luminosity.

Dimensions of the Painting: 180 cm × 180 cm (71 in × 71 in).

Current Location: The Österreichische Galerie Belvedere museum in Vienna, Austria.

Historical and Cultural Context
The work was painted during the height of Klimt's "Golden Phase," characterized by his use of gold leaf in paintings. It was created at a time when Klimt was moving away from the conventions of academic painting and exploring more symbolic and erotic themes.

Subject Matter and Themes
The Kiss portrays an intimate moment between a couple, wrapped in a gold, flowered blanket or robe in a meadow of flowers. Themes of love, intimacy, and sexuality are prevalent in the painting, with the use of symbolic patterns and ornate motifs that suggest a transcendental experience of love.

Artistic Significance
This painting is a symbol of the Vienna Secession's break from traditional academic art. It incorporates Byzantine, medieval, and contemporary influences, showcasing Klimt's unique style that combines the decorative with the erotic.

Critical Reception and Interpretations
The painting was immediately celebrated by critics and the public upon its first exhibition. It is often interpreted as a representation of the perfect union between man and woman or the merging of spiritual and physical love. Some interpretations also suggest it reflects Klimt's personal ideal of a relationship, free from the constraints of society.

Visual Analysis
The Kiss is characterized by its ornate surface, the intricate patterns, and the use of gold, which creates a sacred or magical aura around the couple. The flatness of the composition, the absence of depth, and the almost abstract quality of the figures' robes and the meadow are in stark contrast with the realism of the lovers' faces and hands, creating a focus on the act of kissing itself. The composition is a balance between the figurative and the ornamental, creating a sense of timelessness and universality.

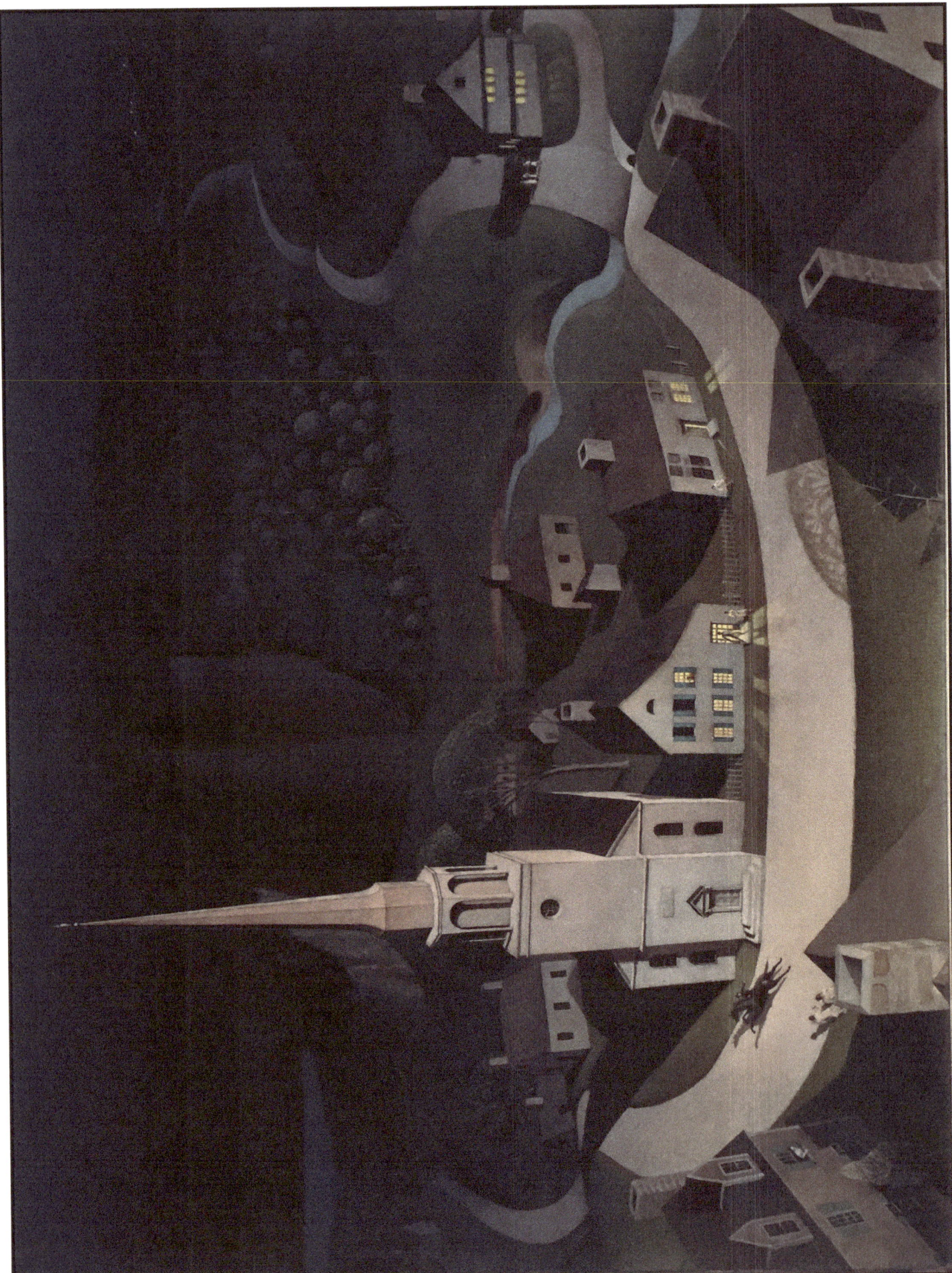

Midnight Ride of Paul Revere

Grant Wood

Date of Creation: 1931

Art Movement or Style: The painting is associated with the Regionalism art movement, which was an American realist modern art movement that was popular in the 1930s. It focused on depicting rural American themes in a figurative style.

Medium and Technique: Oil on Masonite. Wood's technique often involved smooth, finely crafted surfaces with clearly defined forms that reflect his meticulous approach to his subjects.

Dimensions of the Painting: 76 cm × 100 cm (30 in × 40 in).

Current Location: The Metropolitan Museum of Art in New York, New York, USA

Historical and Cultural Context

Midnight Ride of Paul Revere was created after Wood had achieved fame with his painting *American Gothic*. The painting was created during a time of economic hardship in the United States—the Great Depression—and reflects a sense of nostalgia and patriotism, evoking the spirit and values of the American Revolution.

Subject Matter and Themes

The painting is a stylized depiction of the famous historical event where Paul Revere rode at night to warn the American colonial militia of the approaching British forces. Themes include American patriotism, the valorization of the nation's past, and a romanticized view of American history.

Artistic Significance

Grant Wood's painting is significant for its unique style that blends realism with a certain storybook quality. It represents an important moment in American history and reflects the Regionalist art movement's focus on American themes.

Critical Reception and Interpretations

The work has been both praised for its craftsmanship and criticized for its romanticized and historically inaccurate portrayal of the event. It has been interpreted as a symbol of American resilience and self-determination.

Visual Analysis

The painting is characterized by its curvilinear forms, rolling landscape, and the quaint, orderly depiction of the colonial town. The bird's-eye view creates a map-like representation of the scene. The use of light to highlight Paul Revere's figure and the path ahead of him emphasizes the urgency and importance of his midnight ride. The painting's overall composition, with its simplified forms and almost theatrical lighting, imparts a sense of myth to the historical event.

THE ARTISTS

THE ARTISTS

Jan van Eyck

Date of Birth: c. 1390
Place of Birth: Maaseik, Prince-Bishopric of Liège (now Belgium)
Date of Death: July 9, 1441
Place of Death: Bruges, County of Flanders (now Belgium)

Short Biography:
Jan van Eyck was a prominent Early Netherlandish painter active in the 15th century. He is often considered one of the most significant and innovative artists of the Northern Renaissance. Little is known about his early life, but he first appears in historical records around 1422, working in The Hague. By 1425, he was employed by Philip the Good, Duke of Burgundy, as a court painter and valet de chambre, which provided him with a steady income and social status.

Van Eyck settled in Bruges around 1431 and remained there until his death in 1441. His work mainly consisted of religious portraits, altarpieces, and secular portraiture, showcasing remarkable detail and precision. His most famous work is the Ghent Altarpiece (1432), created in collaboration with his brother, Hubert van Eyck, which is renowned for its complexity, vibrant colors, and meticulous detail.

Influence and Significance on Art:
Jan van Eyck is credited with the invention or, more accurately, the perfection of oil painting techniques. His use of oil paints allowed for greater manipulation of color, finer detail, and a depth of realism that had not been seen before in European painting. This innovation significantly influenced the course of Western art, particularly in how artists approached the depiction of texture, light, and space.

Van Eyck's work is known for its incredible attention to detail and realism, with a particular focus on light and surface textures. His portraits are notable for their psychological depth and detailed representation of the sitter's character. He pioneered the use of glazing techniques, which involved applying thin layers of paint to create a translucent effect, enhancing the sense of realism.

Van Eyck's influence extended well beyond his lifetime, impacting numerous artists of the Northern Renaissance, including Rogier van der Weyden and Hans Memling. His innovations in oil painting set a new standard for artists and solidified his reputation as a master of realism and a key figure in the development of early Netherlandish art.

Sandro Botticelli

Date of Birth: c. 1445
Place of Birth: Florence, Republic of Florence (now Italy)
Date of Death: May 17, 1510
Place of Death: Florence, Republic of Florence (now Italy)

Short Biography:

Sandro Botticelli, born Alessandro di Mariano di Vanni Filipepi, was a leading painter of the Italian Renaissance. He was born in Florence around 1445. Botticelli apprenticed as a goldsmith before training under the renowned painter Fra Filippo Lippi. By the early 1470s, he had established his own workshop and quickly became known for his skill in painting religious subjects and mythological themes. Botticelli's art was characterized by its linear grace, attention to detail, and use of vibrant colors.

Botticelli became one of the favorite artists of the powerful Medici family, Florence's de facto rulers. He painted numerous works for them, including the famous Adoration of the Magi. His most renowned masterpieces, The Birth of Venus and Primavera, created in the 1480s, are celebrated for their classical themes, elegant forms, and allegorical complexity. These works highlight Botticelli's fascination with mythology and the idealized beauty of the human form.

Later in his life, Botticelli's style shifted towards a more somber and pious tone, influenced by the reformist preacher Girolamo Savonarola, who advocated for a return to religious piety. Botticelli's later works reflect this religious fervor, focusing more on Christian themes and conveying a more introspective mood. He continued painting until his death in 1510.

Influence and Significance on Art:

Botticelli is considered one of the most important artists of the Italian Renaissance. His work is known for its poetic quality, emphasis on beauty, and elegant linear style. Botticelli's paintings display a mastery of composition and narrative, particularly in his mythological scenes, which are filled with symbolic meanings that resonate with Renaissance humanism and Neoplatonic philosophy.

His depiction of figures, with their graceful poses and flowing drapery, significantly influenced the aesthetics of the time. Botticelli's ability to convey emotion and movement through delicate lines and a harmonious palette set him apart from his contemporaries. His work, especially in The Birth of Venus and Primavera, has become iconic, symbolizing the ideals of Renaissance art—beauty, harmony, and a revival of classical themes.

Although Botticelli's reputation declined after his death as High Renaissance artists like Michelangelo and Leonardo da Vinci rose to prominence, his work was rediscovered in the 19th century and has since been recognized for its profound impact on art history. Botticelli's art continues to be celebrated for its technical brilliance, beauty, and embodiment of the intellectual and cultural spirit of the Renaissance.

Hieronymus Bosch

Date of Birth: c. 1450
Place of Birth: 's-Hertogenbosch, Duchy of Brabant (now the Netherlands)
Date of Death: August 9, 1516
Place of Death: 's-Hertogenbosch, Duchy of Brabant (now the Netherlands)

Short Biography:

Hieronymus Bosch, born Jheronimus van Aken, was a Dutch painter known for his distinctive and imaginative style. He was born around 1450 in the town of 's-Hertogenbosch, from which he took his professional name. Bosch's family were painters, and he likely trained in his father's workshop. He spent most of his life in 's-Hertogenbosch, where he was a respected member of the local community and the Brotherhood of Our Lady, a religious confraternity.

Bosch's works are characterized by their fantastical imagery, intricate detail, and complex symbolism. Unlike many of his contemporaries who focused on religious scenes in a more traditional and realistic manner, Bosch's paintings are filled with surreal, often nightmarish, depictions of heaven, hell, and the moral struggles of humankind. His most famous work, The Garden of Earthly Delights (c. 1490–1510), is a triptych that portrays the creation, the fall of humanity, and a hellscape filled with bizarre creatures and tormented figures, showcasing his vivid imagination and unique vision of human folly.

Bosch's other notable works include The Last Judgment, The Haywain Triptych, and The Temptation of St. Anthony. His paintings often feature moralizing themes, with an emphasis on the consequences of sin and the temptations of earthly pleasures.

Influence and Significance on Art:
Hieronymus Bosch is regarded as one of the most innovative and enigmatic artists of the Northern Renaissance. His work broke away from the conventional religious and moral narratives of his time, introducing surreal, dream-like visions that blend fantasy and reality. Bosch's art is seen as a precursor to later movements that embraced imagination and the subconscious, such as surrealism.

His paintings were highly detailed and filled with symbolism, much of which remains open to interpretation. Bosch's depictions of hell, with their grotesque monsters and vivid portrayal of suffering, were unprecedented and have influenced countless artists over the centuries. His work also reflected the anxieties and fears of his time, particularly the tension between the sacred and the profane.

Bosch's influence is evident in the works of Pieter Bruegel the Elder, who expanded on Bosch's themes of human folly and the grotesque. In the 20th century, surrealist artists like Salvador Dalí and René Magritte drew inspiration from Bosch's imaginative use of dream-like imagery and his exploration of the human psyche. Bosch's art continues to captivate modern audiences with its unique blend of religious allegory, moral critique, and fantastical creativity, making him a pivotal figure in the history of Western art.

Leonardo da Vinci

Date of Birth: April 15, 1452
Place of Birth: Vinci, Republic of Florence (now Italy)
Date of Death: May 2, 1519
Place of Death: Amboise, Kingdom of France

Short Biography:
Leonardo da Vinci was an Italian polymath of the Renaissance period, widely regarded as one of the most diversely talented individuals ever to have lived. Born out of wedlock in Vinci, a small town in the Republic of Florence, Leonardo was the son of a notary, Ser Piero, and a peasant woman named Caterina. He received an informal education in Latin, geometry, and mathematics, but his artistic talents were evident from a young age.

At the age of 14, Leonardo began an apprenticeship with the renowned artist Andrea del Verrocchio in Florence. Here, he learned a wide range of skills, including painting, sculpture, and mechanical arts. By 1478, Leonardo had become an independent master, and he worked on numerous commissions throughout his career, although many remained unfinished.

Leonardo's most famous paintings include The Last Supper (1495–1498), a mural depicting the moment Jesus announces that one of his disciples will betray him, and Mona Lisa (c. 1503–1506), a portrait renowned for its subject's enigmatic expression. In addition to his achievements in art, Leonardo was also an accomplished scientist, engineer, and inventor. His notebooks contain detailed sketches and writings on anatomy, astronomy, hydraulics, and flight, demonstrating his insatiable curiosity and understanding of various scientific principles.

Leonardo spent the last years of his life in France, at the invitation of King Francis I, where he continued his studies and work until his death in 1519.

Influence and Significance on Art:
Leonardo da Vinci is often described as the quintessential "Renaissance man," a symbol of the intellectual and artistic ideals of the Renaissance. His contributions to art are unparalleled; his mastery of techniques like sfumato (the fine shading to produce soft transitions between colors and tones) and chiaroscuro (the use of strong contrasts between light and dark) revolutionized painting. These techniques brought a new level of realism and emotional depth to portraiture and religious scenes, influencing countless artists in his time and beyond.

Leonardo's approach to art was deeply scientific. He meticulously studied human anatomy to accurately depict the human body, resulting in some of the most lifelike figures in art history. His notebooks, filled with observations, sketches, and theories, have provided invaluable insight into his methods and have inspired generations of artists, scientists, and engineers.

Beyond painting, Leonardo's designs for machines, architectural plans, and studies of nature show a visionary understanding of the world that was far ahead of his time. His work laid the groundwork for future scientific discoveries and innovations, bridging the gap between art and science.

Leonardo's legacy endures not only in his surviving artworks but also in his lasting impact on how art, science, and the human experience are perceived. His ability to blend imagination with observation has made him a timeless icon of creativity and intellect.

Michelangelo Buonarroti

Date of Birth: March 6, 1475
Place of Birth: Caprese, Republic of Florence (now Italy)
Date of Death: February 18, 1564
Place of Death: Rome, Papal States (now Italy)

Short Biography:

Michelangelo Buonarroti, commonly known as Michelangelo, was an Italian sculptor, painter, architect, and poet, and one of the most influential figures of the Renaissance. Born in Caprese, a small town near Arezzo, Michelangelo moved to Florence at a young age. His talent was recognized early, and he was apprenticed to Domenico Ghirlandaio, a prominent painter. By 1490, Michelangelo was studying classical sculpture in the gardens of the powerful Medici family, under the patronage of Lorenzo de' Medici.

Michelangelo's first major work was the Pietà (1498–1499), a sculpture of the Virgin Mary holding the dead body of Jesus, which he completed when he was just in his early twenties. His David (1501–1504), a colossal marble statue representing the biblical hero, became a symbol of Florentine freedom and is considered one of the greatest sculptures ever created.

In 1508, Michelangelo was commissioned by Pope Julius II to paint the ceiling of the Sistine Chapel in the Vatican, a task that took four years to complete. The ceiling's iconic frescoes, including The Creation of Adam and The Last Judgment (completed in 1541), showcase Michelangelo's mastery of human anatomy, his powerful compositions, and his ability to convey profound spiritual themes.

Throughout his career, Michelangelo also worked as an architect, most notably on the design of the dome of St. Peter's Basilica in Rome, which became a model for church domes worldwide. His architectural style helped shape Renaissance architecture, blending classical elements with innovative forms.

Influence and Significance on Art:

Michelangelo is widely considered one of the greatest artists in history, and his work has had a profound impact on the development of Western art. His sculptures, characterized by their dynamism, anatomical precision, and emotional depth, set new standards for realism and expressive power. Michelangelo's depiction of the human body, with its idealized proportions and muscular form, was deeply influential, inspiring generations of artists to study and emulate his techniques.

His frescoes in the Sistine Chapel are regarded as some of the finest examples of Renaissance art. They not only display Michelangelo's technical prowess but also convey complex theological ideas through innovative compositions and powerful imagery. His work in the chapel marked a turning point in the history of painting, shifting the focus from the decorative to the expressive, and it helped to elevate the status of painting to that of sculpture and architecture.

As an architect, Michelangelo's influence is evident in the Mannerist movement and beyond, as his designs for buildings like the Laurentian Library and St. Peter's Basilica combined functionality with grandeur, showcasing a mastery of space and form.

Michelangelo's legacy extends beyond his art; his writings, including poetry and letters, offer insights into his thoughts on art, philosophy, and the human condition. His unparalleled ability to merge artistic skill with intellectual depth has made Michelangelo a defining figure of the Renaissance, whose works continue to inspire and resonate across the centuries.

Raphael (Raffaello Sanzio da Urbino)

Date of Birth: April 6, 1483
Place of Birth: Urbino, Duchy of Urbino (now Italy)
Date of Death: April 6, 1520
Place of Death: Rome, Papal States (now Italy)

Short Biography:
Raphael, born Raffaello Sanzio, was one of the leading figures of the Italian High Renaissance, known for his exceptional skills in painting and architecture. Born in Urbino, Raphael was the son of Giovanni Santi, a court painter, from whom he received his early training. After his father's death in 1494, Raphael was apprenticed to the painter Pietro Perugino, from whom he inherited a style characterized by clarity, harmony, and graceful figures.

Raphael moved to Florence in 1504, where he studied the works of Leonardo da Vinci and Michelangelo, which greatly influenced his development as an artist. During this period, he created some of his most famous Madonnas, such as The Madonna of the Goldfinch and La Belle Jardinière, blending Perugino's serene compositions with the dynamism and realism of his Florentine contemporaries.

In 1508, Raphael was invited to Rome by Pope Julius II to work on a series of frescoes in the Vatican's Apostolic Palace, marking a significant phase in his career. His work in the Vatican, including The School of Athens (1509-1511) in the Stanza della Segnatura, is celebrated for its brilliant depiction of classical philosophy and its use of perspective and anatomical accuracy. Raphael's frescoes established him as one of the preeminent artists of his time.

Beyond painting, Raphael was also an accomplished architect and was appointed chief architect of St. Peter's Basilica after the death of Donato Bramante. Raphael's untimely death at the age of 37 in 1520 was widely mourned, and he was buried in the Pantheon in Rome, a testament to his revered status.

Influence and Significance on Art:
Raphael's work epitomizes the ideals of the High Renaissance with its emphasis on balance, clarity, and beauty. His paintings are noted for their grace, harmonious composition, and the idealization of the human form. Raphael's ability to blend elements from his predecessors, such as Leonardo's sfumato and Michelangelo's dynamic figures, allowed him to create a distinct and influential style that represented the culmination of Renaissance artistic principles.

His frescoes in the Vatican, particularly The School of Athens, are considered masterpieces of perspective and humanist ideals. The composition showcases not only Raphael's technical skill but also his intellectual engagement with contemporary philosophical and cultural themes. His portrayal of philosophers like Plato and Aristotle in a grand architectural setting reflects the Renaissance's revival of classical knowledge and learning.

Raphael's influence extended far beyond his lifetime, shaping the development of Western art for centuries. His approach to composition and his idealized representation of the human figure influenced artists of the Mannerist movement and later periods. The clarity and harmony found in his work became a standard for academic art, and his compositions were studied and emulated by generations of artists.

Raphael's legacy is also marked by his contributions to architecture and his role in advancing the integration of painting, sculpture, and architecture into a cohesive artistic vision. His ability to synthesize artistic innovation with classical ideals has solidified his reputation as one of the greatest artists of the Renaissance, whose work continues to inspire admiration and study.

Peter Paul Rubens

Date of Birth: June 28, 1577
Place of Birth: Siegen, Westphalia (now in Germany)
Date of Death: May 30, 1640
Place of Death: Antwerp, Spanish Netherlands (now Belgium)

Short Biography:
Peter Paul Rubens was a Flemish Baroque painter renowned for his vibrant compositions, dynamic figures, and mastery of color. Born in Siegen in 1577, Rubens moved with his family to Antwerp, where he was raised in a culturally rich environment. His father, Jan Rubens, was a lawyer and his mother, Maria Pypelinckx, came from a noble family, which provided Rubens with a well-rounded education that included classical literature and languages.

Rubens began his artistic training in Antwerp under the guidance of prominent painters such as Tobias Verhaecht, Adam van Noort, and Otto van Veen. By 1598, he was admitted as a master painter to the Antwerp Guild of Saint Luke. Seeking to further his skills, Rubens traveled to Italy in 1600, where he studied the works of Renaissance masters like Titian, Michelangelo, and Raphael. His time in Italy, particularly his exposure to the vibrant colors and dramatic compositions of the Venetian school, greatly influenced his style.

Returning to Antwerp in 1608, Rubens quickly became one of the most sought-after painters in Europe. His workshop, which employed numerous assistants and apprentices, produced a vast array of works, including religious altarpieces, mythological scenes, portraits, and landscapes. His major commissions included the Raising of the Cross (1610–1611) and the Descent from the Cross (1612–1614) for Antwerp Cathedral, both of which showcase his skill in depicting movement, emotion, and the human form.

Rubens also played a role as a diplomat, leveraging his international connections and cultural knowledge. His diplomatic missions took him to various European courts, where he negotiated peace treaties and secured commissions. This unique combination of artistic and political involvement earned him widespread respect and influence.

Rubens' personal life was marked by two marriages and the birth of several children. He continued to paint until his death in 1640, leaving behind a legacy that would shape the future of European art.

Influence and Significance on Art:
Peter Paul Rubens is considered one of the foremost artists of the Baroque era, celebrated for his energetic style, dramatic compositions, and sensuous portrayal of the human body. His work is characterized by dynamic movement, rich color palettes, and a masterful use of light and shadow, which conveyed a sense of drama and emotion. Rubens' ability to depict the human figure with anatomical accuracy and expressive force was unmatched, and his paintings often featured voluptuous, robust figures in vibrant, dynamic poses.

Rubens' influence extended far beyond his native Flanders. His work helped to spread the Baroque style throughout Europe, particularly in Spain and France, where artists such as Diego Velázquez and Nicolas Poussin drew inspiration from his compositions. Rubens' prolific output and the establishment of a large workshop allowed his artistic style to reach a wide audience, making him a central figure in the development of Baroque painting.

His contributions to religious and mythological art, with their dramatic intensity and emotional depth, set new standards for storytelling through visual art. Rubens' ability to blend classical themes with contemporary Baroque aesthetics made his work appealing to both religious institutions and secular patrons

Rubens' impact on art extended to his role as a teacher and mentor, training a generation of artists, including Anthony van Dyck, who would become notable figures in their own right. His legacy is one of innovation, vitality, and artistic mastery, making him one of the most influential painters in Western art history. His works continue to be admired for their grandeur, emotional power, and technical brilliance.

Artemisia Gentileschi

Date of Birth: July 8, 1593
Place of Birth: Rome, Papal States (now Italy)
Date of Death: c. 1656 (exact date uncertain)
Place of Death: Naples, Kingdom of Naples (now Italy)

Short Biography:
Artemisia Gentileschi was an Italian Baroque painter, known for her powerful depictions of biblical and mythological female figures. Born in Rome in 1593, she was the daughter of Orazio Gentileschi, a prominent painter who was influenced by Caravaggio. Under her father's guidance, Artemisia showed exceptional artistic talent from a young age, learning to paint in the Caravaggesque style characterized by dramatic lighting and realism.

At the age of 17, Artemisia was sexually assaulted by Agostino Tassi, a colleague of her father. The ensuing trial, during which Artemisia was tortured to test the veracity of her testimony, was a highly publicized scandal. Tassi was convicted but faced little punishment, while the ordeal had a profound effect on Artemisia's life and work.

Following the trial, Artemisia moved to Florence, where she became the first woman to be admitted to the prestigious Accademia di Arte del Disegno. Her reputation as an artist grew, and she received patronage from influential figures, including the Medici family. During her time in Florence, she produced some of her most famous works, such as Judith Slaying Holofernes (c. 1614–1620), which portrays the biblical heroine Judith beheading the Assyrian general Holofernes with striking realism and intensity.

Artemisia's career took her to various Italian cities, including Rome, Venice, and Naples, where she continued to paint religious and historical scenes that often featured strong, assertive female protagonists. In the 1630s, she spent some time in England, working at the court of Charles I alongside her father.

Despite facing the challenges of being a woman in a male-dominated field, Artemisia achieved considerable success during her lifetime and was recognized for her artistic skill and unique voice.

Influence and Significance on Art:

Artemisia Gentileschi is regarded as one of the most important female painters of the Baroque era and a pioneering figure in the history of Western art. Her work is celebrated for its dramatic intensity, realistic depiction of the female form, and its focus on powerful women from biblical and mythological narratives. Artemisia's paintings often convey themes of female strength, resilience, and revenge, which have been interpreted as personal responses to her own experiences.

Her use of Caravaggesque techniques, such as chiaroscuro (the contrast of light and shadow), brought a heightened emotional realism to her subjects, setting her apart from her contemporaries. Artemisia's ability to capture psychological depth and complex emotions in her figures added a new dimension to Baroque painting, challenging traditional portrayals of women as passive or decorative.

Artemisia's legacy extends beyond her artistic achievements; she has become a symbol of feminist art history, inspiring modern interpretations and studies of her life and work. Her success in a predominantly male profession, coupled with her resilience in the face of personal adversity, has made her a powerful icon of women's empowerment in the arts.

In recent years, Artemisia's work has gained renewed attention and appreciation, with major exhibitions dedicated to her art and scholarship re-examining her contributions to Baroque painting. Her life and art continue to resonate, offering insight into the struggles and triumphs of women artists throughout history.

Diego Velázquez

Date of Birth: June 6, 1599
Place of Birth: Seville, Spain
Date of Death: August 6, 1660
Place of Death: Madrid, Spain

Short Biography:

Diego Velázquez was a Spanish painter who is widely regarded as one of the greatest artists of the Baroque period and a master of portrait painting. Born in Seville in 1599, Velázquez showed early artistic talent and began his training at the age of 11 under the tutelage of Francisco Pacheco, a prominent painter and art theorist. Velázquez's marriage to Pacheco's daughter, Juana, in 1618 solidified his connection to the art world.

Velázquez's early works in Seville were primarily genre scenes known as "bodegones," which depicted everyday life, often featuring kitchen scenes with figures. These works demonstrated his skill in capturing realistic details and his keen observation of light and texture. His talent quickly gained him recognition, and in 1623, Velázquez moved to Madrid, where he was appointed court painter to King Philip IV of Spain. This position marked the beginning of a long and illustrious career at the Spanish court, where he painted numerous portraits of the king, the royal family, and other nobility.

One of Velázquez's most famous works is Las Meninas (1656), a complex and enigmatic composition that portrays the young Infanta Margarita surrounded by her entourage, with Velázquez himself depicted at his easel. The painting is celebrated for its masterful use of perspective, light, and its exploration of the relationship between reality and illusion.

Throughout his career, Velázquez traveled to Italy twice, in 1629 and 1649, where he studied the works of the Italian masters and absorbed the influence of the Renaissance and Baroque art. His exposure to Italian art further refined his style, evident in the increased sophistication of his later works.

Velázquez continued to serve as a court painter until his death in 1660. His work not only reflects the grandeur of the Spanish court but also displays a profound understanding of human nature and character.

Influence and Significance on Art:
Diego Velázquez is celebrated for his naturalistic approach to painting, his mastery of light and shadow, and his ability to capture the personality and psychological depth of his subjects. His portraits are renowned for their realism and subtlety, often revealing the inner life of the sitter with a sense of dignity and presence. Velázquez's technical skill in depicting textures, such as the sheen of silk or the coarseness of a servant's clothing, set a new standard in painting.

Velázquez's innovative use of composition, perspective, and the handling of paint influenced many artists both during his lifetime and in subsequent generations. His loose brushwork and the way he captured the effects of light with minimal detail foreshadowed the techniques of later artists, including the Impressionists. Édouard Manet, one of the key figures of the Impressionist movement, famously referred to Velázquez as "the painter of painters" and admired his ability to convey realism with apparent effortlessness.

Velázquez's work had a lasting impact on Spanish art, inspiring artists such as Francisco Goya, who regarded him as a significant influence. His approach to portraiture, with its focus on individuality and the human condition, set a benchmark that has endured through the centuries.

Velázquez's legacy is marked by his contribution to the development of a more naturalistic style of painting, his sophisticated handling of complex themes and compositions, and his role in elevating the art of portraiture. His paintings continue to be studied and admired for their technical excellence, emotional depth, and insight into the world of 17th-century Spain.

Rembrandt Harmenszoon van Rijn

Date of Birth: July 15, 1606
Place of Birth: Leiden, Dutch Republic (now the Netherlands)
Date of Death: October 4, 1669
Place of Death: Amsterdam, Dutch Republic (now the Netherlands)

Short Biography:
Rembrandt Harmenszoon van Rijn, commonly known as Rembrandt, was a Dutch painter and etcher, widely considered one of the greatest visual artists in the history of art. Born in Leiden in 1606, Rembrandt was the son of a miller and came from a relatively well-off family. He attended Latin school and enrolled at the University of Leiden, but his passion for art led him to leave his studies to pursue painting.

He began his artistic training under the painter Jacob van Swanenburgh in Leiden and later studied with Pieter Lastman in Amsterdam, where he was exposed to the Caravaggisti style, which emphasized dramatic lighting and realism. By 1625, Rembrandt had opened his own studio in Leiden, and he gained recognition for his distinctive use of light and shadow, as well as his ability to capture human emotion and character.

In 1631, Rembrandt moved to Amsterdam, where he found great success as a portrait painter, drawing commissions from wealthy patrons and becoming one of the city's leading artists. His marriage to Saskia van Uylenburgh, a cousin of an art dealer, further boosted his social status and client base. During this period, Rembrandt created some of his most famous works, including The Anatomy Lesson of Dr. Nicolaes Tulp (1632) and The Night Watch (1642).

Despite his early success, Rembrandt's later years were marked by personal and financial difficulties. The death of his wife Saskia, a series of unsuccessful investments, and mounting debts led to his bankruptcy in 1656. Nonetheless, he continued to produce masterpieces, exploring deeper psychological themes and developing a more expressive style. His later works, including numerous self-portraits and biblical scenes, reflect a profound understanding of the human condition.

Rembrandt died in 1669 and was buried in an unmarked grave in Amsterdam's Westerkerk. His work, however, has endured, leaving a lasting impact on the history of art.

Influence and Significance on Art:
Rembrandt's influence on art is immense, particularly in his mastery of light and shadow (chiaroscuro) and his ability to convey deep human emotion. His portraits and self-portraits are noted for their psychological depth and the way they capture the character and personality of the subjects. Rembrandt's use of lighting to highlight the emotional intensity of a scene set a new standard in portraiture and narrative painting.

His technique of impasto, applying paint thickly to the canvas to create texture and depth, added a tactile dimension to his work that was innovative for its time. Rembrandt's realistic depiction of human anatomy, expression, and emotion, combined with his attention to everyday details, made his paintings relatable and timeless.

Rembrandt's influence extended beyond his lifetime, inspiring countless artists in the Baroque period and beyond. His approach to narrative in painting, characterized by dramatic compositions and a focus on the human experience, influenced the development of realism in Western art. The way he portrayed biblical and mythological scenes with a sense of humanity and intimacy marked a departure from the more formal and idealized representations of his contemporaries.

His self-portraits, spanning his entire career, provide a unique insight into the artist's personal journey and have been widely studied for their introspective quality. Rembrandt's legacy lives on, not only through his paintings and etchings but also through his profound impact on the way artists capture the complexity of the human soul.

Johannes Vermeer

Date of Birth: October 31, 1632
Place of Birth: Delft, Dutch Republic (now the Netherlands)
Date of Death: December 15, 1675
Place of Death: Delft, Dutch Republic (now the Netherlands)

Short Biography:
Johannes Vermeer was a Dutch Baroque painter, known for his masterful use of light and color in domestic interior scenes of middle-class life. Born in Delft in 1632, Vermeer was the son of a silk weaver and art dealer. His early life is not well-documented, but it is believed that he trained as a painter, possibly under the influence of local artists or through an apprenticeship, though no definitive records of his training exist.

Vermeer married Catharina Bolnes in 1653, converting to Catholicism as part of his marriage. He spent most of his life in Delft, where he joined the local Guild of Saint Luke, a trade association for artists, in the same year he married. Despite producing a relatively small number of works—only about 34 paintings are attributed to him with certainty—Vermeer became a respected member of the artistic community.

His paintings often depict serene, everyday scenes set in domestic interiors, focusing on women engaged in various activities, such as reading letters, playing musical instruments, or performing household chores. Some of his most famous works include Girl with a Pearl Earring (c. 1665), The Milkmaid (c. 1658), and The Art of Painting (c. 1666–1668). Vermeer's attention to detail, use of light to create a sense of intimacy, and composition made his works stand out.

Vermeer's career was not particularly prosperous, and he faced financial difficulties, particularly during the economic downturn in the Netherlands following the Franco-Dutch War. His relatively modest output and the lack of commissions contributed to these hardships. Vermeer died suddenly in 1675, leaving his family in debt.

Influence and Significance on Art:
Johannes Vermeer is regarded as one of the greatest painters of the Dutch Golden Age, celebrated for his ability to capture the beauty of ordinary life with extraordinary sensitivity and realism. His mastery of light and his use of a limited color palette to achieve a luminous, almost ethereal quality in his paintings set him apart from his contemporaries.

Vermeer's approach to painting is noted for its photographic precision and use of perspective, which some historians suggest may have been achieved with the aid of optical devices like the camera obscura. His meticulous technique involved layering paint to build depth and texture, allowing him to render light and shadow with subtle gradations that give his works a sense of tranquility and timelessness.

Though Vermeer was not widely known outside of Delft during his lifetime, his work was rediscovered in the 19th century, gaining widespread admiration. His influence is seen in the emphasis on realism and light in the works of later artists, particularly in the 19th and 20th centuries, including the Impressionists who admired his treatment of light.

Vermeer's paintings have been studied for their compositional balance, the interplay of light and shadow, and their ability to convey a sense of stillness and introspection. His work continues to be celebrated for its beauty and technical brilliance, making him one of the most beloved figures in the history of Western art. The enigmatic quality of paintings like Girl with a Pearl Earring has captured the imagination of audiences worldwide, cementing Vermeer's reputation as a master of capturing the intimate and the everyday,

Jean-Antoine Watteau

Date of Birth: October 10, 1684
Place of Birth: Valenciennes, Kingdom of France
Date of Death: July 18, 1721
Place of Death: Nogent-sur-Marne, Kingdom of France

Short Biography:
Jean-Antoine Watteau was a French painter and one of the leading figures of the Rococo movement. Born in Valenciennes in 1684, Watteau showed an early interest in art and began his apprenticeship with a local artist. In 1702, he moved to Paris, where he initially worked in a painting workshop that produced religious and decorative works. His talent soon led him to study under Claude Gillot, a painter known for theatrical and decorative art. It was through Gillot that Watteau was introduced to the world of theater and commedia dell'arte, themes that would later dominate his work.

Watteau's style evolved as he became associated with the newly fashionable Rococo aesthetic, characterized by its lightness, elegance, and playful themes. By the early 1710s, he had begun to gain recognition for his "fêtes galantes," a genre he popularized, which depicted aristocratic outdoor gatherings characterized by flirtation, music, and dance. His masterpiece, Pilgrimage to Cythera (1717), showcases this genre, portraying an idealized vision of lovers traveling to the mythical island of Cythera, the birthplace of Venus.

Watteau's career was relatively brief due to his fragile health. He suffered from tuberculosis, which ultimately led to his premature death at the age of 36. Despite his short life, Watteau's work had a profound impact on the art world, and he was elected a member of the prestigious Académie Royale de Peinture et de Sculpture in 1717.

Influence and Significance on Art:
Jean-Antoine Watteau is celebrated as a pioneer of the Rococo style and a master of capturing the fleeting moments of pleasure and melancholy. His work is distinguished by its lyrical quality, delicate brushwork, and the subtle interplay of light and color. Watteau's ability to convey both the joy and sadness inherent in human experience, often within the same painting, gave his works an emotional depth that was rare in Rococo art.

Watteau's invention of the fête galante genre allowed him to explore themes of love, beauty, and transience in an innovative way. His paintings often feature elegantly dressed figures in idyllic landscapes, engaged in leisurely pursuits, with a sense of grace and fluidity in their movements. The use of soft, pastel colors and the delicate handling of light create a dreamlike atmosphere, enhancing the sense of escapism and fantasy.

Although Watteau's life was cut short, his influence on the Rococo movement was significant. His approach to composition and his sensitivity to the human condition resonated with later artists, including François Boucher and Jean-Honoré Fragonard, who continued to develop the Rococo style. Watteau's work also foreshadowed Romanticism, with its emphasis on emotion and the individual's experience.

In addition to his paintings, Watteau's numerous sketches and drawings, characterized by their spontaneity and expressiveness, have been admired for their insight into his creative process. His legacy endures as a key figure who captured the essence of early 18th-century French society, blending elegance with a poignant sense of impermanence, and profoundly influencing the direction of European art.

Jean-Honoré Fragonard

Date of Birth: April 5, 1732
Place of Birth: Grasse, Kingdom of France
Date of Death: August 22, 1806
Place of Death: Paris, France

Short Biography:
Jean-Honoré Fragonard was a French painter and printmaker known for his exuberant and sensual paintings that epitomize the Rococo style. Born in Grasse in 1732, Fragonard moved to Paris with his family at a young age. His talent for drawing was evident early on, and he began his artistic training under the renowned Rococo artist François Boucher, one of the leading painters of the time. Fragonard also studied briefly under Jean-Baptiste-Siméon Chardin and later with Carle Vanloo at the French Academy.

In 1752, Fragonard won the prestigious Prix de Rome, which allowed him to study at the French Academy in Rome. His time in Italy had a profound impact on his work, exposing him to the art of the Renaissance and Baroque periods, which influenced his style and subject matter. Upon his return to Paris in the late 1750s, Fragonard established himself as a leading painter of the Rococo movement, gaining fame for his skill in capturing scenes of romance, playful eroticism, and idyllic garden settings.

Some of his most famous works include The Swing (c. 1767), The Stolen Kiss (c. 1786), and The Progress of Love series (1771–1773), which was commissioned for Madame du Barry, the mistress of King Louis XV. These paintings are celebrated for their lush colors, lighthearted themes, and the sensuality with which Fragonard depicted his subjects.

With the onset of the French Revolution in the late 18th century, Fragonard's style fell out of favor, and his career declined. He retreated to Grasse with his family, returning to Paris only in his later years. Fragonard died in relative obscurity in 1806, but his work has since been recognized as some of the finest examples of Rococo art.

Influence and Significance on Art:
Jean-Honoré Fragonard is regarded as one of the greatest painters of the Rococo period, known for his ability to capture the playful, intimate, and sensual aspects of 18th-century French aristocratic life. His work embodies the lightness and elegance of Rococo art, characterized by soft, pastel colors, fluid brushwork, and the depiction of carefree, often flirtatious subjects. Fragonard's paintings are celebrated for their ability to convey a sense of joy and frivolity, often set in lush, romanticized landscapes or opulent interiors.

Fragonard's mastery of color and light, combined with his skill in rendering textures and fabrics, gave his works a sense of vitality and immediacy. His ability to create a narrative within his paintings, often filled with suggestive symbolism and hidden meanings, made his works popular among the aristocracy of his time, who appreciated the blend of sensuality and wit.

While Fragonard's popularity waned with the decline of the Rococo style during the French Revolution, his influence persisted, especially in the 19th century, when his work was rediscovered and admired by artists and collectors. His emphasis on sensuality and emotional expressiveness can be seen as a precursor to the Romantic movement, which followed Rococo.

Fragonard's legacy lives on through his contributions to the development of French painting, his ability to capture the spirit of his age, and his influence on future generations of artists. His works continue to be admired for their technical brilliance, charm, and ability to evoke the pleasures and beauty of life, making him a significant figure in the history of Western art.

Francisco Goya

Date of Birth: March 30, 1746
Place of Birth: Fuendetodos, Aragon, Spain
Date of Death: April 16, 1828
Place of Death: Bordeaux, France

Short Biography:
Francisco de Goya y Lucientes was a Spanish painter and printmaker who is considered one of the most important artists of the late 18th and early 19th centuries. Born in the small village of Fuendetodos in Aragon, Goya moved to Madrid in his youth, where he studied painting. In 1763, Goya applied to the Royal Academy of Fine Arts of San Fernando but was rejected. Despite this setback, he traveled to Italy in 1771 to further his studies and was influenced by the works of the Renaissance and Baroque masters.

Upon his return to Spain, Goya secured work as a designer of religious frescoes and tapestries for the Royal Tapestry Factory, which earned him a growing reputation. His successful tapestry designs for the Spanish royal court led to a series of portrait commissions, and in 1786, he became the official court painter to King Charles III. Under King Charles IV, Goya was appointed First Court Painter, producing numerous portraits of the Spanish aristocracy, including the iconic The Family of Charles IV (1800).

Goya's career took a darker turn during the Napoleonic Wars and the subsequent Peninsular War (1808–1814), which brought devastation to Spain. These events profoundly affected Goya, leading him to create powerful works such as The Third of May 1808 (1814), which depicts the execution of Spanish rebels by French soldiers. This painting is considered one of the first great pieces of modern art for its emotional intensity and stark realism.

In his later years, Goya suffered from illness that left him deaf, which contributed to a period of introspection and the creation of his haunting Black Paintings series. These works, characterized by their dark themes and nightmarish imagery, were painted directly onto the walls of his home. Goya eventually moved to Bordeaux, France, where he continued to work until his death in 1828.

Influence and Significance on Art:

Francisco Goya is often regarded as the last of the Old Masters and the first of the modern artists. His work spans a range of styles, from Rococo to Romanticism, and his ability to convey deep emotion, social commentary, and personal introspection set him apart from his contemporaries. Goya's career marks a transition from the traditional to the modern, and his willingness to explore and portray the darker sides of human nature and society anticipated many of the themes found in later art movements.

Goya's portraits are noted for their psychological depth and realism, capturing not just the physical likeness but also the character and mood of his subjects. His innovative use of light and shadow, combined with expressive brushwork, gave his paintings a powerful immediacy. Goya's work as a printmaker, particularly his Los Caprichos series, utilized etching and aquatint to critique social, political, and religious issues of his time, showcasing his skill as both an artist and a satirist.

The Disasters of War series, depicting the brutality of the Napoleonic invasion of Spain, is a harrowing portrayal of human suffering and remains a powerful anti-war statement. These works, along with The Third of May 1808, are seen as precursors to modernist approaches to depicting conflict and human suffering.

Goya's Black Paintings reflect his existential fears and disillusionment with society, revealing a more personal and subjective approach to art. These paintings influenced the Symbolist and Expressionist movements in the late 19th and early 20th centuries, with their exploration of the subconscious and the grotesque.

Overall, Francisco Goya's versatility, depth of expression, and bold experimentation have left a lasting impact on the development of modern art, influencing artists from Édouard Manet to Pablo Picasso and beyond. His work remains a testament to the power of art to reflect and challenge the human condition.

Caspar David Friedrich

Date of Birth: September 5, 1774
Place of Birth: Greifswald, Swedish Pomerania (now Germany)
Date of Death: May 7, 1840
Place of Death: Dresden, Kingdom of Saxony (now Germany)

Short Biography:

Caspar David Friedrich was a German Romantic landscape painter known for his deeply symbolic and atmospheric works that capture the sublime power of nature and the human experience. Born in Greifswald in 1774, Friedrich experienced personal tragedy early in life, including the deaths of his mother and several siblings, events that would profoundly influence his outlook and art.

Friedrich studied art at the Academy of Fine Arts in Copenhagen from 1794 to 1798, where he was influenced by Danish landscape artists and the ideas of Romanticism, which emphasized emotion, individualism, and the beauty of the natural world. In 1798, he moved to Dresden, which became his home base for the rest of his life. There, he became part of a circle of Romantic writers, poets, and philosophers who shaped his artistic vision.

Friedrich's landscapes are characterized by their contemplative mood, often depicting solitary figures gazing out over vast, mysterious landscapes. His use of atmospheric effects, such as mist, fog, and twilight, creates a sense of melancholy and introspection. Some of his most famous works include Wanderer above the Sea of Fog (c. 1818), which portrays a lone figure standing on a rocky precipice, and The Abbey in the Oakwood (1809-1810), a haunting depiction of a ruined Gothic abbey surrounded by barren trees.

Friedrich's art often incorporates elements of Christian symbolism and the themes of life, death, and the infinite. His work reflects a deep spiritualism and a belief in the transcendental quality of nature. Despite being recognized in his lifetime, Friedrich's reputation declined in his later years, and he struggled financially. He died in 1840 in relative obscurity, but his work was later rediscovered and celebrated as a quintessential expression of Romanticism.

Influence and Significance on Art:
Caspar David Friedrich is considered one of the most important figures of the Romantic movement in Germany, and his work has had a lasting impact on the development of landscape painting. His approach to landscape was revolutionary for its time, moving beyond mere topographical representation to explore the emotional and spiritual dimensions of nature. Friedrich's landscapes invite the viewer to reflect on the sublime and the transcendent, offering a meditative space that encourages introspection and a sense of connection with the infinite.

Friedrich's emphasis on the contemplative experience of nature influenced later artists and movements, including the Symbolists and the Impressionists, who admired his ability to convey mood and atmosphere. His use of light, shadow, and perspective to create a sense of depth and mystery set a precedent for how landscape could be used to express inner emotional states.

In the 20th century, Friedrich's work was rediscovered by Expressionists and Surrealists, who were drawn to his exploration of the unconscious and the metaphysical. His landscapes, with their brooding atmospheres and themes of solitude, also resonated with existentialist thought and the modern exploration of human isolation and the search for meaning.

Friedrich's art remains a powerful testament to the Romantic vision of nature as a source of spiritual and emotional insight. His ability to evoke the sublime beauty and mystery of the natural world continues to captivate audiences, making him one of the most enduring and influential landscape painters in the history of Western art.

Joseph Mallord William Turner

Date of Birth: April 23, 1775
Place of Birth: Covent Garden, London, England
Date of Death: December 19, 1851
Place of Death: Cheyne Walk, Chelsea, London, England

Short Biography:

Joseph Mallord William Turner, often simply known as J.M.W. Turner, was a British painter renowned for his expressive landscapes and seascapes, which are celebrated for their dramatic use of light and color. Born in London in 1775, Turner was the son of a barber and wig-maker. His talent for drawing was evident from an early age, and by the age of 14, he had enrolled in the Royal Academy of Arts. Turner exhibited his first watercolor at the Royal Academy when he was just 15, marking the beginning of a prolific and successful career.

Turner initially trained as a topographical watercolorist, but his work quickly evolved as he explored the possibilities of light, color, and atmospheric effects. He traveled extensively throughout Britain and Europe, drawing inspiration from natural landscapes, architecture, and the sea. Some of his early works, such as Fishermen at Sea (1796), demonstrated his ability to convey the power and majesty of nature.

Throughout his career, Turner experimented with innovative techniques and compositions, often pushing the boundaries of traditional landscape painting. His later works, such as The Fighting Temeraire (1839) and Rain, Steam and Speed – The Great Western Railway (1844), are characterized by their almost abstract treatment of light and color, emphasizing the interplay between natural elements and human endeavor. Turner's fascination with the sublime, the awe-inspiring, and the uncontrollable forces of nature is evident in many of his paintings, which often depict dramatic scenes of storms, shipwrecks, and natural disasters.

Turner's contributions to art extended beyond painting; he was also a respected printmaker and lecturer. He remained deeply involved with the Royal Academy throughout his life, both as a student and later as a professor of perspective. Turner never married and lived a reclusive life in his later years, continuing to paint until his death in 1851.

Influence and Significance on Art:

J.M.W. Turner is widely regarded as one of the greatest landscape painters in Western art history. His innovative approach to capturing light, atmosphere, and motion paved the way for the later developments in Impressionism and abstract art. Turner's ability to depict the transformative power of light and his use of loose, expressive brushstrokes set him apart from his contemporaries, making him a pivotal figure in the transition from traditional representational art to modernist abstraction.

Turner's work had a significant influence on the French Impressionists, including Claude Monet, who admired Turner's ability to convey the fleeting effects of light and weather. His emphasis on color over form and his exploration of the emotional and sensory impact of natural phenomena anticipated many aspects of modern art. Turner's dramatic and emotional portrayals of the natural world also resonated with the Romantic movement's emphasis on the sublime and the power of nature.

Turner's legacy is reflected not only in his groundbreaking paintings but also in his contributions to the understanding of color theory and his impact on subsequent generations of artists. His exploration of natural light and its effects on landscapes inspired artists to see the world differently, breaking away from precise, detailed representations toward a more evocative and atmospheric approach. Turner's influence can be seen in the works of later artists, including the American Hudson River School painters and the broader development of landscape painting in the 19th and 20th centuries.

Turner's work remains highly influential, celebrated for its emotional depth, technical mastery, and innovative vision, cementing his reputation as a pioneer of modern landscape painting.

Jean-Auguste-Dominique Ingres

Date of Birth: August 29, 1780
Place of Birth: Montauban, Kingdom of France
Date of Death: January 14, 1867
Place of Death: Paris, France

Short Biography:

Jean-Auguste-Dominique Ingres was a French Neoclassical painter, known for his precision in drawing and his meticulous attention to detail. Born in Montauban in 1780, Ingres was the son of a successful painter and sculptor, who encouraged his artistic development from a young age. At the age of 16, Ingres moved to Paris to study at the Royal Academy of Painting and Sculpture under the renowned Neoclassical painter Jacques-Louis David, whose influence is evident in Ingres's early work.

Ingres won the prestigious Prix de Rome in 1801, allowing him to study at the French Academy in Rome, where he absorbed the classical ideals of Greek and Roman art, as well as the works of Renaissance masters like Raphael, who remained a lifelong inspiration. His early works during his time in Italy, such as Napoleon I on His Imperial Throne (1806) and The Valpinçon Bather (1808), showcased his skill in portraiture and his ability to depict the human figure with clarity and grace.

Returning to Paris in 1824, Ingres's career flourished with the success of The Vow of Louis XIII, a work that reaffirmed his place as a leading artist of the French school. Throughout his life, Ingres painted numerous portraits of prominent figures of his time, including Madame Moitessier (1856) and Louis-François Bertin (1832), which are celebrated for their realism, attention to detail, and psychological depth.

Ingres also produced a number of notable historical and mythological paintings, such as The Apotheosis of Homer (1827) and The Turkish Bath (1862), which combined his mastery of line with sensuality and rich color. Despite facing criticism from proponents of Romanticism, who saw his style as overly rigid and conservative, Ingres remained a staunch advocate of the Neoclassical ideals of clarity, form, and restraint throughout his career.

Ingres served as the director of the French Academy in Rome from 1835 to 1841 and was a highly influential teacher. He continued to paint until his death in Paris in 1867.

Influence and Significance on Art:

Jean-Auguste-Dominique Ingres is considered one of the leading figures of Neoclassicism, a movement that sought to revive the ideals of classical art, emphasizing line, form, and composition over color and emotional expression. His insistence on the primacy of drawing as the foundation of painting influenced generations of artists, making him a key figure in 19th-century academic art.

Ingres's portraits are renowned for their precision, elegance, and the psychological insight they provide into his subjects. His mastery of line, often described as pure and unerring, set a standard for academic portraiture. Ingres's works, such as The Grande Odalisque (1814), are characterized by their idealized forms and elongation, which create a sense of harmony and balance while subtly introducing an element of sensuality.

While Ingres was initially criticized by some for his adherence to classical ideals, his work influenced not only his contemporaries but also later movements. The clarity and purity of his lines inspired artists associated with the Symbolist and Art Nouveau movements, such as Gustave Moreau and Henri Matisse. Even the Impressionists, who broke away from academic traditions, acknowledged Ingres's technical skill and his ability to convey the beauty of the human form.

Ingres's legacy endures in the way he bridged the gap between classical and modern art, combining rigorous academic training with a unique personal style that continues to resonate with audiences. His emphasis on the importance of line and form in painting laid the groundwork for many future developments in European art, solidifying his place as one of the great masters of the Neoclassical era.

Théodore Géricault

Date of Birth: September 26, 1791
Place of Birth: Rouen, France
Date of Death: January 26, 1824
Place of Death: Paris, France

Short Biography:
Théodore Géricault was a French painter and one of the pioneers of the Romantic movement in art. Born in Rouen in 1791, Géricault moved to Paris with his family when he was a child. He began his artistic training under the classical painter Pierre-Narcisse Guérin, although he soon found himself drawn to more dynamic and emotional styles. He was influenced by the works of Peter Paul Rubens and the Baroque era's dramatic use of light and shadow.

Géricault's early works, such as Officer of the Imperial Guard (1812) and Wounded Cuirassier (1814), exhibited his interest in military subjects and heroic themes, reflecting the tumultuous Napoleonic era. His fascination with dramatic and powerful imagery led him to a study of horses, which became a recurring subject in his art.

Géricault's most famous work, The Raft of the Medusa (1818–1819), established his reputation as a leading Romantic artist. The painting was inspired by a contemporary event: the wreck of the French frigate Méduse and the subsequent abandonment of its crew and passengers on a makeshift raft. Géricault conducted extensive research for the painting, interviewing survivors, studying the raft's design, and even visiting morgues to accurately depict the suffering and desperation of the shipwrecked figures. The monumental canvas, with its realistic portrayal of human agony and suffering, created a sensation when it was exhibited at the Paris Salon in 1819.

In his later years, Géricault explored themes of madness and social isolation, producing a series of portraits depicting the mentally ill, known as The Monomaniacs. These works reflect his interest in psychological realism and empathy for the marginalized.

Géricault's health declined in the early 1820s, partly due to injuries sustained in a horse-riding accident and complications from tuberculosis. He died in Paris in 1824 at the young age of 32.

Influence and Significance on Art:
Théodore Géricault is considered one of the founding figures of Romanticism in French art, characterized by his emotional intensity, dramatic compositions, and focus on contemporary and often controversial subjects. His work marked a departure from the neoclassical tradition that dominated the French art scene, emphasizing emotion, movement, and the sublime rather than calm rationality and idealized beauty.

The Raft of the Medusa is regarded as a seminal work in the Romantic movement, with its focus on human suffering and the raw power of nature. The painting's realism, combined with its social and political commentary, influenced other artists of the time, including Eugène Delacroix, who would become a leading figure in Romantic painting. Géricault's approach to depicting real-life events with emotional honesty and dramatic flair set a new standard for history painting.

Géricault's interest in the human psyche and his compassionate portrayal of the marginalized foreshadowed themes that would become central to later 19th-century art, including realism and early modernist movements. His study of horses and dynamic figures contributed to a new understanding of movement and anatomical accuracy in painting.

Despite his short life, Géricault's impact on the development of Romanticism and his influence on subsequent generations of artists, including Delacroix, Honoré Daumier, and even 20th-century Expressionists, is profound. His legacy is that of an artist unafraid to confront the harsh realities of human existence, using art as a powerful medium to explore and communicate the depths of the human experience.

Asher B. Durand

Date of Birth: August 21, 1796
Place of Birth: Jefferson Village (now Maplewood), New Jersey, United States
Date of Death: September 17, 1886
Place of Death: Maplewood, New Jersey, United States

Short Biography:
Asher Brown Durand was an American painter and engraver, recognized as one of the leading figures of the Hudson River School, a group of landscape painters known for their romantic portrayal of the American wilderness. Born in Jefferson Village, New Jersey, in 1796, Durand initially trained as an engraver. He apprenticed with Peter Maverick, a prominent engraver in New York City, and quickly gained a reputation for his skill, particularly in producing detailed banknote engravings.

Durand's transition from engraving to painting began in the 1830s, influenced by his friendship with the painter Thomas Cole, the founder of the Hudson River School. Durand's early paintings were characterized by precise, finely detailed depictions of nature, reflecting his background in engraving. His work captured the American landscape with a sense of reverence and realism, emphasizing the beauty and spiritual qualities of nature.

One of Durand's most famous works, Kindred Spirits (1849), depicts the artist Thomas Cole and the poet William Cullen Bryant standing on a rocky outcrop in the Catskill Mountains, symbolizing the bond between art, nature, and poetry. This painting became an iconic representation of the Hudson River School's ideals, celebrating the natural beauty of the American landscape.

Throughout his career, Durand traveled extensively, sketching scenes in the Adirondacks, the Catskills, and the White Mountains. His paintings often feature tranquil scenes of forests, rivers, and mountains, marked by their clarity, light, and attention to detail. Durand's essays, published as Letters on Landscape Painting (1855), provided insight into his artistic philosophy, emphasizing the importance of direct observation of nature.

Durand continued to paint and influence American landscape painting until his death in 1886, leaving behind a legacy that celebrated the unspoiled beauty of the American wilderness.

Influence and Significance on Art:
Asher B. Durand is considered one of the central figures of the Hudson River School, playing a crucial role in defining and promoting the movement's aesthetic and philosophical values. His work emphasized the importance of faithfully representing nature, advocating for a detailed and realistic portrayal of the American landscape. Durand's belief that nature was a reflection of the divine influenced his approach to painting, where he sought to capture not just the physical appearance of the landscape but also its spiritual essence.

Durand's meticulous attention to detail and his use of light to convey atmosphere and mood had a significant impact on his contemporaries and later generations of American landscape painters. His landscapes are noted for their serene beauty, clarity, and the sense of peace they evoke, reflecting the Romantic ideal of the sublime as found in nature.

In addition to his paintings, Durand's writings and lectures on landscape painting helped to shape the artistic practices of his time, encouraging artists to study nature directly and develop their individual responses to the natural world. His advocacy for plein air (outdoor) painting and his emphasis on the moral and spiritual value of nature contributed to the broader cultural appreciation of the American wilderness.

Durand's legacy lies in his contribution to American art and the Hudson River School, influencing artists such as Albert Bierstadt, Frederic Edwin Church, and others who followed in his footsteps. His celebration of the natural landscape played a vital role in fostering a sense of national identity and pride in America's natural heritage, leaving an enduring impact on the American artistic tradition.

Eugène Delacroix

Date of Birth: April 26, 1798
Place of Birth: Charenton-Saint-Maurice, Île-de-France, France
Date of Death: August 13, 1863
Place of Death: Paris, France'

Short Biography:
Eugène Delacroix was a leading French Romantic painter known for his expressive brushwork, vibrant use of color, and dramatic compositions. Born in 1798 in Charenton-Saint-Maurice, Delacroix was the son

of Charles-François Delacroix, a government official, and Victoire Oeben, an artistic and literary woman. Delacroix began his artistic training at the Lycée Louis-le-Grand in Paris and later studied under the painter Pierre-Narcisse Guérin, whose neoclassical style influenced his early development.

Delacroix's breakthrough came in 1822 with the exhibition of his painting The Barque of Dante, which depicted a scene from Dante's Inferno with vivid emotion and dramatic intensity. His most famous work, Liberty Leading the People (1830), was inspired by the July Revolution of 1830 in France. The painting features a powerful allegorical figure of Liberty leading a diverse group of people over a barricade, symbolizing the fight for freedom. This work became an icon of revolutionary spirit and remains one of the most recognizable images of the Romantic era.

Throughout his career, Delacroix traveled extensively, including a significant journey to Morocco in 1832, which deeply influenced his work. The vivid colors, exotic landscapes, and depictions of North African culture became recurring themes in his art. Delacroix was also inspired by literature and history, often drawing on the works of Shakespeare, Goethe, and Byron for his subjects. His fascination with dramatic and emotional scenes can be seen in works like The Death of Sardanapalus (1827) and The Massacre at Chios (1824).

In addition to his paintings, Delacroix was a prolific writer and maintained detailed journals, offering insights into his thoughts on art, politics, and society. He continued to paint and exhibit until his death in 1863, leaving behind a legacy as one of the most important figures in the Romantic movement.

Influence and Significance on Art:
Eugène Delacroix is considered one of the greatest Romantic painters, known for his dynamic compositions, expressive use of color, and ability to convey powerful emotions. His style marked a departure from the neoclassical emphasis on order and restraint, embracing instead the energy, passion, and unpredictability of the Romantic spirit. Delacroix's innovative approach to color, using bold contrasts and vibrant hues to create drama and movement, had a profound impact on the development of modern painting.

Delacroix's influence extended to many artists who admired his daring use of color and expressive brushwork, including the Impressionists and Post-Impressionists. Artists such as Vincent van Gogh, Paul Cézanne, and Pierre-Auguste Renoir were inspired by Delacroix's techniques and his belief in the emotional power of color. His works also foreshadowed aspects of Symbolism and even Abstract Expressionism, with their emphasis on emotional depth and expressive use of paint.

Delacroix's fascination with exotic subjects and his portrayal of non-European cultures contributed to the Orientalist movement in 19th-century art. His depictions of North African scenes and people, though sometimes criticized for their romanticized view, opened up new avenues for artistic exploration and broadened the scope of Western art.

In addition to his impact on painting, Delacroix's writings and theoretical ideas about color theory and composition influenced generations of artists. His role as a bridge between the Romantic movement and the later developments in modern art solidified his place as a key figure in the history of art, celebrated for his ability to capture the essence of human emotion and the beauty of the natural world.

Honoré Daumier

Date of Birth: February 26, 1808
Place of Birth: Marseille, France
Date of Death: February 10, 1879
Place of Death: Valmondois, France

Short Biography:
Honoré Daumier was a French painter, sculptor, and printmaker, renowned for his satirical caricatures and social commentary. Born in Marseille in 1808, Daumier moved to Paris with his family in 1816. He initially worked as a legal clerk but soon turned to art, where he found his true calling. Daumier began his artistic career as a lithographer, producing satirical cartoons for various Parisian newspapers, including La Caricature and Le Charivari. His sharp wit and keen observations of contemporary society quickly made him one of the most influential caricaturists of his time.

Daumier's work often targeted the political and social issues of the day, including the corruption and incompetence of government officials, the injustices of the legal system, and the hypocrisies of bourgeois society. One of his most famous lithographs, Gargantua (1831), criticized King Louis-Philippe, depicting him as a giant consuming the wealth of the poor, which led to Daumier's imprisonment for six months. Despite the risks, he continued to use his art as a tool for social criticism, creating over 4,000 lithographs during his career.

In addition to his lithographic work, Daumier was a skilled painter and sculptor. His paintings, such as The Third-Class Carriage (c. 1862–1864), depicted the struggles and dignity of the working class with a realism that anticipated the later Realist and Impressionist movements. His sculptures, like the series of busts titled Celebrities of the Juste Milieu, provided a three-dimensional extension of his caricature work.

Despite his prolific output and influence, Daumier lived much of his life in poverty. His later years were marked by financial difficulties and declining health. He died in relative obscurity in 1879, but his work was soon rediscovered and celebrated for its artistic and social significance.

Influence and Significance on Art:
Honoré Daumier is considered one of the most important figures in 19th-century French art, known for his pioneering role in the development of political satire and social realism. His work had a significant impact on the art of caricature, using humor and exaggeration to comment on societal issues and human behavior. Daumier's ability to blend art with social critique set a precedent for future generations of artists, making him a precursor to modern editorial cartoonists.

Daumier's influence extended beyond caricature; his realistic portrayal of everyday life and the struggles of ordinary people resonated with the Realist movement, led by artists like Gustave Courbet. His use of light, shadow, and composition to convey mood and character also foreshadowed the techniques of the Impressionists, who admired his focus on contemporary urban life and his candid, unidealized approach to his subjects.

Daumier's work, with its emphasis on social justice and empathy for the common people, continues to be relevant and admired for its bold commentary and technical skill. His ability to capture the essence of human nature with both humor and compassion has made him a lasting figure in the history of art. Daumier's legacy lives on through his contributions to visual satire, his influence on later artistic movements, and his enduring power to provoke thought and reflection through his art.

Jean-François Millet

Date of Birth: October 4, 1814
Place of Birth: Gruchy, near Gréville-Hague, Normandy, France
Date of Death: January 20, 1875
Place of Death: Barbizon, France

Short Biography:
Jean-François Millet was a French painter and one of the founders of the Barbizon School, known for his depictions of rural life and peasant laborers. Born in the small farming village of Gruchy in Normandy in 1814, Millet was raised in a humble, rural environment, which had a lasting impact on his work. Initially trained in the classical tradition, he moved to Paris in 1837 to study art, enrolling in the studio of Paul Delaroche. Despite the influence of academic training, Millet was drawn to themes of rustic life and everyday labor.

Millet's early career was marked by struggles for recognition and financial stability. He moved to the village of Barbizon in the late 1840s, where he became associated with the Barbizon School of painters, a group that advocated for plein air painting and the portrayal of nature and rural life. It was during this period that Millet developed his signature style, focusing on the dignity and hardships of peasant life. His paintings depicted scenes of sowing, harvesting, and other agrarian tasks, infused with a sense of solemnity and humanity.

Some of Millet's most famous works include The Gleaners (1857), which shows three peasant women gleaning leftover grain from the field, and The Angelus (1857–1859), depicting two workers pausing for prayer in a field at dusk. These paintings, characterized by their muted color palette, careful composition, and empathy for the working class, resonated with contemporary viewers and critics, though they also faced criticism for their focus on the plight of the rural poor.

Millet's later years were marked by increasing recognition and success, but he remained dedicated to portraying the rural life he knew so well. He continued to live and work in Barbizon until his death in 1875.

Influence and Significance on Art:
Jean-François Millet is considered a key figure in the Realist movement, known for his sympathetic portrayal of rural laborers and his commitment to depicting the realities of peasant life. His focus on ordinary people engaged in everyday tasks marked a departure from the historical and mythological subjects that dominated academic art at the time, contributing to a broader shift towards realism in art.

Millet's work had a profound influence on later artists, particularly those interested in social realism and the representation of the working class. His honest and respectful portrayal of rural life inspired painters like Vincent van Gogh, who admired Millet's ability to capture the dignity and struggles of common people. Van Gogh, in particular, saw Millet as a role model and created numerous works inspired by Millet's themes and compositions.

The emotional depth and simplicity of Millet's paintings also influenced the development of the Symbolist movement and laid the groundwork for later artistic explorations of social issues. His depiction of labor, prayer, and the connection between humans and the land resonated with the Romantic idealization of nature while also providing a realistic portrayal of the challenges faced by rural communities.

Millet's legacy endures through his impact on the evolution of modern art and his ability to convey the universal human experience through the depiction of everyday life. His work continues to be celebrated for its compassionate portrayal of the working class and its influence on the course of 19th-century painting.

Emanuel Leutze

Date of Birth: May 24, 1816
Place of Birth: Schwäbisch Gmünd, Kingdom of Württemberg (now Germany)
Date of Death: July 18, 1868
Place of Death: Washington, D.C., United States

Short Biography:
Emanuel Leutze was a German-American painter best known for his large-scale historical paintings, particularly those depicting American Revolutionary War themes. Born in Schwäbisch Gmünd, Germany, in 1816, Leutze moved with his family to the United States when he was nine years old, settling in Philadelphia. His artistic talents were recognized early on, and after studying under local artists, he returned to Europe in 1840 to further his training at the prestigious Kunstakademie Düsseldorf in Germany.

Leutze's time in Düsseldorf placed him in contact with other artists of the Düsseldorf School, known for their detailed and dramatic historical and genre scenes. His painting style combined the narrative clarity and romanticism of this school with themes that resonated with his American roots. His most famous work, Washington Crossing the Delaware (1851), was painted in Germany but celebrated in the United States. The painting depicts General George Washington's surprise attack on the Hessian forces during the American Revolutionary War. With its dramatic composition and heroic portrayal of Washington, the painting quickly became an iconic representation of American patriotism and courage.

Leutze returned to the United States in 1859, where he continued to paint historical subjects, focusing on themes of freedom, democracy, and American identity. In addition to his paintings, Leutze was active in cultural and political circles, advocating for democratic ideals and the abolitionist movement.

Leutze's later works included murals and portraits, and he was commissioned to create a large mural in the United States Capitol, Westward the Course of Empire Takes Its Way (1861), which celebrates the spirit of American expansion and manifest destiny. Leutze continued to work until his death in Washington, D.C., in 1868.

Influence and Significance on Art:
Emanuel Leutze is best remembered for his iconic painting Washington Crossing the Delaware, which has become one of the most recognizable images in American art. This work exemplifies his ability to combine dramatic narrative, historical accuracy, and symbolic patriotism, making it a powerful representation

of American history and values. The painting's dramatic use of light, color, and composition captures a sense of heroism and determination that resonated with 19th-century audiences, particularly during times of national conflict and identity formation.

Leutze's impact on American art extended beyond his famous paintings. His involvement in the Düsseldorf School helped bridge European and American artistic traditions, and his advocacy for democratic ideals in both his art and personal life influenced the cultural and political landscape of his time. Leutze's work contributed to the development of a distinct American historical painting genre, inspiring other artists to explore themes of national identity, freedom, and democracy.

In addition to his contributions to American history painting, Leutze's role as a cultural figure and advocate for progressive causes, including the abolition of slavery, highlights the intersection of art and social change in his career. His murals in the United States Capitol continue to serve as visual embodiments of the American spirit of exploration and progress.

Leutze's legacy is marked by his ability to capture key moments in American history with both artistic skill and emotional depth, making his work an enduring symbol of American patriotism and the struggle for liberty.

John Everett Millais

Date of Birth: June 8, 1829
Place of Birth: Southampton, England
Date of Death: August 13, 1896
Place of Death: London, England

Short Biography
John Everett Millais was a British painter and one of the founding members of the Pre-Raphaelite Brotherhood, a group of young artists who sought to reform the art establishment by rejecting the academic standards of their time. Born in Southampton in 1829, Millais showed prodigious artistic talent at an early age and was admitted to the Royal Academy Schools in London at the age of 11, making him the youngest student ever to enroll.

In 1848, Millais, along with Dante Gabriel Rossetti and William Holman Hunt, formed the Pre-Raphaelite Brotherhood. The group aimed to return to the detailed, vibrant, and naturalistic styles found in art before the High Renaissance, particularly inspired by the early Italian and Flemish masters. Millais' painting Isabella (1849) was one of the first works to embody the principles of the Pre-Raphaelite movement, characterized by its vivid color, attention to detail, and realistic depiction of the scene.

One of Millais' most famous works, Ophelia (1851–1852), depicts the tragic Shakespearean character Ophelia floating in a river surrounded by flowers. The painting is noted for its meticulous attention to botanical detail, vibrant color palette, and emotional intensity. Ophelia exemplifies the Pre-Raphaelite approach to combining literary inspiration with an almost photographic realism.

In the later part of his career, Millais moved away from the detailed Pre-Raphaelite style, adopting a broader, more painterly approach. He became a highly successful portrait painter and created popular works that appealed to Victorian tastes, such as Bubbles (1886). His shift in style and subjects helped secure his position as one of the leading artists of his time. Millais was elected as a member of the Royal Academy in 1863 and became its president in 1896, shortly before his death.

Influence and Significance on Art:
John Everett Millais played a pivotal role in the establishment and success of the Pre-Raphaelite Brotherhood, which had a profound impact on British art in the mid-19th century. His commitment to naturalism, bright color, and intricate detail helped to redefine the standards of academic painting and inspired a generation of artists. The Pre-Raphaelite emphasis on realism and attention to nature challenged the prevailing trends of the time and laid the groundwork for subsequent movements, including the Arts and Crafts Movement and Symbolism.

Millais' early works, characterized by their meticulous attention to detail and faithful representation of nature, set new standards for narrative painting and influenced the development of British art. His paintings often drew on literary and historical themes, combining a deep appreciation for nature with an emotional depth that resonated with Victorian audiences.

As Millais transitioned to a broader, more accessible style in his later years, he demonstrated his versatility as an artist, gaining widespread popularity and commercial success. His portraits, in particular, are celebrated for their psychological insight and technical skill, capturing the character and personality of his sitters with a sense of immediacy and realism.

Millais' influence extended beyond the visual arts; his work inspired poets and writers of the Victorian era, including his association with John Ruskin, who supported the Pre-Raphaelite movement. Millais' legacy endures in his contributions to the revival of naturalism in painting and his role in challenging the artistic conventions of his time, making him a significant figure in the history of British art.

James McNeill Whistler

Date of Birth: July 11, 1834
Place of Birth: Lowell, Massachusetts, United States
Date of Death: July 17, 1903
Place of Death: London, England

Short Biography:
James McNeill Whistler was an American-born artist known for his innovative approach to painting and printmaking, as well as his influence on the Aesthetic Movement, which emphasized "art for art's sake." Born in Lowell, Massachusetts, in 1834, Whistler spent much of his childhood in Russia, where his father, a civil engineer, worked on railroad projects. After returning to the United States, Whistler enrolled at the United States Military Academy at West Point but was dismissed due to poor academic performance and his rebellious nature.

Whistler moved to Paris in 1855 to pursue a career in art, studying at the École Impériale and under the artist Charles Gleyre. In Paris, he became acquainted with the avant-garde art scene, influenced by the works of Gustave Courbet and the Realist movement. Whistler eventually settled in London in the early 1860s, where he developed his signature style characterized by subtle color harmonies, elegant compositions, and an emphasis on mood over detailed realism.

One of Whistler's most famous works is Arrangement in Grey and Black No.1 (1871), commonly known as Whistler's Mother. The painting, a portrait of his mother seated against a simple, muted backdrop, exemplifies Whistler's interest in tonal harmony and his belief in art's aesthetic qualities. His series of Nocturnes, depicting the River Thames at twilight or night, showcased his ability to capture atmosphere and abstract beauty, using a limited color palette and soft, expressive brushstrokes.

Whistler was known for his combative personality and his strong opinions on art. He was involved in several public disputes, most notably a libel lawsuit against art critic John Ruskin, who had disparaged Whistler's work. Although Whistler won the case, the legal costs led to his financial ruin. Despite these challenges, Whistler remained a central figure in the art world, influencing both contemporary and future artists with his dedication to aesthetic principles.

Influence and Significance on Art:
James McNeill Whistler played a crucial role in the development of modern art by advocating for the aesthetic value of art independent of narrative content or moral instruction. His belief in "art for art's sake" challenged conventional views of art's purpose and paved the way for movements that prioritized form, composition, and the emotional response evoked by visual harmony. Whistler's emphasis on tonal harmony and his use of musical terminology to title his paintings (such as "arrangements" and "nocturnes") highlighted his approach to painting as analogous to musical composition, focusing on mood and atmosphere.

Whistler's innovative techniques and his influence on the Aesthetic Movement impacted artists in both Europe and America. His use of color and light, along with his minimalist compositions, influenced Impressionist and Symbolist painters, including Claude Monet and Edgar Degas. Whistler's interest in Japanese art, particularly the use of asymmetrical composition and delicate line work, also contributed to the broader trend of Japonisme in Western art during the 19th century.

In addition to his paintings, Whistler was a prolific printmaker, producing a significant body of work in etching and lithography that further showcased his technical skill and artistic vision. His contributions to printmaking helped to elevate the medium's status within the art world.

Whistler's legacy endures through his impact on the trajectory of modern art, his role in advocating for the aesthetic autonomy of art, and his influence on the subsequent generations of artists who embraced the principles of visual harmony and abstract beauty. His work remains a cornerstone of collections in major museums worldwide, where it continues to be celebrated for its innovation and subtle elegance.

Claude Monet

Date of Birth: November 14, 1840
Place of Birth: Paris, France
Date of Death: December 5, 1926
Place of Death: Giverny, France

Short Biography:

Claude Monet was a French painter and a founder of the Impressionist movement, known for his innovative use of color and light to capture the transient effects of nature. Born in Paris in 1840, Monet moved to Le Havre with his family as a child, where he developed an early interest in art, selling caricatures and sketches. In the late 1850s, Monet studied under landscape painter Eugène Boudin, who introduced him to plein air painting, a method of painting outdoors directly from nature.

Monet moved to Paris in 1859 to pursue formal art training, studying briefly at the Académie Suisse. He formed friendships with fellow artists, including Pierre-Auguste Renoir, Alfred Sisley, and Camille Pissarro, with whom he shared a desire to break away from the constraints of academic painting. Together, they began to explore new ways of capturing light, atmosphere, and the changing qualities of the natural world.

In 1874, Monet exhibited his painting Impression, Sunrise at the first independent exhibition organized by a group of artists that would come to be known as the Impressionists. The painting's title, derived from a critic's dismissive remark, gave the movement its name. Impression, Sunrise exemplified Monet's approach to capturing fleeting moments with loose brushwork, vibrant colors, and an emphasis on the effects of light rather than detailed representation.

Throughout his career, Monet focused on a series of thematic explorations, painting the same scene multiple times to capture different lighting conditions and seasons. His series of Haystacks, Rouen Cathedral, and Water Lilies are among his most famous works, demonstrating his fascination with the nuances of color and light. In 1883, Monet moved to Giverny, where he created a Japanese-inspired garden that became the primary subject of his later work, particularly his iconic Water Lilies series.

Monet continued to paint until his death in 1926, despite suffering from cataracts in his later years, which affected his vision and use of color.

Influence and Significance on Art:

Claude Monet is widely regarded as one of the most influential figures in the history of Western art, recognized as a central figure in the Impressionist movement and a pioneer in the exploration of color and light. Monet's approach to painting, characterized by loose brushwork, vibrant color palettes, and a focus on capturing the ephemeral qualities of nature, marked a significant departure from traditional academic art.

Monet's dedication to painting en plein air and his emphasis on depicting natural scenes under varying conditions influenced his contemporaries and shaped the direction of modern art. His innovative techniques in handling color and light challenged conventional methods of representation, inspiring subsequent generations of artists to explore new ways of seeing and interpreting the world.

The development of Monet's Water Lilies series, with its emphasis on abstracted forms and reflections, foreshadowed aspects of later art movements, including Abstract Expressionism. His work's focus on mood, atmosphere, and the sensory experience of the viewer also had a lasting impact on the development of visual art in the 20th century.

Monet's contributions to art extended beyond his paintings; he played a vital role in organizing exhibitions that allowed Impressionist artists to showcase their work independently of the traditional Salon. This helped to establish a new market for modern art and laid the groundwork for the diverse and dynamic art scene of the 20th century.

Monet's legacy endures through his innovative approach to landscape painting, his exploration of light and color, and his influence on the course of modern art. His works are celebrated in major museums worldwide, and his garden at Giverny remains a pilgrimage site for art lovers and admirers of his vision.

Pierre-Auguste Renoir

Date of Birth: February 25, 1841
Place of Birth: Limoges, France
Date of Death: December 3, 1919
Place of Death: Cagnes-sur-Mer, France

Short Biography:
Pierre-Auguste Renoir was a French painter and one of the leading figures of the Impressionist movement, known for his vibrant use of color, light, and his depictions of everyday life. Born in Limoges in 1841, Renoir moved with his family to Paris at a young age. He began his artistic career as an apprentice in a porcelain factory, where he painted decorative designs. This early experience with color and form greatly influenced his later work.

In the early 1860s, Renoir entered the École des Beaux-Arts and studied under the academic painter Charles Gleyre, where he met future Impressionist colleagues Claude Monet, Alfred Sisley, and Frédéric Bazille. The group shared a desire to break away from the constraints of academic art and began to explore new techniques for capturing the effects of light and atmosphere. Renoir's early works were influenced by the styles of 18th-century French painters like François Boucher and Jean-Honoré Fragonard, as well as the realism of Gustave Courbet.

Renoir was a central figure in the first Impressionist exhibition in 1874, where his work received both praise and criticism for its fresh, loose brushwork and vibrant colors. Some of his most famous paintings from this period include Luncheon of the Boating Party (1880-1881), Dance at Le Moulin de la Galette (1876), and La Loge (1874). These works captured scenes of contemporary Parisian life, depicting lively gatherings, dances, and the joie de vivre of the bourgeoisie with warmth and immediacy.

In the 1880s, Renoir's style evolved as he moved away from the loose brushwork of Impressionism, seeking greater clarity of form and composition. This period, often referred to as his "Ingres period," was characterized by more structured lines and a focus on classical beauty, as seen in works like The Large Bathers (1884-1887).

Despite suffering from rheumatoid arthritis later in life, which severely limited his mobility, Renoir continued to paint, often having brushes strapped to his hands. His later works are noted for their sensuous and luminous nudes, intimate domestic scenes, and portraits. Renoir died in 1919 at his home in Cagnes-sur-Mer, leaving behind a rich legacy of over 4,000 paintings

Influence and Significance on Art:
Pierre-Auguste Renoir is celebrated for his contributions to the Impressionist movement and his exploration of light, color, and modern life. His work is characterized by its vibrant palette, loose brushwork, and joyful depiction of everyday scenes, which helped define the Impressionist aesthetic. Renoir's ability

to capture the effects of sunlight on figures and landscapes, along with his focus on depicting moments of leisure and pleasure, made his paintings widely popular.

'

Renoir's portrayal of the human figure, especially his nudes, influenced future generations of artists. His emphasis on the beauty of the human form, the sensuality of his brushwork, and the harmony of color and light set a standard for modern figurative painting. His work had a significant impact on artists such as Henri Matisse and Pablo Picasso, who admired his celebration of the human body and the joy of life.

Renoir's shift towards a more classical style later in his career also demonstrated his versatility and commitment to exploring different artistic approaches. This evolution reflected his desire to balance the spontaneity of Impressionism with the structure and permanence of classical art.

Throughout his career, Renoir's work remained a testament to his belief in the beauty of everyday life and the importance of art as a source of joy and pleasure. His paintings continue to be celebrated for their warmth, vibrancy, and ability to capture the fleeting moments of human experience, securing his place as one of the most beloved and influential artists in the history of Western art.

Ilya Repin

Date of Birth: August 5, 1844
Place of Birth: Chuguyev, Kharkov Governorate, Russian Empire (now Ukraine)
Date of Death: September 29, 1930
Place of Death: Kuokkala, Finland (now Repino, Russia)

Short Biography:
Ilya Repin was a Russian realist painter and one of the most prominent figures in the Peredvizhniki (The Wanderers) movement, which sought to bring art to the people and depict the realities of Russian life. Born in 1844 in Chuguyev, a small town in the Kharkov Governorate, Repin showed an early aptitude for art, which led him to study at the Imperial Academy of Arts in St. Petersburg. His training there exposed him to the academic traditions of painting, but he soon became involved with the Peredvizhniki, a group of artists who broke away from the Academy to create art that was more socially relevant and accessible.

Repin's early works, such as Barge Haulers on the Volga (1870–1873), brought him national recognition for their powerful depiction of social issues. The painting portrays a group of laborers struggling to pull a barge along the Volga River, highlighting the harsh conditions and exploitation faced by the working class. Repin's attention to detail, empathy for his subjects, and ability to capture the human spirit made this painting a landmark in Russian art.

Throughout his career, Repin focused on themes of Russian history, society, and culture. His portraits of contemporary figures, such as Leo Tolstoy, Modest Mussorgsky, and Tsar Alexander III, are celebrated for their psychological depth and realism. Other significant works include Ivan the Terrible and His Son Ivan (1885), depicting the tragic and dramatic moment after Ivan the Terrible has mortally wounded his son, and Reply of the Zaporozhian Cossacks (1880–1891), a vivid and dynamic portrayal of Cossacks mocking a Turkish sultan.

Repin was deeply engaged in the cultural and intellectual life of his time, contributing to discussions on art, literature, and politics. Despite his success, he faced cri

cism from both conservative and radical factions. In his later years, Repin moved to Kuokkala (now Repino, Russia), where he continued to paint and write until his death in 1930.

Influence and Significance on Art:

Ilya Repin is considered one of the greatest Russian painters of the 19th century, known for his masterful technique, attention to detail, and commitment to depicting the social realities of his time. His work played a crucial role in the development of Russian realism, a movement that sought to portray everyday life and social issues with honesty and empathy. Repin's paintings are characterized by their emotional depth, dramatic compositions, and ability to capture the essence of his subjects, whether depicting scenes of historical significance, portraits of cultural figures, or scenes of ordinary life.

Repin's involvement with the Peredvizhniki movement was instrumental in challenging the conventions of academic art and promoting a more socially conscious approach to painting. His work resonated with a broad audience, bridging the gap between the artistic elite and the general public. By focusing on the struggles and joys of ordinary people, Repin's art became a powerful vehicle for social commentary and national identity.

His influence extended beyond Russia, inspiring artists across Europe who were interested in alism and social themes. Repin's ability to convey the psychological complexity of his subjects and his mastery of color, light, and texture set a standard for portrait painting and narrative art.

Repin's legacy continues to be celebrated in Russia and around the world. His works are housed in major museums, such as the Tretyakov Gallery in Moscow and the Russian Museum in St. Petersburg, where they remain a testament to his vision, technical skill, and commitment to capturing the human experience.

Henri Rousseau

Date of Birth: May 21, 1844
Place of Birth: Laval, France
Date of Death: September 2, 1910
Place of Death: Paris, France

Short Biography:

Henri Rousseau, often referred to as "Le Douanier" (The Customs Officer) due to his day job, was a French post-impressionist painter known for his naïve or primitive style. Born in Laval, France, in 1844, Rousseau moved to Paris, where he worked various jobs, including as a toll collector for the city government, a position he held until he retired in 1893. Although he had no formal training as an artist, Rousseau began painting in his spare time and devoted himself fully to his art after his retirement.

Rousseau's style was characterized by its flat, graphic forms, vivid colors, and meticulous detail, which stood in contrast to the more polished and technically advanced styles of his contemporaries. His most famous works are his jungle scenes, such as The Sleeping Gypsy (1897) and The Dream (1910). Despite never having traveled outside of France, Rousseau created these exotic landscapes using his imagination, inspiration from illustrated books, botanical gardens, and visits to the zoo.

His art often depicted fantastical scenes with a dreamlike quality, blending reality and imagination. Rousseau's lack of formal training led to an unconventional approach to perspective and proportion, which critics initially derided as simplistic or childish. However, his work gradually gained recognition and was admired by avant-garde artists for its originality, sincerity, and the sense of wonder it conveyed.

Rousseau exhibited regularly at the Salon des Indépendants, where his work attracted the attention of prominent artists such as Pablo Picasso and the poet Guillaume Apollinaire, who became his supporters and friends. Despite facing financial difficulties and skepticism from the art establishment, Rousseau continued to paint until his death in Paris in 1910.

Influence and Significance on Art:
Henri Rousseau is celebrated for his contribution to the development of modern art, particularly through his unique and imaginative style that challenged the conventions of academic painting. His work is a precursor to the Surrealist movement, influencing artists such as Salvador Dalí, Max Ernst, and Joan Miró, who admired his dreamlike compositions and exploration of the subconscious.

Rousseau's use of bold colors, simplified forms, and imaginative subject matter also resonated with the Fauves and early modernists, including Henri Matisse and Wassily Kandinsky, who were inspired by his expressive use of color and the emotive power of his imagery. His approach to painting, characterized by a disregard for traditional perspective and a focus on symbolic and emotional content, paved the way for the emergence of primitivism and a broader acceptance of non-academic art styles.

Rousseau's ability to create a sense of mystery and narrative through his seemingly naïve technique has made his work enduringly popular. His art evokes a sense of innocence and wonder, capturing the imagination of viewers with its fantastical landscapes and intriguing scenes. Rousseau's legacy is evident in the continued fascination with his life and work, which remains a source of inspiration for artists exploring the boundaries between reality and fantasy.

Henri Rousseau's contribution to art history lies in his role as a self-taught artist who, through sheer originality and vision, helped to shape the course of modern art. His work continues to be celebrated for its charm, inventiveness, and its profound impact on the development of 20th-century avant-garde movements.

John William Waterhouse

Date of Birth: April 6, 1849
Place of Birth: Rome, Papal States (now Italy)
Date of Death: February 10, 1917
Place of Death: London, England

Short Biography:

John William Waterhouse was a British painter known for his depictions of classical, historical, and literary subjects, often featuring ethereal, idealized female figures. Born in Rome in 1849 to English parents who were both painters, Waterhouse spent his early childhood immersed in the rich cultural environment of the Italian capital. The family moved to London in the late 1850s, where Waterhouse continued his artistic training.

In 1870, Waterhouse enrolled at the Royal Academy of Arts in London, where he quickly gained recognition for his talent. His early works were influenced by the classical themes and styles of Lawrence Alma-Tadema and Frederic Leighton, characterized by their attention to detail, use of vibrant colors, and interest in antiquity. Waterhouse's fascination with mythological and literary themes, particularly those drawn from ancient Greek mythology, Arthurian legend, and the works of poets like Alfred, Lord Tennyson, became central to his artistic career.

One of Waterhouse's most famous paintings, The Lady of Shalott (1888), is based on Tennyson's poem of the same name, depicting the tragic figure of the Lady of Shalott drifting down a river in a boat. This painting exemplifies Waterhouse's romantic style, with its focus on emotion, intricate composition, and the haunting beauty of the subject. Other notable works include Hylas and the Nymphs (1896), Ophelia (1894), and Circe Offering the Cup to Ulysses (1891).

Waterhouse's work is characterized by its dreamy, atmospheric quality and the artist's ability to convey narrative through lush, detailed landscapes and expressive figures. Despite the rise of modernism in the late 19th and early 20th centuries, Waterhouse remained committed to the themes and style of Romanticism and the Pre-Raphaelite Brotherhood, blending realism with fantasy to create captivating and timeless images.

Influence and Significance on Art:

John William Waterhouse is often associated with the later phase of the Pre-Raphaelite movement, although he developed his distinct style that combined elements of Romanticism, classicism, and the Pre-Raphaelite aesthetic. His work is renowned for its technical proficiency, especially in the depiction of light, texture, and detail, as well as its evocative use of narrative and symbolism.

Waterhouse's paintings are celebrated for their exploration of mythological and literary subjects, often focusing on the inner lives and emotions of women. His portrayal of female figures, marked by their grace, beauty, and emotional complexity, has been both admired and critiqued for its romanticization and idealization of femininity. Nonetheless, his ability to capture the emotional and psychological depth of his subjects made his work resonate with audiences and continues to captivate viewers today.

Waterhouse's commitment to traditional techniques and his resistance to the modernist trends of his time positioned him as both a preserver of past artistic ideals and a bridge to future generations who would look back to the narrative power and aesthetic beauty of his work. His paintings remain iconic representations of Romantic and Pre-Raphaelite art, inspiring contemporary artists and illustrators who draw on similar themes of myth, legend, and literary inspiration.

The enduring popularity of Waterhouse's work, with pieces like The Lady of Shalott and Hylas and the Nymphs still widely recognized and reproduced, attests to his lasting impact on the world of art. His legacy is marked by his ability to blend beauty and narrative, creating art that transcends its historical moment to speak to universal themes of love, fate, and the human experience.

Vincent van Gogh

Date of Birth: March 30, 1853
Place of Birth: Zundert, Netherlands
Date of Death: July 29, 1890
Place of Death: Auvers-sur-Oise, France

Short Biography:
Vincent van Gogh was a Dutch Post-Impressionist painter whose work has had a profound impact on the development of modern art. Born in Zundert, Netherlands, in 1853, Van Gogh was the son of a Protestant minister and showed an early interest in art. However, his path to becoming an artist was not straightforward. Before dedicating himself to painting, Van Gogh worked as an art dealer, a teacher, and a preacher. It wasn't until his late twenties that he decided to pursue art seriously, studying at the Académie Royale des Beaux-Arts in Brussels.

Van Gogh's early works were characterized by dark tones and somber themes, focusing on the lives of peasants and the working class, as seen in The Potato Eaters (1885). In 1886, Van Gogh moved to Paris, where he was influenced by the vibrant colors and dynamic techniques of the Impressionists and Neo-Impressionists, such as Claude Monet, Georges Seurat, and Paul Signac. This exposure led him to adopt a brighter color palette and more expressive brushwork.

In 1888, Van Gogh moved to Arles in the south of France, where he produced some of his most famous works, including Sunflowers, The Bedroom, and Starry Night. His time in Arles was marked by prolific creativity but also by increasing mental instability. During this period, he famously cut off part of his own ear after an argument with fellow artist Paul Gauguin. Despite his struggles with mental health, Van Gogh continued to paint, creating bold and emotive works that conveyed his deep connection to nature and his inner turmoil.

In 1890, Van Gogh moved to Auvers-sur-Oise, near Paris, where he continued to paint, focusing on landscapes and portraits. On July 27, 1890, he suffered a gunshot wound, believed to be self-inflicted, and died two days later. His death marked the end of a brief but intensely productive artistic career.

Influence and Significance on Art:
Vincent van Gogh is regarded as one of the most influential figures in the history of Western art, despite achieving little commercial success during his lifetime. His work is celebrated for its emotional depth, bold use of color, and distinctive brushwork, which convey a sense of movement and intensity. Van Gogh's approach to painting was deeply personal and innovative, often using color and form to express his feelings and experiences.

Van Gogh's technique of applying thick, expressive strokes of paint, known as impasto, and his use of vivid, non-naturalistic colors, were revolutionary at the time and laid the groundwork for Expressionism and

Fauvism. His ability to infuse everyday scenes and landscapes with emotional resonance and psychological insight has made his work timeless and universally relatable.

Van Gogh's letters, particularly those to his brother Theo, provide valuable insight into his artistic process, thoughts on color theory, and personal struggles, offering a unique glimpse into the mind of a creative genius. His life and work have inspired numerous biographies, films, and exhibitions, solidifying his status as a cultural icon.

Today, Van Gogh's paintings are among the most famous and valuable in the world, housed in major museums such as the Van Gogh Museum in Amsterdam and the Musée d'Orsay in Paris. His legacy continues to influence artists and captivate audiences, making him one of the most beloved and enduring figures in art history.

Georges Seurat

Date of Birth: December 2, 1859
Place of Birth: Paris, France
Date of Death: March 29, 1891
Place of Death: Paris, France

Short Biography:
Georges Seurat was a French post-Impressionist painter known for pioneering the technique of pointillism, a method of painting in which small, distinct dots of color are applied in patterns to form an image. Born in Paris in 1859, Seurat showed an early interest in art and attended the École Municipale de Sculpture et Dessin, followed by the prestigious École des Beaux-Arts. His formal training focused on classical techniques, but he was also exposed to contemporary developments in color theory and optics, which profoundly influenced his artistic direction.

Seurat's most famous work, A Sunday on La Grande Jatte (1884-1886), marked the culmination of his interest in color theory and scientific approaches to painting. This large-scale painting, depicting Parisians leisurely enjoying an afternoon on an island in the Seine, utilized his pointillist technique to achieve a luminous, harmonious effect. Seurat spent over two years on the painting, meticulously applying small dots of pure color that, when viewed from a distance, blend together to form cohesive shapes and scenes.

Throughout his career, Seurat was committed to the idea that scientific principles could be applied to the creation of art. He developed a systematic approach to color and composition, believing that by using precise dots of color and organizing them according to scientific theories of harmony, he could evoke specific emotional responses from viewers. His work often focused on scenes of contemporary Parisian life, the leisure activities of the middle class, and the effects of light and atmosphere.

Despite his relatively short life—he died at the age of 31, possibly from meningitis or pneumonia—Seurat's influence on the art world was profound. His innovative techniques and ideas paved the way for future developments in modern art.

Influence and Significance on Art:

Georges Seurat is considered one of the most influential artists of the post-Impressionist movement, known for his systematic and scientific approach to painting and his development of pointillism (also known as divisionism). By breaking down color into its component parts and applying it in precise, calculated dots, Seurat introduced a new way of thinking about color, light, and the process of visual perception.

Seurat's work, particularly A Sunday on La Grande Jatte, had a significant impact on the trajectory of modern art. His methodical approach and use of color theory influenced contemporaries and future artists, including Paul Signac, who became one of the leading proponents of pointillism, and Henri Matisse, who explored similar ideas in his own way. The emphasis on color harmony and the emotional impact of color seen in Seurat's work also resonated with the Fauves and later with abstract artists.

In addition to his technical contributions, Seurat's emphasis on the artist's intellectual control over the creative process challenged the spontaneity and emotional immediacy of Impressionism. His work represents a bridge between the naturalism of the 19th century and the abstract explorations of the 20th century, making him a key figure in the evolution of modern art.

Seurat's exploration of the relationship between art and science laid the groundwork for further innovations in visual art, particularly in the study of how the human eye perceives color and form. His legacy endures through the continued study and admiration of his paintings, which are celebrated for their precision, beauty, and the innovative spirit that defined his approach to art.

Gustav Klimt

Date of Birth: July 14, 1862
Place of Birth: Baumgarten, near Vienna, Austrian Empire (now Austria)
Date of Death: February 6, 1918
Place of Death: Vienna, Austria

Short Biography:

Gustav Klimt was an Austrian symbolist painter and one of the most prominent members of the Vienna Secession movement. Born in Baumgarten, near Vienna, in 1862, Klimt was the second of seven children. He showed early artistic talent, which led him to enroll in the Vienna School of Arts and Crafts, where he received formal training in architectural painting. Klimt initially worked as a decorator, creating murals and ceilings for public buildings with his brother Ernst and fellow artist Franz Matsch.

In the 1890s, Klimt began to move away from academic painting, embracing a more personal and experimental style that combined symbolism, eroticism, and an exploration of the human psyche. This shift in his work was marked by the founding of the Vienna Secession in 1897, a group of artists who sought to break free from the constraints of academic art and explore new artistic ideas. Klimt served as the first president of the group, which became known for its embrace of Art Nouveau and its promotion of modern art.

Klimt's most famous period, known as his "Golden Phase," featured works that incorporated gold leaf, intricate patterns, and rich symbolism. One of his most iconic paintings from this period is The Kiss (1907-1908), which depicts a couple locked in an intimate embrace, surrounded by a shimmering, golden background. Other notable works include Portrait of Adele Bloch-Bauer I (1907) and Danaë (1907). Klimt's use of gold, inspired by Byzantine mosaics and the decorative arts, created a sense of opulence and timelessness.

Klimt's work often focused on themes of love, eroticism, and the female form, and his paintings are known for their sensuousness and psychological depth. Although he faced criticism and controversy for his explicit depictions of sexuality, Klimt remained committed to exploring the boundaries of art and challenging societal norms.

Klimt died in 1918 due to a stroke and pneumonia, leaving behind a legacy that would influence future generations of artists.

Influence and Significance on Art:
Gustav Klimt is considered one of the most important figures in modern art, known for his distinctive style that combined symbolism, eroticism, and a decorative aesthetic. His role as a founding member of the Vienna Secession helped to establish Vienna as a center of avant-garde art and culture at the turn of the 20th century. Klimt's embrace of Art Nouveau, with its emphasis on natural forms, flowing lines, and decorative patterns, played a significant role in shaping the visual language of the movement.

Klimt's innovative use of gold leaf, mosaic-like patterns, and symbolic imagery influenced not only painters but also designers and architects of his time. His ability to merge fine art with decorative art blurred the boundaries between different artistic disciplines, paving the way for later modernist movements that sought to integrate art into everyday life.

His focus on the female form and exploration of themes such as sensuality, fertility, and the subconscious anticipated the work of later Expressionists and Surrealists. Klimt's portrayal of women, often depicted with a sense of both strength and vulnerability, challenged traditional representations and offered a more complex view of femininity.

Klimt's impact on art continues to be felt today, with his works celebrated for their beauty, emotional depth, and technical innovation. His paintings are housed in major museums worldwide, and his influence can be seen in contemporary art, design, and fashion. Klimt's legacy endures as a symbol of the artistic and cultural flourishing of Vienna at the turn of the century, and as a testament to the power of art to transcend conventional boundaries.

Edvard Munch

Date of Birth: December 12, 1863
Place of Birth: Loten, Hedmark, Norway
Date of Death: January 23, 1944
Place of Death: Oslo, Norway

Short Biography:
Edvard Munch was a Norwegian painter and printmaker whose work is associated with the Symbolist and Expressionist movements. Born in Loten, Norway, in 1863, Munch faced a series of personal tragedies

from a young age, including the death of his mother when he was five and his sister shortly thereafter. These early experiences of illness and loss profoundly influenced his outlook on life and art, leading him to explore themes of death, anxiety, and existential dread.

Munch began his formal art training at the Royal School of Art and Design in Kristiania (now Oslo) in the 1880s. His early work was influenced by the Symbolist painters, Impressionism, and Post-Impressionism, but he soon developed a distinctive style characterized by bold colors, swirling lines, and a focus on emotional and psychological content. Munch's work often dealt with themes of love, fear, and human vulnerability, capturing the angst and alienation of modern life.

His most famous painting, The Scream (1893), is an iconic image of existential anxiety and is considered one of the most important works of modern art. The painting depicts a figure standing on a bridge, holding its head in its hands, with a sky that seems to pulsate with vibrant, swirling colors. The Scream became a symbol of human anxiety and existential despair, resonating with audiences around the world.

Throughout his career, Munch produced numerous paintings, prints, and woodcuts exploring similar themes of isolation, illness, and emotional turmoil. His Frieze of Life series, which includes The Scream, Madonna, and The Dance of Life, reflects his ongoing preoccupation with the stages of life, love, and death. Despite struggling with mental health issues, including a nervous breakdown in 1908, Munch continued to work prolifically, gaining recognition both in Norway and internationally.

Munch spent his later years living in relative isolation, focusing on his art and occasionally engaging in exhibitions. He left a significant portion of his work to the city of Oslo, which became the foundation for the Munch Museum, established after his death in 1944.

Influence and Significance on Art:
Edvard Munch is regarded as one of the pioneers of modern Expressionism, known for his ability to convey deep psychological and emotional states through his art. His exploration of themes such as existential dread, fear, love, and death set him apart from his contemporaries and laid the groundwork for future developments in modern art. Munch's use of vivid color, dynamic composition, and symbolic imagery to express inner turmoil and psychological experiences influenced the direction of 20th-century art, inspiring artists like German Expressionists Ernst Ludwig Kirchner, Emil Nolde, and others.

Munch's innovative approach to printmaking, particularly his use of color lithography and woodcuts, helped to redefine the medium, making his work more accessible and expanding its reach. His ability to convey raw emotion and his focus on the darker aspects of human existence resonated with the burgeoning Expressionist movement and other avant-garde artists seeking to break away from traditional representational art.

The Scream remains one of the most recognized and reproduced images in the world, symbolizing the universal experience of anxiety and existential despair. Its impact extends beyond the art world, becoming an iconic symbol of modern human experience and a reference point in popular culture.

Munch's legacy is celebrated in museums and galleries worldwide, where his works continue to captivate viewers with their emotional power and timeless exploration of the human condition. His contributions to the development of Expressionism and his influence on modern art secure his place as one of the most important and influential artists of the late 19th and early 20th centuries.

Henri de Toulouse-Lautrec

Date of Birth: November 24, 1864
Place of Birth: Albi, Tarn, France
Date of Death: September 9, 1901
Place of Death: Saint-André-du-Bois, Gironde, France

Short Biography:

Henri de Toulouse-Lautrec was a French painter, printmaker, and illustrator known for his depictions of Parisian nightlife and his role in the development of modern poster art. Born into an aristocratic family in Albi, France, Toulouse-Lautrec suffered from genetic health problems, exacerbated by two childhood accidents that left his legs permanently stunted. Unable to participate in many physical activities, he turned to art as a form of expression and solace.

Toulouse-Lautrec moved to Paris in the early 1880s to study art, training under academic painters like Léon Bonnat and Fernand Cormon. He quickly became involved in the bohemian circles of Montmartre, an area known for its vibrant nightlife, cabarets, and cafés. He was a frequent visitor to establishments such as the Moulin Rouge, where he observed and befriended many of the performers, dancers, and patrons. These settings provided the inspiration for much of his work.

Toulouse-Lautrec's paintings, drawings, and prints captured the energy and atmosphere of Montmartre's nightlife with a unique blend of realism and caricature. His works often featured vivid colors, bold outlines, and a keen sense of movement, influenced by Japanese ukiyo-e prints and the flat perspective of Impressionism. Some of his most famous works include At the Moulin Rouge (1892-1895), The Dance at the Moulin Rouge (1890), and his iconic posters for performers like Jane Avril and Aristide Bruant.

Toulouse-Lautrec's lifestyle and excessive alcohol consumption led to deteriorating health, and he was committed to a sanatorium in 1899. He continued to work until his health further declined, and he died at his family's estate in 1901 at the age of 36.

Influence and Significance on Art:

Henri de Toulouse-Lautrec is considered one of the most important figures in the Post-Impressionist movement and a pioneer in the art of the modern poster. His work provided a vivid portrayal of Parisian nightlife, capturing the spirit and characters of the bohemian world with both humor and empathy. His unique perspective, influenced by his physical condition and social outsider status, allowed him to observe and depict the lives of entertainers, prostitutes, and patrons with a sense of authenticity and intimacy.

Toulouse-Lautrec's innovative use of color, line, and composition had a lasting impact on both fine art and commercial art. His posters for the Moulin Rouge and other venues revolutionized advertising, combining artistic quality with mass appeal, and laid the groundwork for modern graphic design and visual communication. His embrace of the graphic arts and the use of lithography brought a new level of sophistication to the medium, influencing later artists such as Alphonse Mucha and the Art Nouveau movement.

Beyond his technical contributions, Toulouse-Lautrec's work challenged societal norms and preconceptions, offering a compassionate and often candid view of the marginalized and unconventional aspects of society. His portrayal of Parisian nightlife, with its blend of glamour and grittiness, captured the essence of the Belle Époque and provided a valuable historical record of the period.

Toulouse-Lautrec's legacy continues to be celebrated for its impact on modern art and culture. His paintings and posters are exhibited in major museums worldwide, and his life and work have inspired numerous films, books, and exhibitions, solidifying his place as a key figure in the history of art.

Grant Wood

Date of Birth: February 13, 1891
Place of Birth: Anamosa, Iowa, United States
Date of Death: February 12, 1942
Place of Death: Iowa City, Iowa, United States

Short Biography:
Grant Wood was an American painter best known for his iconic work American Gothic (1930), which has become one of the most recognized and parodied images in American art. Born in Anamosa, Iowa, in 1891, Wood spent his early years on a farm before moving with his family to Cedar Rapids after his father's death. His rural upbringing and deep connection to the Midwest greatly influenced his artistic style and subject matter.

Wood showed an early talent for art, and after high school, he studied at the Minneapolis School of Design and Handicraft and later at the Art Institute of Chicago. He spent time in Europe in the 1920s, where he was influenced by Impressionism, but it was his exposure to the works of the Northern Renaissance artists, particularly Jan van Eyck and Albrecht Dürer, that had a lasting impact on his approach to painting. These influences led Wood to develop a style characterized by meticulous detail, clarity, and a focus on the American Midwest.

In the late 1920s, Wood co-founded the Stone City Art Colony in Iowa, where he aimed to create a supportive environment for regional artists. During this period, he adopted a style known as Regionalism, which emphasized realistic depictions of rural American life and landscapes, often portraying the simplicity and values of small-town life. His works, such as American Gothic, Stone City, Iowa (1930), and Daughters of Revolution (1932), reflect his commitment to representing the American heartland.

American Gothic, featuring a stern-faced farmer holding a pitchfork next to a woman (modeled by Wood's sister and his dentist) standing in front of a Gothic Revival house, became an instant sensation and sparked numerous interpretations, ranging from a celebration of American values to a satirical critique of rural conservatism.

Wood served as a faculty member at the University of Iowa in the 1930s, where he continued to paint and teach until his death from pancreatic cancer in 1942.

Influence and Significance on Art:
Grant Wood is considered one of the leading figures of the American Regionalist movement, which sought to depict the everyday lives and landscapes of rural America in a period marked by the Great Depression and a search for national identity. His work, characterized by its precise realism, attention to detail, and use of American subjects, stood in contrast to the abstract and modernist trends of the time,

offering an alternative vision rooted in the nation's heartland.

Wood's American Gothic remains a defining image of American art, symbolizing both the strength and resilience of rural Americans and a nuanced critique of traditional values. The painting's iconic status has made it a cultural touchstone, inspiring countless parodies, adaptations, and interpretations.

Wood's influence extended beyond his paintings; his role as an educator and advocate for Regionalism helped to promote the idea that American art should reflect American themes and experiences. His belief in the importance of local culture and identity resonated with artists during a time of economic hardship and social change, contributing to the development of a distinctly American art form.

While Regionalism fell out of favor with the rise of Abstract Expressionism after World War II, Wood's work continues to be celebrated for its contribution to American art and its enduring relevance. His legacy is evident in the ongoing appreciation for art that reflects the everyday lives and landscapes of ordinary people, making him a key figure in the history of 20th-century American painting.

Printed in the USA
CPSIA information can be obtained
at www.ICGtesting.com
JSHW061919071024
71237JS00002B/2